The author

Michael Fry has spent several years of his life in the United States, mainly New England and California, twice as a visiting fellow at Brown University, Providence, Rhode Island. Much of the research for two of his major books, *The Dundas Despotism* and *The Scottish Empire*, was carried out in American archives. After completing his studies at the universities of Oxford and Hamburg, he started his writing career as a journalist on *The Scotsman* where he served as Economics Correspondent and Brussels Correspondent, as well as the paper's restaurant critic. For nearly twenty years he has been a freelance, a regular columnist in a variety of newspapers and a contributor to many more in Britain, Europe and America. His main intellectual interest lies in modern Scottish history, in which connection he has written books, articles and political pamphlets. He has stood as candidate for the British and Scottish Parliaments. When not travelling, he lives in Edinburgh.

D1056754

'Bold, Independent, Unconquer'd and Free'

How the Scots Made America Safe for
Liberty, Democracy and Capitalism.

MICHAEL FRY

FORT PUBLISHING LTD

First published in 2003 by Fort Publishing Ltd, Old Belmont House, 12 Robsland Avenue, Ayr, KA7 2RW.

© Michael Fry, 2003

All rights reserved. No part of this publication may be reproduced, stored in a retrieval system, or transmitted, in any form or by any means, electronic, mechanical, photocopying, recording or otherwise, without the prior permission of the publishers and copyright holders.

Michael Fry has asserted his rights under the Copyright, Designs and Patents Act, 1988 to be identified as the author of this work.

The 'two flags' chapter illustration by Michael Esk, Edinburgh

Typeset by S. Fairgrieve, Edinburgh

Printed by Bell and Bain Ltd, Glasgow

ISBN 0-9544461-3-5

A catalogue record for this book is available from the British Library

Thus bold, independent, unconquer'd and free,
Her bright course of glory for ever shall run:
For brave Caledonia immortal must be . . .

From 'Caledonia: A Ballad' by Robert Burns.

CONTENTS

PREFACE

M y greatest debt of gratitude is owed to James McCarroll, the managing director of Fort Publishing, for asking me to write a book about Scotland and America. It has turned out to be an enjoyable and satisfying project, above all intellectually useful to me, as I hope it will prove to others. My previous work *The Scottish Empire* grew vast and sprawling during the several years of its composition, in which the maintenance of some order in the mountains of material I had gathered became a major task in itself. I did not want this to dissolve into a history of the Scots abroad, of the Scottish diaspora generally, because that seemed to me too diffuse an organising principle. At all times, so far as I could, I kept in view the concept of Empire as something to give structure to the whole. Sacrifices had to be made in consequence. The history of the Scots in Japan is interesting, for example, yet Japan never came under any kind of external imperial rule, so Japan was left out. The history of the Scots in Latin America is even more interesting, and a good argument can be made for claiming Latin America as part of Britain's informal Empire in just the same way as certain other regions of the globe which were never coloured pink on the map. Still, that continent consisted of formally independent countries so, with much regret, I left it out as well.

But the biggest and most grievous omission I imposed on myself was the US. The period from 1707 to 1776, the seventy years or so that Scotland and America spent together under the British Crown, mutually enriched both nations. It was galling for me to break off the story of their relationship at what seemed to be the most promising point, simply because the Americans seceded from the Empire. With grim resolve, this was what I did all the same. The mutilation did not, of course, alter the fact that in the two succeeding centuries the US continued to exert a fascination on Scots quite as great as any British colony or dominion

did. Whether as a destination for emigrants or a locus for investment, they treated America in exactly the same manner as they
treated Canada or Australia. I make the point in the relevant
chapter below that during late-Victorian times there developed a
sort of North Atlantic free-trade area, where a man with skills to
sell could do so as readily in Glasgow as in New York as in
Montreal. It was a vigorous, spontaneous development only
brought to a halt by the economic and political disasters of the
twentieth century, which caused Scotland to withdraw into a
dispiriting parochialism while America slowly and reluctantly
took on the imperial role it plays now. It may be that the
renewed phase of globalisation under way at the turn of the millennium will temper the fates of both countries in such a fashion
as to bring them closer together again.

Angus Calder's review of *The Scottish Empire* saw it as in
essence the story of how the Scots used the British Empire for
their own purposes. Their cultural autonomy could be taken for
granted; they passed through a strait gate to acceptance by the
English as full and equal partners in the imperial enterprise
(something which the Irish, by contrast, never achieved); and so
the scene was set for significant Scottish contributions in particular
aspects of the Empire. When we compare to that the relationship
between Scotland and America it is obvious that things had to
run a different course. Though Scottish ideas proved useful to
the Founding Fathers of the US, Scots could not contribute to the
further development of the Republic in any collective sense
because, as a collectivity, they did not belong to it. Only individuals could contribute and they had, like the rest of the
American population, to take their chances in a system of political
and economic liberty where all were equal and nobody was
privileged. That so many Scots did so well out of it is a tribute
to their talents and energies and also, in my view, a confirmation
of the strength of the cultural autonomy posited by Calder. One
benefit of Scottish culture for those brought up in it was that,
incidentally, it gave them the capacity to prosper in America if
this was what they wanted to do. We may at any rate note how
their contribution fell away as the national culture grew frag-
mented and enfeebled during the twentieth century. Now

America influences Scotland rather than the other way round. Perhaps, in this as in other spheres, it is time for a cultural revival to redress the balance.

In that sense, the present book is a complement to *The Scottish Empire*. It is the story of the spread of Scottish influences inside a different system of values, American rather than imperial. So this is a study of differentiation, though some things remain the same. For example, in the US too the Scottish influences went to form a greater entity but then faded away as distinct elements. The exchange finally reversed and now a new culture exerts its own stronger pull on an older culture it has grown from and displaced. American culture today colours Scottish culture more deeply than any other single culture does – even English culture, to which Scots anyway dislike becoming indebted while remaining quite happy to imitate Americans in numberless aspects of ordinary life. Little is nowadays sent in return, apart from one or two global superstars. Scots, before they can offer much more, will have to become a good deal clearer in their own minds about what from now on they want for themselves and their country. My own hope is that the harmless labours of historians can be of help. With a recent shift of focus from a depressing internal history to a rather more encouraging external history, we are doing something to break down the unnecessary limits which Scots imposed on themselves with the embarrassing provincialism and mediocrity of the twentieth century. 'What do they know of Scotland who only Scotland know?' I asked in *The Scottish Empire*. It seems to me that interaction with the outside world has done at least as much as any domestic development to maintain the cultural autonomy which is the most interesting fact about the modern nation, and has proved to be the foundation for any other sort of autonomy.

This book was never intended to carry a great weight of scholarly apparatus but to present some ideas about aspects of the relationship between Scotland and America on the basis of readily available facts (certain of which, however, will have to be sought out in journals rather than in books by readers interested in pursuing the subject further). It would in any event be churlish of me not to record here my gratitude to authors who have preceded and, in one or two cases, worked with me in this field of study. It was opened up half-a-century ago by two eminent historians who were then young instructors at Harvard University, Bernard Bailyn and John Clive, with their article 'England's Cultural Provinces, Scotland and America' in the *William and Mary Quarterly* (1954). Bailyn's *Voyagers to the West* (1986) makes an equally distinguished contribution to another aspect of the topic, emigration. On this see also Ned Landsman's *Scotland and its First American Colony, New Jersey 1685-1765* (1985). On the relative importance of emigration, insufficient account has as yet been taken of Alan Karras's *Sojourners in the Sun, Scottish migrants in Jamaica and the Chesapeake* (1992).

The debate about the Scottish intellectual origins of the American Revolution was launched by Gary Wills's *Inventing America, Jefferson's Declaration of Independence* (1978). The resulting lively controversy illumined later and more general surveys, such as Richard Sher's and Jeffrey Smitten's *Scotland and America in the Age of the Enlightenment* (1990), a work itself placed in still wider context by Stewart J. Brown's *William Robertson and the Expansion of Europe* (1996). Wills also allowed reassessment of earlier studies, including G. S. Pryde, *The Scottish Universities and the Colleges of Colonial America* (1957). That book reminds us that interest in all these matters has not been entirely confined to the American side. Among Scottish contributions are W. R. Brock's *Scotus Americanus* (1982) and Tom Devine's classic study of *The Tobacco Lords* (1975).

There are so far few studies of the Scottish-American relationship in the nineteenth and twentieth centuries, but fortunately they include penetrating surveys such as Arthur Herman's *The Scottish Enlightenment* (2001) – which traces its influence into later periods – and two collections of essays by Andrew Hook, *Scotland and America, a study of cultural relations* (1975) and *From Ganderscleuch to Goose Creek* (1999), the latter being a literary history. The work of Sir Alec Cairncross referred to in the text below is *Home and Foreign Investment 1870–1913* (1953). I should mention also my debt to Neal Ascherson's *Stone Voices* (2002) for some specific points. Duncan Bruce's *The Mark of the Scots* (1996) is, and is likely to remain, a quarry for anyone interested in its subject. This subject is spreading beyond the book. I gathered valuable information from the website www.scotsinthecivilwar. When all else fails there is word of mouth, and I should thank Brian Monteith MSP for his advice on aspects of popular culture of which I am wholly ignorant.

Scottish-Canadian history has been better served. There are several general surveys, some by now quite venerable: A. L. Fraser, *The Mission of the Scot in Canada* (1903); G. Bryce, *The Scotsman in Canada* (1911); J. A. Roy, *The Scot and Canada* (1947); W. S. Reid, *The Scottish Tradition in Canada* (1976). The romance of the North West Company continues to attract both readers and writers, with books such as those by G. C. Davidson (1918), W. S. Wallace (1934) and M. W. Campbell (1957). There is also a wide range of other more specialist volumes, among which my own favourites are D. Campbell and R. A. MacLean, *Beyond the Atlantic Roar* (1975), on the Scots of Nova Scotia, and J. M. Bumsted, *The People's Clearance* (1982), a book of Scottish history by a Canadian scholar which makes me think native Scots ought to be banned from writing about the Highlands.

Michael Fry
Providence, Rhode Island
February 2003

INTRODUCTION

T he time will come at the end of this book for conclusions
about Scotland and America. It is enough for now to set
down a couple of simple points which have gone a long way to
determining their relationship and which will colour much of its
story in the pages that follow.

First, Scotland is an old country and America is a young
country. According to the accepted historical account, the union
of the four peoples occupying what is now the national territory
of Scotland began in 834. At that date, Kenneth MacAlpin, King
of Scots – a people in the West of the country descended from
Irish invaders – gained the throne of Pictland, the kingdom of
older indigenous tribes covering most of the North and East. In
1018 Kenneth's descendant, Malcolm II, conquered the
Lothians, where the peasants' Northumbrian dialect of Anglo-
Saxon was to change over the ages into the modern Scots
tongue. His grandson, Duncan, who was already ruler in
Strathclyde, the territory of ancient Britons in the south-west,
became king of a united Scotland in 1034, within boundaries
that have hardly changed during a thousand years.

The process of forming Scotland had taken two centuries
and in some ways it is not complete even yet. The different
regions of the country – Highlands and Lowlands, East and
West – maintain a rugged individuality, while the local patriotism of cities and towns often gives rise to intense rivalry with a
neighbour. Still, despite the diversity within such a tiny territory,

1

a rock-solid sense of Scottish identity overrides it all. This was first forged in the Wars of Independence, the desperate struggle against the imperialism of England which ended with its being crushed at the Battle of Bannockburn in 1314 under the leadership of King Robert Bruce. Again and again, Scots vindicated their freedom in battle against English aggression. In 1560, John Knox inspired the Reformation, which gave them the gruff, Presbyterian side of their character. The construction of Great Britain started in 1603, when James VI, King of Scots, succeeded his cousin, Elizabeth I of England, and brought about the Union of Crowns. But it would take another hundred years of mistrust, tension and war between the two nations before the Union of Parliaments followed in 1707.

Scotland and England have ever since formed one country in a political sense. But despite the three centuries of Union, Scotland is still Scotland, recognisable and distinct from all other nations. Only this can have allowed it to re-emerge, in a political sense, with the establishment of a devolved Scottish Parliament in 1999. A number of small European nations just disappeared inside some larger entity during those three centuries, yet it is not hard to see why Scotland escaped the same fate.

The Union of 1707, if driven along by coercion and bribery, was in crucial respects the outcome of a genuine negotiation. Under it the Scots, though losing their Parliament, kept the other national institutions they most valued: the Church, the law and the educational system. So a frame of nationality survived, and a tenacious popular memory of the Scottish past made sure the frame was not a matter of bare bones, but of flesh and blood. Almost everything that happens in Scotland today reflects in some way those thousand years of Scottish history.

By contrast, America is a young country. Nowadays, it may be senior to most members of the United Nations, yet it retains the aura of youth, a freshness, optimism and vitality which older nations find it hard to summon up even with the best will in the world. Two hundred years of history do not weigh on Americans as they would do on Scots. That makes it easier to change things, and to deal with failure. In Scotland it is quite hard to change things, and Scots may well prefer persistence in failure to any sort of change. They would often rather keep things as they are for the sake of the past, unless really forced to change by the depth of failure. The things that fail may well embody some aspect of the past which is especially cherished by Scots, something which makes them feel more Scottish.

For instance, Glasgow and its River Clyde in the West of Scotland formed during the nineteenth century the biggest centre of shipbuilding in the world, and were the focus of a whole way of industrial life with a typically Scottish system of values in honest toil and sturdy independence. The shipbuilding industry began to collapse about 1920, though it took till 1980 for most of it to vanish; some final fragments survive even yet. The main reason why the disappearance was so slow lay in the ferocious opposition to it by the workforce. British governments usually opted to subsidise the shipyards rather than face down the resistance. The result has been to retard the growth of a more modern industrial structure on Clydeside. Yet hardly anyone in Scotland ever questioned whether this was the right way to deal with economic change: the general assumption was that the resistance had an overwhelming moral force behind it, because of the Scottish values it represented.

Any comparable American city or region would have regarded it as absurd to argue that it possessed a moral right to produce the same things in 1980 as it did in 1920. Everyone would have moved on and adapted to economic forces as they came along. It has often been said in recent times that Scots and Americans share certain values, and without doubt one of them is enterprise, which both peoples admire. But it has to be remembered that Scots in many circumstances admire failure too, because failure can be heroic and success is not always the measure of moral worth. That is a product of Scottish history. Scots who did not share this view among their countrymen could always go to America.

Secondly, Scotland is a small country and America is a big country. For the record, Scotland could fit into the territory of the continental United States one hundred times; it is about the size of South Carolina. Every year, the US population increases

3

by as much as the entire Scottish population, which remained more or less static at five million or so right through the twentieth century. Just as there is a cult of newness in America, so there is a cult of bigness, in everything from the thickness of steaks to the dimensions of refrigerators to the length of cars to the height of buildings.

By contrast, the scale of Scottish life is small and intimate. Even the vaunted Highlands, with their highest point on Ben Nevis at 4,406 feet, are mere hillocks by the standards of Colorado or Alaska. The most Scottish of Scotland's communities are the small towns, places like Forfar or Kelso, which are unequivocally themselves, and not any other place, quite unlike an anonymous suburb. The central area of Edinburgh can be crossed on foot in half an hour; almost certainly, any citizen of it who does this will meet on the way somebody he knows. So even the capital city often has the feel of a village.

This intimacy of Scottish life brings further cultural effects. Scots have often been described as a restless, wandering race, but that is true only of a minority – obviously an able minority, because they always made their presence felt wherever they went. The experience of the majority has been different. Though there is no compulsion about it, most Scots live and die within a few miles of where they were born: they show little of the typical American readiness to leave everything behind and migrate 3,000 miles from New England to California in pursuit of some opportunity.

And because Scotland is such a small country the Scots, especially those within a particular professional sphere, will often know everything about each other: character, parentage, educational attainments, state of marriage and so on. As there are not many secrets in Scotland, the real secrets will only be of the darkest. So it can seem a claustrophobic kind of country. This has always ensured that some Scots will want to get out, because they cannot stand it, and seek their fortunes in America or another continent of wide open spaces.

But the majority who stay behind do not necessarily feel stifled. On the contrary, the close-knit nature of Scotland has been a condition of the survival of Scottish culture, in a not too friendly

4

historical environment where it could easily just have dissolved. A culture has to be deeply rooted and strongly bonded if it is to survive across many generations. By a sort of spontaneous consensus, this is what Scots have achieved. There is a price to be paid: a bit of intolerance, quite a lot of reluctance to change. Still, for most Scots, now and in the past, the bargain has been worth it.

Even so, this is not a culture capable of export. In the eighteenth and nineteenth centuries, there were occasional attempts to create little Scotlands beyond the seas in distant parts of the British Empire. When the Jacobite heroine, Flora Macdonald, and her husband, Alan Macdonald of Kingsburgh, emigrated to North Carolina with a large number of their dependants in 1769, they hoped to recreate on the opposite side of the Atlantic Ocean a more hospitable setting for the life of their clan than was available on the Isle of Skye. What they had not reckoned with was the American Revolution, which was to establish a system of popular government not easy to reconcile with the rule of chieftains in the old way. They came home again.

Some symbols of these efforts to transplant Scotland remain, in the fashion for Highland games and Scottish dancing in North America, in the wearing of kilts and tartans, and so on. As yet, however, it is rare for anyone to go beyond that and take an interest in deeper aspects of the cultural autonomy which have preserved Scotland through three centuries. Much of this will remain completely unknown even to enthusiasts for things Scottish, though I hope a good deal of it will be revealed in the following pages. A big country like America, especially in its present superpower's position, can readily put its cultural stamp on the world. For a small country like Scotland that is impossible: it is a real achievement if the culture survives at all. It survives not as something universal, but as belonging to one place and time. This, too, has marked the behaviour of Scots who have gone out into the world. They expect to have to fit in with the strange places where they end up, to conform to a way of life which they have not determined. All the same, it is remarkable how much good they have often quietly been able to do in line with Scottish conceptions.

This is all very different from America, where the past has little value except as entertainment, and where any deeper questions of identity have melted away into the shallow nostrums of multiculturalism. With all that said, it is time to take a closer look at the encounter between one small country in the Old World and the big country of the New World.

1

PIONEERS

Nowadays nobody believes that Christopher Columbus was the first man to sail across the Atlantic Ocean from Europe to America in 1492. It has long been known, since the lost information was recovered from their sagas, that the Vikings made it 500 years before him. Even before then, Saint Brendan and other Irish monks are supposed to have established hermitages on remote islands of the northern seas. From Spain before Columbus the Basques, too, were probably regular voyagers to Newfoundland, where they fished the cod that was and is a staple of their diet; but they were a people who survived by keeping themselves to themselves. European archives have thrown up other occasional references to odd, forgotten voyages which may or may not have succeeded in reaching the opposite side of the ocean.

Scots belonged to this medieval world of seafaring nations along the eastern seaboard of the North Atlantic. To all intents and purposes their own country was an island. With the English frontier closed to them, they were forced to sail to any foreign country they wanted to get to. And so they did, across to Scandinavia and Germany, through the Sound to the Baltic countries, down to Holland and France, even as far as Spain and the Mediterranean region. But did they ever turn outwards from the narrow seas to the ocean?

It would be surprising if they had not. In fact, we hear of Scots on the very first oceanic voyages, as members of Viking crews. For a couple of centuries before Scotland was united in the eleventh century, Norsemen dominated large parts of the North and West of the country. Scotland is the nearest landfall for any ship sailing out from Scandinavia. The Orkney and Shetland Islands were thickly settled by Vikings, whose descendants still spoke a Norse dialect till the eighteenth century which echoes yet in the local lilt. Similar settlements sprang up in the Western Isles and in other places accessible by sea right down to the Isle of Man, together with a good deal of the mainland. Place-names of modern Scotland such as Thurso and Stornoway are Norse, not Celtic, in origin. So are the names of rivers such as the Helmsdale or mountains such as Hecla and Helaval. Except in Orkney and Shetland, the Vikings did not supplant the native peoples. No doubt they were sworn enemies at first, but gradually they merged to form a mixed race of Norsemen and Gaels. These faced the wide Atlantic together.

One of the sagas tells the story of Herjulf the Viking, the captain of a longboat which just before the year 1000 got lost in a storm on its journey round Greenland, where a Norse colony had been established. When the weather cleared, he and his crew found themselves becalmed amid icy, barren wastes. They were afraid, but they happened to have on board a man from the Hebrides, the long line of islands to the west of Scotland, where the people remain musical to this day. To cheer his companions up, this nameless fellow composed a prayer, the 'Song of the Tidal Wave', and encouraged them to get on their way again. Once they reached safety, Herjulf recounted his experience to his friend Leif Eriksson, the most intrepid of Norse explorers. That inspired Leif to set out on the fabled voyage which took him through the islands where Herjulf had been to a mainland beyond – and to a brief, hostile encounter with a native people firing arrows at the intruders. Leif had reached America.

Other Vikings followed him. One was Thorfin Karlsefni, who had two Scots on board his ship, a man and a woman. This time the saga gives their names, Hake and Hekja. When he arrived at the American coastline, he put them ashore. He ordered them to scout southwards and see what sort of country it was. He would meet them at an agreed point three days later. The feelings of Hake and Hekja as they ran off into the primeval American forest can only be guessed at. But they came to no harm. On the contrary, they stopped to gather the wheat and grapes they saw growing in the clearings. When they handed their finds over to Thorfin, he decided to call the country Vinland, Land of Wine, which became the usual Norse name for this mysterious country and appears on a European map of the fifteenth century. From such evidence, modern scholars have argued that the Vikings must have penetrated as far south as Cape Cod or Long Island Sound. The trouble is that the facts in the saga are too sketchy to allow any certainty, and the whole episode may have been inserted later to bolster Thorfin's reputation. Yet a single word gives this charming tale a ring of authenticity. For some reason, mention is made of Hake's and Hekja's clothing, a *kjafal*, a sleeveless tunic with a hood. The word is found nowhere else in Old Norse literature, and probably represents the Gaelic *cabhail*, the body of a shirt, or *gioball*, a garment. How could the detail have been recorded at all if it was not genuine? If this confirms the story, Scotland can fairly count Hake and Hekja among the first Europeans to have set foot in the New World.

With the Vikings present in Iceland and Greenland, the transatlantic traffic at the northern end of the ocean remained quite busy all through the Middle Ages. The Icelanders are still there today, while the Greenlanders did not abandon their settlement till the turn of the fifteenth century, probably because their environment grew more hostile as the global climate entered what is now known as the Little Ice Age. Parts of Scotland continued to belong to the wider Norse community: the islands of Orkney and Shetland were not finally ceded by Denmark till 1469. While Orkney owed allegiance to the Danish Crown, to all intents and purposes it retained its independence under the rule of a native dynasty founded by the martyr, St Magnus. This dynasty was gradually scotticised. In the late fourteenth century, an heiress of it married Henry Sinclair, whose family were overlords of Caithness, the nearest territory on the Scottish mainland. He inherited the earldom of Orkney.

What makes Earl Henry Sinclair worth remembering here is the accident of a shipwreck which brought to his little palace at Kirkwall a bedraggled Venetian, Niccolo Zeno. Visitors from Italy were exotic but by no means unfamiliar figures in these remote reaches of northern Europe. They often acted as bankers, providing for payments among the traders of the various ports and so sustaining the hazardous international trade of the period. Though they usually stayed in some comfortable city such as Bruges in the Netherlands, on occasion they had to undertake voyages to more distant places, and sometimes these voyages ended in misfortune. Zeno came of a noble family in Venice, wealthy and enterprising, as skilled in finance as in seafaring. Sinclair would have been impressed, and received him hospitably. Niccolo Zeno soon died of his hardships, but he left behind his son Antonio who, now unable to get home, took up employment under the Earl. For him, the sudden acquisition of foreign expertise was a windfall. He had heard from his own Orcadian fishermen of a land across the ocean. Now he set out with the young Italian to find it. According to the manuscript which Zeno eventually left behind him, they landed there on 2 June 1398 – perhaps in Nova Scotia. If this is true, they preceded Columbus by almost a century. Unfortunately there is no other evidence to confirm the story, and medieval Italians were rather given to tales of risky journeys in places where their observations were unlikely to be disputed: even the authenticity of Marco Polo's travels to China is less than certain.

It was the penalty of a period when communication remained primitive. Any early knowledge of America remained locked in the minds of the seamen who had been there, or at most in the circles of their families and friends in the ports whence they sailed. Even if somehow this knowledge came to be written down, it would not necessarily be spread: the Church monopolised information about the world, on parchments laboriously copied out by monks. It was not an age when news passed round quickly. If Columbus stood at the end of a line of transatlantic explorers, the difference by 1492 was that printing had been invented, so all over Europe people could soon read books about the discoveries by him and the others who soon followed him. The printed word opened minds that had been closed. Europeans mentally prepared themselves to move outwards in the great expansion which, over the next three or four centuries, would see them come to dominate the globe.

The first of the overseas empires were Spanish and Portuguese. Scots had long had links with these nations: it was in Spain that the soldiers taking the heart of King Robert Bruce to Jerusalem, after his death in 1329, turned aside to fight the Moors and so had to give up their crusading quest. No doubt in any Iberian port it would have been possible to find the odd Scot. One, Thomas Blake, married a Spanish lady and made his way in the early days to America, where he spent twenty years in Mexico and Colombia. The Spaniards were still getting to know the New World. From their base in the conquered capital of the Aztecs, Mexico City, they sent out parties to make the first explorations of what was clearly a vast continent to the north. They set off in the confident expectation that untold riches would be there for the asking, as Hernan Cortes had found in Mexico and Francisco Pizarro in Peru. One such expedition was headed by Francisco Vasquez de Coronado in 1540, and Blake joined it. Its goal was the fabled Seven Cities of Cibola, with their gates of turquoise. Coronado's soldiers rode up through Arizona and New Mexico, Texas, Oklahoma and Kansas. They discovered the Grand Canyon, but otherwise just miserable Indian villages. Blake did not make his fortune, but saw sights no other Scot would see for a couple of centuries.

The nations of northern Europe followed Spain and Portugal slowly. It was hard to catch up with the head start they had won. They gained, or appeared to gain, fabulous wealth. And, whether in the East Indies or West Indies, they dug themselves into their possessions with enough military strength to repel rivals. It took more than a hundred years for these rivals to start competing in any serious fashion. The Dutch were the most successful, mainly in the Orient. After a couple of false starts, England established Jamestown in Virginia in 1607. France founded Quebec in Canada in 1609.

Scotland was already sending out individual trading ships to America, but the records have not survived to give us a complete picture of these efforts. In any event, the most important event in Scottish history during this period was the accession of King James VI to the throne of his English cousin, Elizabeth, after her death in 1603. He moved to London and left Edinburgh behind him, returning only once to the city of his birth before he died in 1625. This was the Union of the Crowns. While Scotland and England continued as separate kingdoms, they had one monarch. James VI and I, as he now was, wanted to bring the two countries still closer together and unite their Parliaments as well. But the Scots were too proud of their independence, and the English did not want them anyway because of their poverty. What the thwarted King James could do was promote joint expeditions overseas by Scots and Englishmen. This, he hoped, would make them feel no longer just Scottish or English, but British.

One opportunity lay close at hand over in Ireland, more especially in Ulster, which is actually visible across the narrow waters from the south-western coast of Scotland. Green and fertile Antrim looks inviting compared to wild and windswept Wigtownshire. The English had first attacked Ireland back in 1170, but during the Middle Ages, with help from the Scots under King Robert Bruce, the Irish managed to push the invaders back till they were confined to little more than the city of Dublin. Then, under Queen Elizabeth, there had been a serious English effort at complete conquest of Ireland. It just about succeeded, but at an enormous cost in lives and money.

This was the situation the Queen left to her cousin, James. He had to bring some stability to a situation of inherent instability, with an occupying army trying to hold down a hostile population. To James it seemed a problem that Ireland remained full of Irishmen. He considered both the Scots and the English to be more civilised peoples. It would help if they went to live among the Irish to set them a good example or, if they would not follow it, to push them off their lands. Ulster offered a convenient setting for this policy because the province's native nobility had just been forced into exile, in the Flight of the Earls in 1607. James handed their forfeited lands to loyal followers of his own, including many Scots gentlemen, who began to bring in the settlers to their so-called plantations.

Such was the origin of the population which went by the

unlovely name of Scotch-Irish when it later began to emigrate to America, where it was to play such a huge role in the development of the US. Though settlers from Scotland and England had arrived in Ulster in about equal numbers, somehow the province acquired more of a Scottish than an English character. It was, and remains, the chief centre of Presbyterianism in Ireland, and Presbyterianism is the established religion of Scotland. These Presbyterians not only fought with the native Roman Catholic population, but were also subjected to persecution by the English authorities in Dublin. The history of the Scotch-Irish is one of adversity, bloodshed and hardship, all overcome by the steadfast faith of the people. It gives the Northern Irish of today that indelible stubbornness which often exasperates others who have to deal with them.

Yet, while marked by their Scottish heritage, they have grown apart from their Scots kinsmen. When Presbyterianism is an established religion, as in Scotland, nothing could be more sedate and orderly; when it is put in a position of dissent, as in Ireland, it turns uncontrollably rebellious. This is the difference between the Scots of Scotland and the Scots of Ulster and, oddly, that difference came out at its clearest in America. When the moment arrived to take sides in 1776, the Scots of Scotland living in the Thirteen Colonies stayed by a great majority loyal to the British Crown. The Scots of Ulster, or Scotch-Irish, stood in the forefront of the American Revolution.

King James had had a hard enough time trying to promote a British identity in Ireland but at a longer distance, in North America, the task proved beyond him. During his reign his subjects founded three colonies on the eastern seaboard: Virginia in 1607; Massachusetts in 1620; and Nova Scotia in 1624. The first two were English and the third was Scottish. The first two survived and the third did not, though this could hardly be blamed on the Scots involved. As always in these early expeditions there was a problem of finance. James sought to solve the problem by selling land in Nova Scotia which had not yet been occupied, or even seen, and allowing the men who bought it to bear the title of Sir, for themselves and their male heirs, in all time coming. Many bought the titles, but few showed any desire to go and live across the Atlantic.

James turned for help to one of the Scots courtiers who had gone with him to London in 1603, Sir William Alexander of Menstrie, whom he would eventually make a peer as Earl of Stirling. Alexander had a son, also William, who was willing to lead an expedition to Nova Scotia. He made several attempts. Finally in 1629 he and his men succeeded not only in getting there but also in wintering at Port Royal (now Annapolis) on the Bay of Fundy. This was at or near an exposed French outpost which had been given up because England and France were now at war, through the foolishly aggressive policy of James's son and successor, Charles I. Conditions at Port Royal were crude, and the ferocity of the first Canadian winter came as a shock even to Scots used to being buffeted by the weather.

Yet the Scots hung on. Unlike in Virginia, which saw horrible massacres during these years, they befriended rather than fought the Native American nation of the area, the Micmacs, and purchased furs from them to ship home. The Scots did not suffer the internal religious wrangling of Massachusetts either. They remained a trading rather than farming settlement, living communally in a blockhouse rather than individually on plots of land round it. How all this might have developed we cannot know, because they were forced to abandon Port Royal after three years. The war between England and France came to an end in 1632, and as the price of peace the French insisted the Scottish colony had to go, even though Scotland took no part in the fighting. This was a penalty of having one king for two countries whose interests might differ. The Scots departed, but they left behind them the name of Nova Scotia, New Scotland, which has stuck ever since to the large peninsula at what is now the eastern extremity of Canada.

The Scots' efforts at colonisation might have continued, but the following period proved to be the most troubled in their national history. By 1640 they were at war with England, after an offensive by Charles I to get rid of Presbyterianism. The Covenanters, those who banded together to defend it, ruled Scotland for the next few years. Then the country was overrun by the armies of Oliver Cromwell. Independence was regained only in 1660, but under the rule of Charles II who embarked on the bloody persecution of Covenanters known grimly as the Killing Time. Not till the 1680s could Scotland summon up the energy or resources to turn outwards once again.

In that decade two new Scottish colonies were founded in America, both to some extent a result of religious persecution. One succeeded up to a point, but the other failed completely. The more successful was in East New Jersey, at that time a separate English colony. The man who organised it was Robert Barclay of Urie, a big landowner in Aberdeenshire. He had also joined the Quakers, a sect which, perhaps for its very gentleness, suffered excessively from the intolerance of the time. His friend William Penn was already establishing Pennsylvania. Barclay tried to emulate him on the tract of territory which runs down the western side of the Hudson Valley, for which he obtained a grant from the Crown. It is now an industrial desert, but in those days it was rich farmland, attractive to settlers who first made New Jersey the Garden State, with a reputation for producing beautiful fruit. In the event, only a few Quakers came over and Barclay sold off the land to other gentlemen from the north-east of Scotland. There was a question whether they should import slaves to work their estates. One of the Scots Quakers, George Keith, objected to this and wrote the first protest against slavery to be published on American soil. He persuaded the proprietors of East New Jersey to employ only free labour. Gradually they and their tenants became absorbed into the general population of the area as it was more densely settled. But the towns they founded, Elizabeth and Perth Amboy (the latter named after a Scottish nobleman, the Duke of Perth) are still there today.

The second Scottish colony of the 1680s was also founded on English territory, but at the other, southern end of the Atlantic seaboard. This area remained in dispute between England and Spain. In fact Spain still claimed the whole of North America, though without being able to make good its claim. All the same the Spaniards, from their base at St Augustine in Florida, had been able to keep the neighbouring region subdued, through the work of missions backed up by occasional military intervention. This fragile control now came under threat as the English inched down the coast. In 1670 they founded Charleston in South

Carolina. The Scottish colony was intended to take another step southwards – as well as solve the problem of what to do with Covenanters still fighting the royal government in Scotland. It seemed a good idea to ship them to America and let them fight the Spaniards instead. One of their leaders, Henry Erskine, Lord Cardross, was offered immunity from prosecution if he would head the expedition.

In 1683 Cardross set off with a couple of hundred men, some with their families. They founded a settlement called Stewart's Town at a fine natural harbour on Beaufort Island. Today it is a resort, but then it was the furthest outpost of a military frontier, which the Spanish authorities feared would serve also as a base for pirates to attack convoys carrying the precious metals of the New World back to their mother country. As in Nova Scotia, the settlers showed an uncanny knack for befriending the local tribes of Native Americans, some of which had risen up against Spanish domination. The Spaniards had no option but to act. Without warning, an expeditionary force appeared one day and overran Stewart's Town. Most of the Scots, unused to a sub-tropical climate, were sick and could put up no resistance. They were lucky to be allowed their escape to Charleston.

Scotland as an independent nation mounted one more major colonising effort, in 1698–1700. This was at Darien in the present republic of Panama, on the isthmus which joins the two Americas. In conception the plan looked brilliant. Here a great emporium was to be set up through which the commerce between the Atlantic and the Pacific Oceans would flow. The Scots, as a small nation, had no pretensions to bringing the region around it under their rule. They wished only to provide a place where all the world could come to trade in peace, and to cream off a little profit for themselves.

So brilliant was the Scots' scheme that it blinded them to some obvious problems. This period saw growing competition among the imperial powers, and Panama was a place of obvious strategic significance. It already belonged to the Spanish Empire, but the last thing other powers wanted in a time of tension was to see Spain upset by some madcap scheme of the Scots. One particular person who did not want to see that was

William of Orange, King of Scotland but also King of England, and counting English interests as of far greater importance to him: again the Scots suffered under the Union of the Crowns. Without English co-operation the colony stood little chance anyway, and William actually banned his English subjects from trading with it. When the Scots at Darien heard of this they just gave up, tired as they were of the non-stop rain, the pestilent conditions and the futility of the whole business. A second expedition fared no better. Spanish soldiers sent the would-be colonists on their way; most perished trying to get home. The cost to Scotland in lives and above all in money had been so enormous as to affect the destiny of the nation. Darien gave one of the main incentives for Scots to enter into a full incorporating Union, a Union of the Parliaments, with England in 1707.

Then a new era opened for Scotland in many respects, including relations with America. The previous English Empire became a British Empire. In the course of the eighteenth century it would grow into the world's biggest, and even survive the apparently catastrophic loss of the Thirteen Colonies in 1783. Before then, it had opened a field of enterprise to Scots such as they always wanted. Before they had been hampered in exploiting opportunities overseas by the smallness and weakness of their own country. Now that problem was solved: instead of facing constant obstruction from England, a much bigger and stronger country, Scots had its support. This proved to be the key which unlocked the world to them.

A prime purpose of the Scots on entering into the Union of 1707 was to increase their trade. Up to now they had prided themselves as a fighting race, who had maintained their independence against all comers for more than 2,000 years, according to national legends. But in modern Europe this was not quite such a point of pride as it once had been. Scots could see that similar small nations for which they had a fellow feeling – the Dutch or the Swiss – no longer relied on military prowess to maintain their independence. On the contrary, these had become peaceable, trading nations and were better off for it. At any rate, they had grown much richer than the Scots, who remained dirt-poor. The question arose of how to get in on expanding international commerce. Trade needed money, and Scots had none. Darien disposed of the idea that a beginner could simply set up in trade and wait for the profits to roll in. But in the British Empire the Scots had the next best thing to the free trade which was most suited to their interests. Oceans to the east and to the west now stood open to them, though they still thought the British Empire not free-trading enough: that would be a basic theme in the founding text of modern economics, *The Wealth of Nations*, published by Adam Smith from Kirkcaldy in 1776.

Smith learned all he knew about trade among the merchants of Glasgow, where he had been a student and professor early in his career. There the effects of greater trade on Scotland were most obvious. A seaborne traffic to the West Indies and North America had long flourished, often illicitly. From time to time, before the Union, the English had banned Scottish ships from colonial ports, but then Glaswegians just smuggled what they were not allowed to carry officially. This transatlantic trade had already grown so big by 1668 that the city fathers paid for a new deep harbour to be built at Port Glasgow down river on the Clyde.

A reason why this commerce flourished despite the obstructions was that, on the Great Circle, Glasgow lay nearer to, say, Virginia than any English port. A voyage from England lasted six weeks but from Scotland a ship could get there in a month – and therefore turn round twice in the normal sailing season. Scottish ships also passed through distant northern waters where they were less vulnerable to pirates or foreign navies. Virginia's major crop of tobacco had been coming to Glasgow since at least the 1640s. After 1707, it started coming in larger and larger volumes. Just before the American Revolution, Glasgow was the world's greatest emporium for the trade in tobacco. It landed more than any English port and it re-exported all over Europe, especially to France where a lucrative deal was struck with the officials of the royal monopoly. Little of the tobacco stayed in Glasgow, but enough to give Glaswegians a permanent addiction to the deadly weed.

Tobacco was the first big business in Scotland and it had crucial effects. It turned Glasgow, once a pretty little town girt with blossoming orchards, into a commercial port with enough capital to adjust rapidly to new activities as economic forces dictated.

This was exactly what happened after 1776, when the trade in tobacco was lost: the merchants built factories to manufacture cotton which they brought from India and later again from the US. The foundations for one of the world's great centres of industry in the nineteenth century were laid.

In America the Scottish success in this business also had its effects. Scots came late to Virginia and were obliged to make their way without the help of established English networks. For their voyages to be profitable, they needed cargoes outwards as well as homewards. They filled the hold with pots and pans, or cheap textiles and paper: just about anything that could be sold in the back country where luxuries were few. They set up stores and got to know the local farmers. Then they could also act as agents for their kinsmen in Glasgow. They were shrewd and struck deals: small growers found they could compete with the owners of big plantations in exporting their crops. The Scots readily extended credit. In fact, the huge amount owed them by 1776 was one incentive for the American Revolution. Scots acted as a catalyst for extending the area of cultivation and making Virginia, together with Maryland and the Carolinas, colonies with many prosperous independent farmers, not just a few wealthy gentlemen. This would have its political consequences.

The second new opportunity presented to Scots inside the British Empire was emigration. Though today we tend to think of Scotland as a classic land of emigration, like Ireland or Sicily, this did not really become true till the nineteenth century. For at least the first half of the eighteenth century, few Scots took up their new opportunity. They had long been a wandering race, and some of those who wandered did settle down elsewhere. But for most the purpose of wandering had been to make a fortune and return with enhanced status to the close-knit society of Scotland. This remained true even now that America was open to Scots. Of course a trickle of them emigrated for good, with no intention of ever coming home. But the traders in the back country, and even more those among them who grew rich enough to buy a plantation, regarded themselves as temporary residents. They did not turn into Americans but remained Scots. This would mark them out when the Revolution came.

The numbers of Scots in America was still quite small till after the Seven Years War (known in the US as the French and Indian War), which ended with the Treaty of Paris in 1763. It represented a triumph for Britain, confirming the conquest of Canada and much of India and for the first time establishing an ascendancy as a global power over France. This may have made emigration to America more attractive, because the British army could better protect settlers on the frontier: up till then the French in Canada had often incited Native American nations to attack remote outposts. But probably more important causes of emigration in this period were to be found in the growing population and general social progress at home in Britain. These causes began to exert pressure especially on the peripheral regions, on the Highlands of Scotland and on Ireland. A growing population could not be supported by the limited area of fertile land amid the moors and the mountains. Better health, better transport, better awareness of the outside world meant the population was readier to try its chances somewhere else.

In the Scottish Highlands there was the special problem that the old structure of clans and chieftains had finally been shattered by the failure of the Jacobite rebellion of 1745, and the British army's defeat of the heroic Gaels at Culloden. The government in London then set about systematically removing what it identified as the causes of the rebellion, which meant ultimately changing Highland society from a feudal into a commercial one. Soon the chieftains who survived, after proofs of their loyalty, were vaunting themselves not on the numbers of warriors they could summon for battle with the fiery cross but on the income they could accumulate from their tenants' rents. With a growing population, the rents rapidly rose and the people began to think of moving rather than pay them.

We have graphic testimony to this turning point in Highland history from the accounts of their journey to the region in 1773 by Dr Samuel Johnson, the gruff, bear-like compiler of the first English dictionary, and his faithful Scottish companion, James Boswell. Johnson took pleasure in showing himself blatantly anti-Scottish; this was to him a land of barbarism. Boswell made excuses for it. At their first meeting in London he had admitted he was a Scot but said, 'I cannot help it.' The doctor had replied, 'That, Sir, is what I find a great many of your countrymen cannot help.' All the same he managed to persuade Johnson to embark on a journey northwards not only to Edinburgh, centre of the Scottish Enlightenment, but also out to the remote Highlands and Islands, where travelling was difficult and comforts were few. During their visit to Skye, Boswell confided this entry to his journal:

> In the evening the company danced as usual. We performed, with much activity, a dance which, I suppose, the emigration from Skye has occasioned. They call it *America*. Each of the couples, after the common involutions and evolutions, successively whirls round in a circle, till all are in motion; and the dance seems intended to show how emigration catches, till a whole neighbourhood is set afloat.

Dr Johnson, not as boorish a man as he made out, enquired with care why the people should want to emigrate, something he regarded as by nature an unpleasant experience. And he learned this of recent Highland history:

> Whole neighbourhoods formed parties for removal; so that their departure from their native country is no longer exile. He that goes thus accompanied, carries with him all that makes life pleasant. He sits down in a better climate, surrounded by his kindred and his friends; they carry with them their language, their opinions, their popular songs, and hereditary merriment: they change nothing but the place of their abode.

That seems to be an accurate report about the motives of many emigrants. If a way of life came under pressure from hostile social and economic forces, then one plausible answer – rather than change the way of life – was to remove it to a place where those forces would no longer operate. In other words, if there was a shortage of land on Skye, then the people might go to North Carolina, for example, where land was unlimited, and take their way of life with them.

As it happened, that was precisely the path shortly to be chosen by two of Johnson and Boswell's hosts on Skye. Alan Macdonald of Kingsburgh was a leading member of his clan who farmed on one of the island's outer peninsulas. His wife Flora Macdonald was famous as a Jacobite heroine because of the help she had given to Bonnie Prince Charlie when he was on the run after Culloden. To elude his pursuers, he crossed disguised as her female servant, under the name of Betty Burke, from North Uist to Skye: the adventure gave rise to the song, 'Speed, Bonnie Boat'. But celebrity was no guarantee of prosperity. Along with everybody else on the island, Alan and Flora Macdonald now felt the pinch. Not long after the visit by Johnson and Boswell they and a large number of their clansmen emigrated to the country on the Cape Fear River round a township by the name of Cross Creek, later known as Fayetteville. They exchanged a rocky terrain and a cool climate for fertile flatlands which they must have found unpleasantly hot in summer. But they had no doubt in their minds that conditions would be easier here, and they settled down to recreate the life of their clan. We shall see in the next chapter what happened to them.

In Ulster, meanwhile, many of the same hostile social and economic forces were at work as in the Scottish Highlands. They were if anything made worse by the disabilities under which the Presbyterians and other Protestant dissenters suffered. They were not as downtrodden as the Roman Catholic Irish, but still the government took the absurd view that they were a danger. They were reckoned a danger in particular to the established Anglicanism, as represented by the Church of Ireland, perhaps because the country actually contained more Presbyterians than Anglicans. In any event the descendants of the original Scots immigrants were excluded from any civil office and from higher education – though this had the advantage that they continued to go to university in Scotland.

While the Irish Presbyterians had proved their loyalty over and over again during the various political and religious upheavals in the British Isles around the turn of the eighteenth century, they could still see little prospect of decisive improvement in their condition. So more and more of them opted to go to America and seek the freedom denied them at home. By this time there was not much room for them in the established colonies of Virginia or New England. Generally, after landing at somewhere like Philadelphia, they made their way through the passes of the mountains to the unsettled Ohio and Tennessee Valleys beyond. After 1763 this became illegal, because the British authorities did not want colonists going to regions where they might come into conflict with the Native Americans, and have to be rescued at great expense and danger by the army of King George III, always with the chance of a general war breaking out in consequence. The Ulstermen or Scotch-Irish completely ignored this prohibition. They expected nothing of any government. They were ready to defend themselves. They asked only to be left alone. This spirit of independence meant they were ready for the Revolution when it came.

It is a reasonable estimate that between 1763 and 1776 more than 50,000 people of Scottish blood, from both Scotland and Ulster, crossed the Atlantic Ocean to settle permanently in the Thirteen Colonies. More would no doubt have followed if peace between Britain and America had been maintained. Despite what can plausibly be called this mass emigration, Scots remained fairly thinly scattered in the New World. There were a few places, mentioned above, where a concentration of settlement took place. But otherwise the Scots were dispersed like other groups from the Old World – Germans, Dutch, French, Swiss and so on – among a population overwhelmingly English in origin. This would make a difference during the coming struggle for independence. For now, the Scots could not be said to have had much impact on America. That would soon change.

2

REVOLUTIONARIES

T he relationship between an old country and a new country, which is also a relationship between a small country and a big country, has to be a complicated one when it comes down to the events of real life. So it is in the case of the American Revolution and the part that Scots took in it, usually by opposing it. Modern Americans often appear surprised at this, as do modern Scots. Today the democratic values of Scotland and the US seem close and intertwined to such an extent that it may be hard to imagine how the two nations could ever have regarded themselves as enemies in a struggle over the fundamental principles on which society is founded. Yet that is how things were back in 1776, and we should try to understand why.

Let us start with a single example. On 4 July 1776, William Panton was a merchant in Savannah, Georgia, who had done well since arriving there from Aberdeenshire a decade before. As one of a farmer's seven children, he could never have expected so much at home. He ran a flourishing trade to Britain and owned extensive properties. He was a respected citizen, and there is no reason to suppose he had anything but friendly relations with his American neighbours. As the transatlantic crisis built up, he supported their point of view. On 13 June 1775, a public meeting had been held in Savannah against the efforts of the Parliament at Westminster to raise tax in America. Panton went along and voted for the protest, which the meeting passed. At that stage, Savannahians still blamed all the trouble on English politicians rather than on King George III himself. So they also addressed a petition to their sovereign. It was to be signed by every adult male in the colony, which had a population of just a few thousand. Such a demonstration of unanimity, the meeting hoped, would help both the British and the Americans to see the need for compromise. But events moved too fast for that. Panton was at last forced to choose sides. Though he understood American grievances, he had to consider his own position. Revolutions overthrow the social order and seldom benefit rich men. His riches arose from the existence of the British Empire. He stayed loyal to the Crown.

The case for loyalty seemed just as clear-cut to Scots much poorer than Panton. Up at Cross Creek in North Carolina, the Highlanders who settled along with Alan and Flora Macdonald were cultivating their first crops, or even still clearing the forest, when the Revolution broke out. They had come from Skye with high hopes just a year or two before, looking forward to recreating the life of their clan and spending the rest of their days in America. These clansmen were of Jacobite stock, rebels or sons of rebels against the succession of King George's Hanoverian dynasty and in favour of restoring the Stewarts, the ancient royal house of Scotland. Yet now they had no doubt where their loyalties lay. Alan Macdonald sent round the fiery cross, just as he would have done at home in the Highlands to call out his men for the king. Flora Macdonald, seated on a white horse, addressed them in eloquent Gaelic before they marched down to Wilmington, capital of the colony. There, patriots had taken over and forced the royal governor to seek refuge on a ship in the Cape Fear River. The Highlanders were to attack them from the rear and restore legitimate authority in North Carolina. They set off wearing their tartans and playing their bagpipes, their claymores at their sides. On the morning of 18 February 1776, they approached the bridge which crossed Moore's Creek on the trail to the coast. The patriots were waiting. They had dug trenches on the further side of the bridge, removed its cross-planks and greased the supports. When the Highlanders attempted a charge across it, they slipped into the water or were shot down if they did manage to get over. Their expedition in the name of the king came to a sorry end.

But what interest did these Highlanders, many of them unable even to speak English, have in the integrity of the British Empire? Some were indeed indifferent to it, and only followed the call of their clan. Once captured, if they would promise not to take up arms again, they were allowed to return and live quietly on their farms at Cross Creek, where their descendants often remain today. Yet for others the call of the clan was the most important thing in their lives. It had been so in Scotland and it was still so in America. They belonged to a hierarchical society where it was automatic for a man to defer to his chief – who in turn deferred to the paramount chief, the king. If men did not follow these calls, society would collapse. On such reasoning, American revolutionaries were out to destroy society, and to secure victory would have to destroy the sort of society in which the Highlanders wished to live. So these remained loyal. Alan and Flora Macdonald, with others, returned to Skye rather than stay in revolutionary America.

The attitude of Scots in America reflected the attitude of their countrymen at home. Nobody was more hawkish than the Scots of Scotland in calling for the firmest possible military action against the Americans, who were to be forced back into their true allegiance at all costs. We can detect two obvious motives for this hard line. One was that the Scots themselves, or rather the Jacobites, had during the eighteenth century staged two uprisings against the British state, in 1715 and 1745 – and much good it had done them. Both were crushed, leaving behind huge problems which loyal Scots had to struggle to solve. After 1745 they had just escaped seeing their cherished national institutions – Church, law and universities, all guaranteed under the Union of 1707 – taken away from them by vengeful Englishmen. So there was no mileage for the Scots in siding with revolt in another part of the British Empire. The second motive lay in the benefits which the Empire was bringing the Scots. Their trade had expanded, and the economy of their country was moving forward. They thought that much of the improvement depended on the imperial connection. Loud commitment to this connection could bring its own rewards if, as most Scots expected, the Americans were soon defeated.

Underneath these calculations, we might also detect a deeper instinct at work. Scotland was an old country, which maintained its traditional ways of life by conservative defence of them: revolution could do no good, but on the contrary was likely to wreak harm. By contrast America was a new country, where ways of life were still being formed, and had no need to be bound by the interests of an imperial government 3,000 miles away: some kind of revolution, whether violent or peaceful, would be inevitable in the end. Again, Scotland was a small country, not in command of its own destiny, which had to accommodate itself as best it could to powerful forces in the world around it. By contrast America was a big country, with as yet just a scattered population, to be sure, even so one which the British could not control when challenged; and some sense of the vastness of the continent was already drawing that population westwards into the wilderness, where it could only be left to rule itself.

Another interesting comparison is between the Scots of Scotland and the Scots of Ulster. The Scots of Scotland had everything to lose by siding with the Americans; the Scots of Ulster had nothing to lose. To them, England's difficulty was Ireland's opportunity. They found their opportunity as the transatlantic conflict turned into a general European war, after France, Spain and Holland entered on the American side. British resources became overstretched and a militia was raised for defence against possible attacks on the homeland from hostile fleets. Ulstermen joined up with enthusiasm in these companies of Volunteers – but, once organised and armed, they presented a list of political demands to the Government in London. It could not afford to risk an Irish rising as well. So, for a few years, Ireland won more freedom under the Crown.

The same spirit of independence was at work among the Ulstermen's kith and kin on the other side of the ocean. To begin with, the war did not affect them much, because most lived in the back country far from where hostilities first broke out in New England. There the two sides fought themselves to a standstill in the initial stage of the conflict. The British occupied New York and Philadelphia but could not bring the rebellion to an end anywhere else. In 1780, they tried a new strategy, directed at the southern colonies, which they reckoned to be more loyal, not least because that was where most Scots in America lived. They captured Charleston and called on colonists to return to their allegiance. The response to this was gratifying: enough Carolinians and Georgians flocked to the royal colours for a militia to be formed and for an attack to be planned on Virginia, the most populous colony and home of leading revolutionaries. These forces were placed under British commanders, one of them a Scotsman, Patrick Ferguson.

Ferguson led his troops inland. By October 1780 he reached King's Mountain on the border between North and South Carolina. He knew that the Scotch-Irish settled beyond in the Appalachian valleys were, now war had come home to them, organising resistance. He meant to overawe them and block any move by their forces into the low country. But 3,000 of them came to meet him. While he was camped on the mountain, they surrounded him and attacked. Ferguson's militiamen were out-numbered but they fought gallantly, while he galloped back and forth across the summit conspicuous in a tartan shirt and blowing a silver whistle to direct them amid the din of battle. Suddenly he was hit by a bullet and dragged along the ground with a foot caught in his stirrup, till halted and propped against a tree, where he died. His terrified and disordered soldiers gave up at once. But the raging rebels ran amok and massacred a quarter of them as they tried to surrender. Many of these were doubtless loyal Scots, falling to the blades and bullets of Scotch-Irish patriots. Nothing brings out the contrast between them so clearly.

So deep was the contrast that we can even seek its roots in philosophy. It had been about 1740, while as yet British people knew nothing and cared less what Americans thought or wanted, that Francis Hutcheson, professor of moral philosophy at Glasgow, tackled the question in one of his books 'when it is that colonies may turn independent'. Hutcheson was a Presbyterian Ulsterman who, like many of his community, had crossed to Scotland for his higher education. In adult life he returned to become a popular teacher, not least because he switched from lecturing in Latin to lecturing in English. Hutcheson's answer to his question about the colonies hinged on misgovernment by the mother country, deriving from the venerable Calvinist doctrine of a right to resist tyrannical rulers. If administration was severe or legislation oppressive, or even if a colony felt ready for self-sufficiency, then it might in justice break away.

When Hutcheson made the point he was not preaching rebellion, something which would have landed him in trouble with the academic authorities; he had problems enough with his philosophical views. He was preaching liberalism, and this made him stand out in the Scotland, indeed in the Europe, of his time. He advocated liberty in every sphere of life because it would make people happy. It would not dissipate into selfishness because free people could use their reason for moral purposes and make other people happy too. Just as they could tell right from wrong among the facts in the world about them, so they could tell right from wrong in their behaviour. That was why God had given them their reason: God's wisdom and goodness guaranteed their virtue. As a rule of conduct Hutcheson invented a phrase which became famous in Victorian times: 'Action is best, which produces the greatest happiness of the greatest number.' It was not a rule which could easily be used to justify British efforts to suppress the American Revolution.

Hutcheson was dead by the time the Revolution came and clearly, given the Scottish hostility to it, he had not been able to exert much influence on opinion in his adopted country. But one blot on the picture of seamless loyalty among the Scots of Scotland was that the nation's two greatest minds, David Hume the philosopher and Adam Smith the founder of economics, believed it was wrong to use force against the colonists. Both knew Hutcheson's writings, and Smith had been one of his students.

Hume died in 1776, while the transatlantic conflict was still unfolding, but before his death he said: 'I am American in my principles, and wish we would let them alone to govern or mis-govern themselves as they think proper.' He had always dis-liked empires and imperialism. He was somewhat anti-English, and not only because from the time he had spent in London he knew that Scots in England could still be targets of abuse: he wrote of 'the barbarians who live by the banks of the Thames'. He also believed the English had been corrupted by their acquisition of an empire. He thought their vaunted ancient constitution was a sham. It kept up a pretence of rule by the king, yet to all intents and purposes England had turned into a republic where power depended on money, and the most money lay at the disposal of imperial interests, financiers in London who ran the trade to America and to other colonies. They veiled their power by whipping up nationalism in the masses and browbeating any opposition. They were destroying culture and liberty.

Like most educated men of his time, Hume drew for his own political philosophy on the literature of the ancient world. Rome had gone through the same experience of empire. The Roman virtues of the original republic were undermined by acquisition of an empire, till this too collapsed. History now repeated itself. Empires were bad for people. From this we see that Hume was not a revolutionary in politics but, on the contrary, rather conservative. He preferred systems of politics that preserved culture and liberty. He was, however, a revolutionary of the mind: his preference was formed from basic questions he posed about the way the human mind works. He argued that our ideas originate from repeated association of one event with another – when the sun rises, we sense light and heat – not from any perception of objective truth. From that particular association, for example, it had once been taken as objective truth that the sun goes round the earth, and men were burned at the stake for denying it; now we know that the earth goes round the sun. We rely on habits and conventions of thinking because in the end we cannot reach any certain knowledge of reality. With his argument, Hume heaved a huge rock into the tranquil pool of western philosophy, where it had hardly ever been doubted that in principle the mind can see truth: the question was how, not if. In the practical politics of the immediate crisis in 1776, Hume concluded that it would be futile for the British to impose their ideas of sovereignty on the Americans. They had their own ideas which, given that they were the ones who had to form a new society on the other side of the ocean, were likely to prevail.

On 4 July 1776, Smith was meanwhile finishing off his great work, *The Wealth of Nations*. He hauled it back from the printers so he could add his comments about the hottest issue of the moment. They were to the effect that he had always known this trouble would happen. Britain imposed such unjust commercial rules on the Americans – banning their manufactures, forcing them to trade with the mother country – that they were bound to react. The best thing would be independence for the colonies. Then the two sides could develop relations to their mutual benefit in freedom and peace.

As a pupil of Hutcheson, Adam Smith had shown his master's influence in his first book, *A Theory of Moral Sentiments* (1759), yet he also went beyond it. Hutcheson said morality was inborn, but Smith thought civility and compassion might not be enough when in our relations with others we had to deal with the darker side of human nature. In our social life we also required tougher qualities, the ability to discipline, restrain, moralise and rebuke. Smith was working his way towards an idea of moral sense more basic and instinctual, and less abstract, than Hutcheson's. Smith found it in what he called sympathy, a natural sense of identification with others. When we see them suffer, we feel sorry for them. When we see them happy, it gladdens us. To belong to society is to experience others' joy and sorrow, pleasure and pain. In later writings Smith extended his analysis to the more practical spheres of life. In politics, he decided there was no need for heavy-handed intervention by government if, given a basic framework of the rule of law, the moral sentiments of citizens made them restrain their fellows from hurting or disturbing the happiness of one another. The same argument applied to economics, as set out in *The Wealth of Nations*: if governments did not interfere, an 'unseen hand' would lead those engaged in economic activity to act for their mutual benefit. But British policy in America was contrary to all this.

Scotland is a disputatious nation and, famous as Hume and Smith became on both sides of the Atlantic Ocean, their brother Scots by no means always agreed with them. They objected especially to Hume and the fact that his philosophy made him not just a sceptic but also an atheist, refusing to accept revealed truth. Much of Scottish intellectual activity over the next century was taken up with finding answers to Hume. Those seeking the answers tried to restore a basis for human knowledge through human experience, experience of a material universe which in their view was more powerful than all the axioms of philosophy: this evidence of the senses could not be reasoned away because it was itself the starting point of reason, given to us by God. The leader of this school of thinking was Thomas Reid, who succeeded Smith in the chair of moral philosophy at Glasgow in 1764 and later moved to Aberdeen. He wrote: 'The evidence of sense, the evidence of memory, and the evidence of the necessary relations of things, are all distinct . . . To reason against any of these kinds of evidence is absurd . . . They are first principles, and as such fall not within the province of reason, but of common sense.' The last phrase stuck. The teachings of these Scots became known as the philosophy of Common Sense: it was the real basis of the Scottish Enlightenment. It had a remarkable impact in America too, as the revolutionaries set out to found their republic on enlightened principles.

This was why the few American Scots who did support the Revolution, though they formed a minority of a minority in the Thirteen Colonies, proved so important. They were channels into America of Scottish thinking. Two of the fifty-six men who signed the Declaration of Independence in Philadelphia on 4 July 1776 had been born in Scotland. What were they doing there and what did they want to achieve?

John Witherspoon had arrived as a delegate of New Jersey. He was the sole ordained clergyman to sign. As president of the College of New Jersey (later Princeton), he had become a successful and respected man with, it might have been thought, a big stake in the existing order of things. The reasons for his personal rebellion have to be traced back to his roots in Scotland. He was born not far from Edinburgh, but after his education at its university he spent most of his Scottish career at the village of Beith in Ayrshire. It lay in old Covenanting country which, a century before, had also resisted King Charles II's persecution of Presbyterians. Though this region of the West of Scotland had long been at peace, that spirit still survived. Christianity was simple to the point of being stark: the people came to a bare church to hear their preacher and, after singing a psalm or two, went home again, fortified only by the word of God. There were no raiments or rituals to distract their minds from that. They might take Communion once a year. When they died, they were shoved in the earth without ceremony. Their preacher told them that most of them were damned.

The beetle-browed Witherspoon's loyalty to this old-time religion aroused much popular admiration at a time when the Church of Scotland had otherwise turned more refined and gentlemanly under the impact of enlightened ideas. He was a fine preacher, he wielded a sharp pen and he did not compromise. He published satires of his backsliding brethren and their efforts, as he saw it, to subject the Kirk to a polite elite. For the public at large, he wrote a tract against the theatre, condemning the passions it aroused as hostile to religion. Eventually he was called to a new parish at Paisley, a growing industrial town, where under him the faith flourished amid much ungodliness. There he received the invitation to the vacant presidency of Princeton, a college which trained Presbyterian clergy for the Thirteen Colonies. It came as a surprise to him, and he was probably not even aware that his reputation reached across the ocean. Nor did he have any obvious reason to abandon his established if controversial position in Scottish society, especially as his wife feared America would be too uncivilised. Yet he was never a man to shirk a challenge. In 1768, he left Scotland for ever.

America enthralled him. When he looked back to Scotland, he remembered how he had been forced to wage a constant and often losing battle against efforts to subvert true religion. In an old country, there were too many vested interests corrupted by worldliness. But here in the New World a society was being built afresh. It filled him with hope that this society could be so imbued with Christian virtue that it would never be corrupted. That was work he set about at Princeton in training his students for leadership. For instance, one innovation he brought with him from Scotland was to set up debating societies where students 'may learn, by early habit, presence of mind and proper pronunciation and gesture in public speaking'. As for their formal education, he gave them among other things a thorough grounding in the Scottish philosophers, including Smith and Hume, though he disapproved of the latter. Still, Witherspoon thought the best way to set about defeating objectionable arguments was to gain an understanding of them, so he took care to introduce his students to ideas he himself did not agree with. In this way his influence extended far beyond his own views and led in directions he could not foresee.

Witherspoon struck a deep chord among Americans who felt with him that they were an elect people called by God to build the City on the Hill. In this inspiring environment, Witherspoon concluded that a British Government trying to control and subdue the colonists was another corrupting influence stretching out its tentacles across the Atlantic. He espoused the American cause with a whole heart. His ardour and eloquence were a great asset to it. He recalled how, in Scottish history, allegiance to a king was never taken for granted: it had to be earned by good and just government, for lack of which the king might be deposed. That was why he came to the Continental Congress at Philadelphia in 1776. He gave it, in uncertain and dangerous times, the revivalist fervour it needed. That kind of fervour persists as an element in American society to this day.

The second born Scot to sign the Declaration of Independence was of a different stamp. James Wilson represented another American prototype, the smart lawyer, precise, tight-lipped and bespectacled but doing well out of life, sometimes none too scrupulous in his dealings, yet with a sharp eye for how the mechanisms of a well-ordered society can be made to work. He had been born the son of a farmer in Fife and educated at the universities of St Andrews and Glasgow, before setting off at once to seek his fortune in America. In 1765 he disembarked in Philadelphia and first earned a living as tutor at the city's college (later the University of Pennsylvania). Then he studied for the bar, set up a practice and waxed fat on speculations in land. Within ten years he was rich enough to be dabbling in politics, and in 1776 came to the Continental Congress as a delegate of Pennsylvania.

From the outset, Wilson was outspoken in advocating

American rights, though he showed none of the rancorous hyperbole of certain others in the Congress. He still set great store by the connection with the mother country, and in this did not differ from other Scots in the colonies. But he thought, in his lawyer's way, that this connection imposed obligations on both sides. The British Government, he insisted, must allow the same freedoms to the peoples of all its dominions – and it was treating America unfairly. These sentiments made him a moderate, perhaps none too popular among the rest of the delegates. The difficulty was solved for him as it became clear that the British were not prepared to accept the principle he had set out for their dealings with Americans. Wilson drifted towards the more radical element in the Congress. And so he came to sign the Declaration of Independence.

Wilson played a worthy part, like the rest of the nineteen delegates who hailed from Scotland and Ulster or had ancestors there. Scotch-Irish outnumbered native Scots: Matthew Thornton from New Hampshire, Thomas McKean from Delaware, James Smith and George Taylor from Pennsylvania, the last having sold himself as an indentured servant to pay his passage from Ireland but now helping to decide the fate of his new country. There were descendants of previous Scottish immigrants: Thomas Hooper of North Carolina, whose father had settled in Boston, and wealthy Philip Livingston, of a family which had gone a century before to the upper Hudson Valley, where they made money from trading in furs and intermarried with earlier Dutch landowners. Scots blood, which he does not seem to have been proud of, also ran in the veins of a Virginian delegate, Thomas Jefferson: his mother, Jane Randolph, claimed descent from Thomas Randolph, Earl of Moray in the time of King Robert Bruce.

Jefferson was the author of the Declaration of Independence, though the draft he put to the delegates did not pass unscathed. Into it he wrote an insulting mention of 'Scotch and foreign mercenaries' sent by King George III to coerce the colonies, but the others made him take it out. If proud of his descent, he did not at all regard himself as a Scot, and would have been annoyed to be described as such when he knew that most Scots opposed the revolutionaries. More important was that the future president had received a Scottish education from William Small, his tutor at William and Mary College; Jefferson later said it 'fixed the destinies of my life'. Small was a graduate of Marischal College, Aberdeen, the most progressive of the Scottish universities. To students from a range of backgrounds, some very poor, it gave a broad general education, not just one in classical languages, as in England. The focus lay in moral philosophy. Small taught this philosophy at William and Mary too. So when Jefferson included 'the pursuit of happiness' among the rights of man in the Declaration of Independence, he was probably making a reference to Hutcheson. And when Jefferson wrote, 'we hold these truths to be self-evident', he was probably making a reference to Reid.

Except for Jefferson it was, of all the delegates at the Continental Congress, Wilson who would have the biggest influence on the future of America. But he showed his true mettle after 1776. The sequence of events in the dozen years from the Declaration of Independence to the framing of the Constitution in 1787–8 seems with hindsight so logical that it is hard now to appreciate how few of the Founding Fathers could follow that logic then. Wilson saw that Americans had in effect committed themselves not just to breaking the link with Britain but to creating a new nation. He understood that it would not do for the Thirteen Colonies to act as if they were individually independent. They accepted loose Articles of Confederation but, when the war with Britain ended in 1783, it was already clear that such a vague arrangement for limited common action could not offer a solution to the daunting political and economic problems by which the Americans, to their dismay, found themselves at once beset. A closer union was needed but, as the Constitutional Convention gathered in 1787, again in Philadelphia, nobody could be sure a closer union would be achieved.

For the success of that Convention, Wilson can claim a huge share of credit. Jefferson had meanwhile gone to be the American ambassador to France and, somewhat unexpectedly, it was now Wilson who stood out for his political knowledge and wisdom. He stressed that the foundation of a new form of government, the fount of authority for Constitution, President and

Congress, had to be 'the people of the United States'. He advocated a single executive in the presidential office. He urged that equal representation should rest not on parity of the states but on the size of their population (a Congress with two chambers embodied both ideas). Above all, he conceived of the Supreme Court as a central element of the Constitution, placing it in a more powerful position than any court in the world even today, let alone in the eighteenth century. Perhaps the nearest equivalent then was the Court of Session, the highest civil court in Scotland. After the Union of 1707, that court took over a general guardianship of Scots law, adapting it to changing needs while preserving its basic values. It was still not superior to the British Parliament in London, and could not strike down Scottish legislation, though there was little enough of that. In other words, separation of powers existed in practice rather than principle, and was not guaranteed. Wilson proposed to the Philadelphia Convention to make the separation of powers formal and explicit, so that the independence of the judiciary from the legislature and the executive would be absolute, and the rule of law in the new nation unshakeable.

Wilson had firm ideas but, being a lawyer, accepted sound compromise with his colleagues in adjustment of the different states' genuine interests. Nobody was more active in seeking compromise, for he spoke on the floor of the convention more than anyone else. Even so, the deal which at last came through the long and wearisome negotiations, preserving unitary and democratic elements which had at first shocked many Americans, was in essence Wilson's. His battle was not finished. He had to exert himself all over again to persuade his own Pennsylvania to ratify the result: without the Keystone State a union of the rest would scarcely have been possible. He then sat for eight formative years as an inaugural Justice of the Supreme Court, though when he died in 1797 few Americans realised what they owed him. He was a technician rather than a leader like George Washington or Thomas Jefferson. Still, history has granted Wilson his due as the man who did most to give the young Republic what made it unique, its Constitution.

Even so, Wilson's efforts might have gone for nothing without powerful support. Two groups of wealthy men in the independent colonies dominated their politics, the merchants of New England and more especially the planters of Virginia. It was among the latter that Wilson found his crucial ally, James Madison. He was a youngster in the revolutionary generation, aged only 25 at the time of the Declaration of Independence, but he had inherited a high place in colonial society. His was one of the foremost Virginian families, living in splendour at Montpelier. They had not a drop of Scots blood in their veins, yet Madison, like Jefferson, shows how Scottish influence in America might depend not on genes but on force of ideas. Wilson, the practical native Scot, brought his lawyer's industry and expertise to the task of constructing a workable political mechanism; Madison, imbued with Scottish ideas, was to provide a convincing philosophical framework for the mechanism and to set it on a firm foundation by rallying the Virginians to it.

How had Madison absorbed these ideas? The short answer is through Witherspoon. Most sons of the slave-owning Episcopalian gentry of Virginia were sent to study at William and Mary but the precocious Madison had heard of Witherspoon and wanted to be taught by him. So in 1769 he opted to go to the College of New Jersey instead. He and Aaron Burr, one day to be US vice-president, were Witherspoon's favourites in their class. He did whatever he could to bring them on. They were the orna-ments of their debating society, soon well-versed in political debate. And through Witherspoon's teaching Madison found a great affinity to Hume. Whatever his views on religion, the Scot was a most attractive thinker, free of crude prejudice, charming and humorous, yet with a deadly intellectual style which left his opponents looking foolish more than anything else. This was the distinguished public persona that the bright but shy boy from the Virginian plantation decided to adopt.

It served Madison well at the Philadelphia Convention in 1787. In an essay, 'The Idea of a Perfect Commonwealth', Hume had tried to work out how the process of imperial growth and expansion could be stopped from turning into corruption and decay. A basic problem with both the British and Roman Empires had been that they were centralised. Power rested with governing cliques in the imperial capitals. Still, if power could be dispersed, into what Hume called an 'extended republic', there was hope yet. He wrote: 'In a large government which is modelled with masterly skill, there is compass and room enough to refine the democracy.' This democracy had to be refined because 'the people as a body are unfit for government', too easily swayed by their emotions and prejudices. But in a decentralised system, 'when dispersed in small bodies,' as Hume put it, 'they are more susceptible both to reason and order; the force of popular currents and tides is, in great measure, broken'. The governing cliques then have to direct their energies to co-ordinating the different parts of the whole, rather than conspiring to subvert it or control it. In Hume's words, 'the parts are so distant and remote, that it is very difficult, either by intrigue, prejudice, or passion, to hurry them into any measures against the public interest.' Madison thought Hume's words fitted the American situation. The 'small bodies' were the individual colonies or states, and Hume had suggested how they could be welded into one political system that would remain stable if it gave scope to expression of their individual interests. By the time the Convention opened, Madison had already set out how all this might be applied to America in his 'Notes on the Confederacy'.

Once the framers of the Constitution had completed their work, Madison defended its principles in the *Federalist Papers*. This classic of political literature is remarkable for the way it conducts at the highest intellectual level a debate intended to exert direct effect on public opinion: a pity it is not more of a model for modern times. In the tenth number of the series, Madison turned to the concept of the extended republic, showing that this could be realised in America by the separation of powers among executive, legislature and judiciary, by careful limitation of federal power as against the states, by deference to the disparate interests of jealous ex-colonies strung out over 2,000 miles of Atlantic seaboard. Historians have quipped that the real author of the tenth *Federalist Paper* was Hume. Here, certainly, Madison clothes himself in the sceptical philosopher's garb and remarks, as Hume might have done while passing the claret over dinner in Edinburgh, 'If men were angels, there would be no need of government.'

39

Once approved by the Convention, the Constitution had to be ratified by the legislatures of the states. It had some close shaves there, but in 1789 the new Republic was launched and the clockwork mechanism of its procedures set running. Through the genius of the Founding Fathers, Scottish fears about the effect of revolution on this society – that it would descend into chaos and mayhem – had been demonstrated as unfounded. America was indeed a revolutionary society in the sense that no society like it existed in the entire world. It was destined to develop into a powerful nation but it had the opportunity, before matters advanced too far, of shaping and determining its future – so different from any of the European nations, with the burden of their centuries of history.

It was Scottish philosophy that showed the Founding Fathers, themselves bewigged paragons of prudence, how this development could be held within bounds. The strong moral sense which pervaded and modified their revolutionary politics is the clear sign of a Scottish presence. If an upheaval was needed to achieve independence, they could then take immediate refuge in the most cautious revolutionary position available. Unlike the French Revolution which erupted in that same year of 1789, and did descend into chaos and mayhem, the American Revolution brought order and liberty. Americans decided one revolution was enough. A stable system had to be the first call on their energies afterwards, before anyone got round to the perfection of humanity, that sure project for bringing out the worst in us.

Estimates from the returns of the first US census in 1790 yield the result that about one in fifteen out of more than two million citizens of the infant Republic were Scots. Almost certainly that was a smaller proportion than in the Thirteen Colonies in 1776. Emigration from Scotland to America had been banned during the war, and many Scots already settled there fled. In Virginia the Scottish traders were tarred and feathered by their indignant neighbours. Georgia excluded all Scots from its territory, and confiscated the property of any who owned it. Where there had been enough Scots living in these southern colonies to organise loyal support for Britain, they had been beaten, as at Moore's

Creek Bridge and King's Mountain. Some, like Alan and Flora MacDonald, returned to Scotland, but others had nothing much to return to and, if they had lost everything, could anyway not afford the transatlantic passage. So an exodus of Scots took place to other regions of the Americas: the West Indies, Nova Scotia and Upper Canada, today Ontario, where many soldiers of the Highland regiments which fought in the war were given grants of land if they wanted to stay and try their luck in the New World.

As Adam Smith predicted, trade between Britain and America afterwards flourished even though the political connection between them was ended. Americans could now, of course, carry on commerce with any country they liked, but in practice the British long remained their principal trading partners. Despite the war, the colonial connections and habits of two centuries were not so easy to break. Besides, Britain led the industrial revolution and many manufactures had to come from there, even though Americans started up in competition. An example of subsequent development can be taken from Glasgow, which had suffered the complete collapse of its business in tobacco during the hostilities. Though that now resumed, it never did so with the same vigour as before. But the city had plenty of capital, and switched to cotton. Before long huge imports of cotton came from the southern states of the US and Glasgow turned into a major producer of textiles to be exported back across the Atlantic. Further south still, Florida and the Gulf Coast, ceded by Spain to Britain in 1763, were returned by the treaty which ended the American war in 1783. During those twenty years Scots appeared to trade with Native American nations, and now with white settlers penetrating the region. The Spanish hold was slack, the political outlook uncertain. More to the point, Spain had little concept of free trade. It was found that the commerce of the Gulf had to be left in Scottish hands. William Panton, former merchant of Savannah, was one of those who exploited it.

As for Scots remaining in the US, they just became Americans. Being Scottish was now no great advantage, after all that had happened. Either those who stayed were committed to

America, or else they did not much mind what government they lived under so long as they could get on with their lives. The Scotch-Irish had had no problem with the Revolution anyway, and formed one of the most dynamic elements in the new Republic. The Presbyterians formed, or rather reformed, their American synod. As a minority, they rested content with a system where Church and state were separated, as one denomination among many. Scots had set up other local institutions, such as St Andrew's Societies in New York, Charleston and elsewhere, or Freemasons' lodges practising the Scottish rite. They survived the Revolution, indeed flourished, but as nothing more than social clubs, and not as a focus for ethnic politics. Only in the nineteenth century would new immigrant groups start to organise themselves in that way, first in self-defence, then for political spoils. Scots, usually educated and successful people, had no need for any such thing. They merged into the American melting pot. At most their names marked them out from the general population.

Scotland and America had spent only a few decades together under the British Crown, from the Union of 1707 to the Declaration of Independence in 1776. Their relations developed in a fruitful manner during this short period. But now they went their separate ways. America chose an independent future, Scotland an imperial one. Even so, their relations would develop still more fruitfully from now on.

PRESIDENTS

T he inauguration of George Washington, the first US president, took place in April 1789 in New York, the temporary capital of the new Republic. He arrived off a ship, landed at a pier on the East River, then walked in procession along Wall Street. The inaugural ceremony itself took place on the balcony of Federal Hall, before a large crowd, near where the New York Stock Exchange stands today. The oath of office was administered by the chancellor of the state of New York, Robert Livingston, a descendant of Scots pioneers who had settled near Albany more than a hundred years before and grown rich on the trade and agriculture of the upper Hudson Valley.

Washington's family, which originated in County Durham in the North of England, had a few Scottish ancestors but this was not something he ever cared to boast about. He, too, knew that most of the Scots in the Thirteen Colonies had stayed true to the British Crown during the American Revolution, though he always counselled his comrades-in-arms, often in vain, to treat the loyalists leniently. The absence in him of any harsh prejudice is shown by his readiness to rely on men whose Scottish connections were stronger than his own, of which the role played by Livingston in the first inauguration was a small symbol.

Washington always preferred to work with an inner circle of close confidants, and two of the secretaries he appointed to his

Cabinet were men of recent Scottish ancestry. The Secretary of the Treasury was Alexander Hamilton, whose father had come from Ayrshire and settled on the Caribbean island of Nevis. He was following a well-trodden path for Scots, many of whom sought their fortunes in the West Indies during the eighteenth century (another son of Ayrshire, Robert Burns, the national bard, was toying with the idea just about this time but never managed to get further than the nearest port of Greenock). The West Indies was the richest part of the British Empire, where investment could produce large and fast returns from the production of sugar and other exotic crops on plantations worked by slaves. Their white masters led a languid, if uneasy life. A black uprising was their constant fear, and few intended to remain as permanent colonists: the rest hoped to take their money back to Scotland and buy a landed estate to raise their status in the homeland. Hamilton was illegitimate, born to one of his father's mistresses, and he had an inborn rootlessness which perhaps accounted for his financial acumen. Aged only 17, he left his native Nevis for New York, where he was to make his fortune as a lawyer and banker.

Hamilton's importance to the infant Republic can hardly be underestimated. He had dedicated himself to the American cause at the outset of the Revolution, and from his writings in support of it he attracted the notice of Washington, who made Hamilton his secretary and aide-de-camp. The young man also fought in the field and distinguished himself at the Siege of Yorktown, where the surrender of Lord Cornwallis's British army in effect brought the War of Independence to an end in 1781. Hamilton remained at the heart of the effort to unite the colonies, always favouring a strong central government, stronger than the one that emerged. It faced huge economic problems. The war had caused destruction of property and disruption of trade. So much paper money was issued by the Continental Congress as to lose almost all its value – there was once a saying, 'It's not worth a continental', referring to the hopelessly depreciated early American notes. And now a government had to be set up with no system of public credit. Hamilton made it his job to establish one, to start coining dollars in 1794 and to found the

Bank of the United States. Without the shrewdness Hamilton inherited from his Scots ancestors, the new nation might have sunk almost before it began.

Washington's Secretary of War was Henry Knox, of a Scottish family which had come by way of Ulster and settled in Boston. He was a bookseller to trade, a fat fellow weighing 280 pounds with a lively sense of humour – an excellent foil to his more fastidious leader, who was also a big man, though tall rather than plump. Despite Knox's corpulence and his previous sedentary life, he proved to be a fit and strong soldier. He stayed at Washington's side throughout an arduous, often disappointing war and there was no officer the commander-in-chief trusted more. So he became a natural choice to join the first American Cabinet. The Republic stayed at peace during Washington's two terms of office, though in constant anxiety that it would have to fight once again. Hostilities broke out all over Europe after 1789 as revolutionary France turned on its neighbours and steadily subdued them, except for Britain, which remained secure behind the wooden walls of the Royal Navy. Thomas Jefferson, the Secretary of State, would have been glad to join in the war on the French side; Hamilton, on the other hand, was determinedly pro-British. While Washington took the view that America should keep out of European conflicts, military vigilance was necessary all the same. Knox carried out the second part of this policy.

For its first half-century or so, the US was dominated politically by two groups, the social elites of Virginia and New England, the one agricultural and the other commercial; the first contained a certain Scottish element, the second next to none. Washington was succeeded in the presidency by John Adams of Massachusetts and he in turn by Thomas Jefferson, the anti-Scot who had been schooled liked a Scotsman. Under him, the US took its next great step forward with the Louisiana Purchase of 1803. To negotiate this from France, Jefferson sent to Paris two American Scots, Robert Livingston and James Monroe, the future president. With their success, the US acquired a vast tract of land from the Mississippi River to the Rocky Mountains and doubled the size of its territory. So far the great majority of Americans had remained living within 100 miles of the eastern seaboard: they inevitably kept a kind of colonial mentality, conscious that they had but recently crossed the ocean and still in part dependent on links back to the other side. From now they would look westwards rather than eastwards. The future of the US – the Manifest Destiny, as it would come to be known – was continental.

Jefferson knew what he was doing. He pushed through the (possibly unconstitutional) purchase with the intention that the land should be settled by thousands and one day by millions of farmers with moderate land-holdings, independent and egalitarian in spirit; the native nations dwelling there could either be fully Americanised or go somewhere else. Meanwhile the territory was a social, cultural and political void, but in Jefferson's view all the better for that. It meant the population arising on it could follow a rather abstract philosophical ideal. These citizens of the Republic would owe little or nothing to their past. They would be motivated by a self-confident individualism. They would form a new social ethos. They would come together in a novel kind of civic community. And they would be inspired by the ideals for humanity offered in the Scottish Enlightenment which Jefferson had absorbed through his education. He called it the 'empire of liberty'.

James Madison succeeded Jefferson in the presidency in 1809. Compared to the glories of his youth, this climax of his career proved disappointing. He had been Secretary of State for eight years, and his own term at the top was largely spent in facing the consequences of policies he followed before he got there. This was for a politician an unusual and unpleasant fate, made worse by the fact that Madison felt burned out after more than thirty years of public life. The chief problem he faced arose from the continuing war in Europe, especially between Britain and France, and the restraints both had placed on the trade of the neutral Americans. US policy was that if one would lift the restraints, it would impose an embargo on the other. Madison received some unconvincing assurances from the French, and put an embargo on the British. This set off a drift to the War of 1812, egged on by members of the Congress who thought it would be a chance to conquer Canada.

Madison now had to face a different set of Scotsmen from

those he had met in his books at the College of New Jersey. The British suffered some reverses, but for them the highpoint of the hostilities came when they were able, against no resistance, to land an expeditionary force in Chesapeake Bay and march on Washington. The commander of the fleet carrying the force was Admiral Alexander Cochrane, of a family wild even by Scottish standards. He had informed the US government of his intention 'to destroy and lay waste such towns and districts upon the coast as may be found available'. It ought not to have been so much of a surprise that he assaulted the new capital of the Republic. The landing itself was led by Admiral George Cockburn and the troops, once ashore, came under the command of General Robert Ross. The members of the US administration fled; the President's wife, Dolley, was seen 'in her carriage flying full speed through Georgetown, accompanied by an officer carrying a drawn sword'.

Ross's regiments entered the undefended city on 24 August 1814. They fired a volley through the windows of the Capitol, went inside and set it on fire. They proceeded to the President's official residence, put all the furnishings in the parlour and set them alight too; afterwards the building had to be painted to hide the scorches, and so became the White House. The Treasury Building and the Navy Yard went up in flames also, till a thunderstorm put them out. The cyclone and torrential rain made life a misery for the fugitive American politicians and soldiers, not to speak of thousands of refugees, wandering aimlessly round Maryland. At one tavern crowded with the homeless Dolley Madison was turned away and told her husband should be held to blame for all this. President Madison had already become unpopular as the cause of this calamitous war, and after the burning of Washington he never recovered his standing.

James Monroe followed Madison. He was the great-grandson of a Scot who had come in shackles to America. This was during the Civil War in Britain, actually a complex series of conflicts nowadays better named as the Wars of the Three Kingdoms, that is, of Scotland, England and Ireland. It centred on the struggle between King Charles I and his English Parliament, while the Scots played a perilous game allied first to one side then to the other. Their aim was to maintain their independence and uphold the National Covenant which pledged them to their Presbyterian religion. By 1648 the king had accepted the Covenant, so the Scots were willing to fight for him. They invaded England, only to be defeated by Oliver Cromwell at the Battle of Preston. Andrew Monroe was one of many Scottish soldiers taken prisoner there. Had they been Irish, they would probably have been slaughtered; the easiest other way to get rid of them was to ship them off to the plantations. So Monroe arrived in Virginia, soon escaped his captors, went to the back country and eventually prospered as a farmer.

His descendant James inherited this fighting spirit. In 1776 he was only 18, but he left the College of William and Mary and joined the American army, to be wounded at the Battle of Trenton. At home in Virginia, Jefferson was a neighbour. He took the young man under his wing, and a political career followed. Monroe served in the US Senate, as Governor of Virginia and as envoy to France, negotiating the Louisiana Purchase. Under Madison he was Secretary of State and heir-apparent for the presidency. He easily won the election; when re-elected in 1820 he would have been chosen unanimously, except that one member of the electoral college decided Washington ought to be the sole man ever to have been accorded that honour and cast his vote against Monroe. He was not an impressive figure: people quipped that he looked like an eel standing on its tail. Tall and thin, with stooped shoulders, he was a laboured thinker, earnest and diligent. His own Secretary of State, John Quincy Adams, wrote: 'There is a slowness, want of decision, and a spirit of procrastination in the President.'

All the same, Monroe's turned out to be an important administration. US territory continued to expand with the acquisition of Florida from Spain. The President supported the creation of Liberia in West Africa as a refuge for freed slaves, and is commemorated in the name of that nation's capital, Monrovia. But at home the fateful struggle between North and South, between free states and slave states, began to take shape. The issue crystallised around the admission of Missouri to the Union in 1820; the question was whether it should come in slave or free. Long wrangling resulted in the Missouri Compromise, under which one new slave state was to be admitted for every new free state. The South could then maintain its position in the US Senate, where all states have equal votes (in the House of Representatives the North already enjoyed a majority), and block any legislation to abolish slavery. The compromise removed an immediate difficulty but institutionalised the sectional conflict that was to lead to the American Civil War. The other milestone of the presidency was the Monroe Doctrine, which its author included in a message to Congress in 1823. Its aim was to deter Spain from any bid to recover the republics of South America which had just thrown off the imperial yoke. The doctrine stated that the two American continents were closed to European colonisation; that the US did not intend to interfere in European affairs; that America was for Americans; and that any attempt to conquer the South American republics would be a 'manifestation of unfriendly disposition towards the United States'.

By now the day of the Founding Fathers was almost done. The next president, John Quincy Adams, had been too young to fight in 1776, but with a father who had signed the Declaration of Independence and became president himself, he belonged to the passing generation. At the election of 1824 he faced two rivals, Henry Clay and Andrew Jackson, and none had a majority in the electoral college. It fell to the House of Representatives to decide. There Clay supported Adams, even though Jackson had won a plurality of the popular vote; and Adams, once in the White House, made Clay his Secretary of State. The outcry was deafening. In any European country this sequence of events would have been perfectly normal, but Americans prided themselves on the moral superiority of their system. A whiff of corruption dogged Adams's administration. At the following election in 1828 Jackson, the wronged candidate last time, swept all before him.

Jackson opened a new era in US politics. Power vanished from the old revolutionary elite. Now candidates for the White House would have to harness popular forces. This was what Jackson did. He was the first President from beyond the original Thirteen Colonies. He hailed from Tennessee, and campaigned as an outsider against the establishment in Washington: it would become a familiar strategy. Striking also is the part the Scotch-Irish played in this transformation of the country. Jackson was Scotch-Irish himself. His father had been a luckless draper from near Belfast who came over in 1765 but died a couple of years later, just before his son was born in a log cabin somewhere on the border between North and South Carolina; both states claim him as a native son. His widowed mother had to find work as a servant, and life was harsh. But so it was for nearly all the Scotch-Irish. Hardship tempered them and endowed them with their special character, democratic and defiant, no less here on the American frontier than back in their homeland of Ulster. It turned them revolutionary, made them the cutting edge of the Republic's westward expansion and now, half a century on from 1776, gave them a sort of fulfilment. For the period ahead, up to the Civil War, they above all came to typify the new political populism.

Of course, the Scotch-Irish remained only a minority within the general American population. They did not act collectively, unlike later immigrant groups; they were far too individualistic for that. It is all the same remarkable that three of the next presidents up to 1861 rose from their ranks. And in a sense the Scotch-Irish shaped the course of American history over these years. They made fine frontiersmen, hardy and dauntless. So the frontier was pushed ever further to the west, to the River Mississippi and beyond. But another frontier lay close to their hearts, the frontier between North and South, between slave and free, which ran first along the Mason–Dixon Line, then along the River Ohio. As such, it split the main area of settlement by the Scotch-Irish, which they had opened up as they flooded through the Cumberland Gap in the eighteenth century. They lived on both sides, with perhaps more of them in the South than in the North. Even so, it gave them an interest in the maintenance of the Union. This frontier met the other frontier, and the crossing had more significance than any mere line on the map. In order to maintain the Union, under the Missouri Compromise, the western frontier had to be pushed ever further so that the frontier between North and South could be extended, and parity between them preserved. This ultimately doomed balancing act was in many ways the work of the Scotch-Irish.

The new age arrived with a vengeance when Jackson went to be inaugurated in Washington in 1829. He was a man of the people and he brought the people with him. The message was that they had created the nation: it was now theirs, and Jackson was their man. His status as popular hero he owed to his fighting qualities. He had never lost the hatred of the British he first found as a boy soldier, enlisted at the age of 12, in the War of Independence; captured, he was ordered to clean an enemy officer's boots and cut across the head with a sabre when he refused. He finally got his revenge by defeating the British at the Battle of New Orleans in 1814, before waging a cruel campaign against their allies, the Native Americans, and for good measure turning the Spaniards out of their remaining posts on the Gulf of Mexico. The presence of two new states in the Union, Alabama and Mississippi, was essentially owed to him.

Now his supporters descended on Washington almost as a conquering army: nothing like it had been seen since the British burned the city down. At least the ceremonies went off without a hitch. Jackson, a tall, loose-limbed, grey-headed man with clear blue eyes, made a fine impression with an eloquent, moderate speech. But he had invited everyone back to the White House for a party. High and low, old and young, the wheelers and dealers in sharp suits together with the rough frontiersmen in coonskin caps, all followed him there. This riotous mob broke the furniture and squirted tobacco juice on the rich carpets. Glass was smashed and whisky punch was spilled on the floor to form a soup with crushed pastries and sweetmeats. The rooms were crammed to bursting, and to get a glimpse of the President people stood on the exquisite damask of the chairs in their muddy boots. Through the mayhem a handsome and elegant Jackson moved at his ease, greeting friends and urging everyone to eat, drink and be merry. When he tired of it, he left by a back window, but some of them had to be carried out. This memorable scene was, we may be sure, not wholly accidental: Jackson wanted to show he despised official Washington and the genteel, exclusive habits it had drifted into. The people were reclaiming it.

Jackson's administration reflected the character of a lusty, energetic nation in all its growing diversity, which meant in the end he had few definite achievements to his credit. His term was a long uproar of controversy, a period of unresolved restlessness and of purposeless movement, above all a time when repressed enmities started ominously to surface. It saw the dispute between federal power and states' rights staked out. Legislation on tariffs defined the differing economic interests of North and South. Repeated banking crises ruined the foolish or unlucky and left the clever or fortunate unscathed. Enormous trouble was stored up for the future, though little of it rubbed off on Jackson, the popular hero.

One of Jackson's strongest supporters back home in Tennessee was James Knox Polk, who would become the second Scotch-Irish president of this era. Polk is a contraction of Pollok or Pollock, a name familiar in the West of Scotland. The contraction perhaps indicates in the history of the family a period when they were illiterate, as they passed through poverty after going to Ireland and then to America; they lost the memory of the old spelling and when they climbed the social ladder again they started writing their name just as they said it. After crossing the Atlantic they made their way with thousands of their countrymen over the western mountains. Unlike many of them, Polk grew up a quiet and colourless man. In adulthood he was a dutiful Congressman and Governor of Tennessee. At the presidential election of 1844, he became the first dark horse in American history to win the race. He insisted he would only serve one term.

But, as in the case of Monroe, Polk's unpromising presidency took on an unexpected importance. Under him the West was won. As he came into office in 1845 the US signed a treaty of annexation with Texas, which had been an independent republic since 1836, largely under the leadership of American Scots. They had broken free from Mexico, but Mexico did not recognise their independence, still less the right of the US to admit Texas to the Union. Fighting broke out on the Rio Grande in 1846, and full-scale war followed. US forces invaded Mexico from the north and by a landing further south followed up with an advance on

Mexico City, which was captured in September 1847. Many soldiers who were later to become famous in the American Civil War had their first experience of combat in this campaign. Among them was a junior officer of Scottish descent, Lieutenant Ulysses S. Grant. In his memoirs, written many years later, he said: 'I do not think there was ever a more wicked war than that waged by the United States on Mexico. I thought so at the time, when I was a youngster, only I had not moral courage enough to resign.'

Texas was now American, but there had never been any chance of its going back to the Mexicans anyway. The real object of these campaigns and manoeuvres was California. It remained as yet a Mexican province, but Mexico's presence consisted of little more than missions and haciendas. This sunny land lay in effect open to everyone. And everyone, from Scots to Russians, appeared there. But it was the Americans that had the most designing schemes on California. Those of them who looked with pride on the steady westward movement of settlers, and the Manifest Destiny it represented, believed the only logical place for it to stop was at that other shining sea, the Pacific Ocean. The Mexican war gave them their opportunity. President Polk sent out a military expedition overland from Missouri but, before it arrived, California had already been seized by simple dint of landing a naval force at Monterey, the Mexican capital of the province, and claiming it as American. Mexico formally ceded Texas, New Mexico and California to the US by the Treaty of Guadalupe in 1848.

That required in turn the urgent solution of another problem, but one that showed that the British and Americans were, for the first time since 1776, learning to settle their differences without fighting each other. The problem was the border between the US and Canada, which up to now had ended at the western tip of the Great Lakes. How was it to be drawn across the rest of the continent? The British claimed everything north of the forty-second parallel of latitude, while the Americans wanted everything up to 54° 40'. If the British had got their way both Oregon and Washington would now be part of Canada, as the forty-second parallel is the northern boundary of California. If the American claim had prevailed the border would have been drawn eastwards from the southern extremity of Alaska, and Canada would have had no access to the Pacific Ocean. The Foreign Secretary in London was a Scot, George Gordon, Earl of Aberdeen, a man of peace and, according to his colleague William Gladstone, 'a very just man'. Aberdeen proposed to split the difference and draw the border along the forty-ninth parallel, except where it crossed Vancouver Island, which was to be wholly Canadian. Polk agreed to this just as he invaded Mexico: war on two fronts would anyway not have been sensible. It was the last territorial dispute between the US on one side, and Britain and Canada on the other.

If only relations within the US could have been so amicable. But neither territorial expansion nor numberless compromises could cure the cancer of slavery. It completely dominated political life and clogged up the Congress. In such inauspicious circumstances the last Scotch-Irish president of the era was elected in 1856. James Buchanan's ancestors had originated in Stirlingshire in Scotland, and gone via Ireland to America. He was from Pennsylvania, a free state, but he followed a policy of appeasing the slave states, arguing in effect that the Union could be held together only if the North gave way to the South. What this meant in practice was immediately and dramatically underlined by the judgement of the Supreme Court in the case of Dred Scott only two days after Buchanan's inauguration. Scott was a slave belonging to a military surgeon posted from Missouri to Wisconsin, from a slave to a free state. His lawyers contended that he thus became free: free soil makes a free man. After a long legal process, the Supreme Court disagreed. But that meant slaves might be owned, assuming their owner had legitimate rights of property over them, even in free states, and more especially in free territories which therefore, when the time came to admit them to the Union, might have to be admitted as slave states. The whole North was outraged.

What few saw at the time was that this case brought the US a giant step nearer the Civil War. If the Constitution and due legal process could not curb slavery, then some other means would have to be found. Buchanan did not seem to understand this. He was a pleasant, well-groomed, elderly bachelor who liked to spend his time reading books, when he was not reading the Constitution for some answer to the country's problems which it did not contain. The national temperature steadily rose outside the walls of the White House, sometimes not far outside: fistfights regularly broke out in Congress. There was already a shooting war in Kansas, between those disputing whether it should be admitted to the Union as a free state or a slave state. More and more slaves simply ran away from their masters in the South, and attempts to recapture them in the North proved futile. In 1859, John Brown and a few other militant abolitionists seized the federal arsenal at Harper's Ferry in Virginia and called on slaves to rise in revolt with the arms he could now supply: the local militia easily rounded them all up and Brown was hanged. His cause now had a martyr.

The trouble was a product of the backlash in the North, the increasingly violent moral indignation aroused there by slavery as something not just undesirable or distasteful but intolerable. It offered fertile soil for the rise of the Republican Party, whose candidate Abraham Lincoln won against the odds in the presidential election of 1860. At once the southern states started seceding from the Union. Buchanan thought they had no right to do this. But he could not discover any constitutional authority to coerce a seceding state and bring it back into the Union by force of arms. Even if he had been able to decide on this point he would still have hesitated because Lincoln was coming in, and he did not want to embarrass his successor. Meanwhile, the American Civil War broke out.

The war gave a rebirth to the US, bloody and absolute. The structures of the Constitution survived, but federal authority became paramount and out of that authority a centralised modern state was to grow. It would be hard to point to any Scottish or Scotch-Irish influence on this process. American Scots submitted to it along with everyone else, but a surprising number of them continued to reach the White House.

It is possible, though unproven, that Lincoln himself had Scots blood. The district round his birthplace in the backwoods of Kentucky housed many Scottish settlers to whom his family might have been related. A link seems more likely in the case of his wife,

Mary Todd. She attended the Presbyterian church in their hometown of Springfield, Illinois, and as a widow was to go in 1870 for a consoling visit to her former minister, now back in Edinburgh. The Lincolns called one of their four sons William Wallace, whose death as a child in 1862 added to their afflictions in wartime.

Andrew Johnson, the vice-president who succeeded Lincoln after his assassination on 15 April 1865, was Scotch-Irish through his mother, Polly McDonough. Born in North Carolina, he moved as a young man to Tennessee and, by dint of hard work, prospered; at one stage of his life he had actually owned slaves. He became a candidate of the Republicans because they wanted a Southerner, yet they had no reason to think he would soon, or ever, be president, because Lincoln was still a relatively young man. Thrust into power in tragic circumstances, Johnson carried on with Lincoln's proclaimed policy of treating the defeated South with generosity. But the bitterness which had poisoned political life before the war lost nothing of its venom after victory. There was a large faction in Congress disinclined to show mercy to Southerners, and disapproving of Johnson's measures for reconstruction of the South. However well meaning, he was a dogmatic, ill-tempered man. He made such enemies of his opponents in Congress that they combined to impeach him, the first presidential impeachment in US history. He escaped a verdict of guilty by a single vote.

Johnson had no chance of re-election. His successor was Ulysses S. Grant, whom we saw above tormented by his conscience in the Mexican War of 1846. The scrupulous young officer had meanwhile become a hero of the Civil War. The odds were stacked against the Confederacy from the start, but it kept going for four years on the brilliant generalship of Robert E. Lee, Stonewall Jackson and others. The Union had a sequence of mediocre generals, the despair of Lincoln. But Grant brought that sequence to an end. He spent the early part of the war in the backwater of the West, where the Union's few successes came. Lincoln at length promoted him to the command in the main theatre of Virginia; told that Grant drank, the President replied that he wished all his generals did. Grant concentrated his forces in the Tidewater area south-east of Richmond, the Confederate capital. After what was in essence a long siege, he broke through and captured the city in April 1865. The surrender of the South was then a matter of time. Grant did not carry this distinction in the field into the White House. A straightforward military man, or reasonably so, he let himself be surrounded by unsavoury characters. Business in the country boomed, making vast fortunes for some. The money was often used to suborn government. Constant vigilance has ever since been required to keep Washington clean, and even so it has not always succeeded.

Chester Alan Arthur, the next Scotch-Irish President, shows this well. His family were relatively recent immigrants; his father, a Presbyterian minister, had arrived from Ballymena in Ulster in 1815. Arthur grew up in New York to become a Republican machine politician. This did not in itself provide an income, so he was made Collector of the Port of New York in the US Customs. His custom-house employed a thousand clerks, several hundred more than were needed. Most had nothing to do, some were so illiterate they could not write their names, but all were good Republicans. It was normal to deduct from their salaries a percentage for the party's campaigning fund. A previous president, Rutherford B. Hayes, had decided to clean things up a little; he ordered Arthur to sack incompetent officials and stop using his payroll for political purposes. Arthur evaded these instructions and Hayes dismissed him. Even so, at the Republican convention of 1880, Arthur was chosen as vice-presidential candidate, to balance the ticket of James Garfield of Ohio.

As in most elections during this period, the Republicans carried all, or nearly all, the states outside the South. But, within six months of entering the White House, Garfield was dead, the victim of an assassin's bullet, and Arthur was president. The spoilsmen of the Republican Party thought the good old days of unrestrained looting were back. They got the surprise of their lives. An unexpected change came over Arthur. He dropped the methods of machine politics and portrayed himself as a champion of honesty, efficiency and good government. He has even been called the first modern president, governing for all the people and for all sections of the country, regardless of party. That meant he had no chance of being re-elected either.

The dominance of the Republican Party continued up to and beyond the end of the nineteenth century, though its rivalry with the Democratic Party gradually changed in character. Straight after the Civil War, the rivalry had been, or had been depicted, as one of absolute loyalty to the Union against lukewarm loyalty or even disloyalty. As memories of the war faded, the two great American parties took more conventional places on the political spectrum, the Republicans to the right and the Democrats to the left, though the differences between them were much more fuzzy and variable than in any European country. The Republicans, with money and office behind them, were usually in and the Democrats usually out.

By the turn of the twentieth century, the circumstances of the US imposed more definite commitments to policy than Americans had been used to. In the presidency of William McKinley, for example, the Republicans had a clear yet elaborate programme of imperialism, the gold standard and a protective tariff, designed to strengthen the US both internally and externally. McKinley was of Scotch-Irish descent, his family having come from Ulster in the eighteenth century. He was re-elected but assassinated in 1901, when he had hardly begun his second term. His vice-president, Theodore Roosevelt, succeeded him.

Roosevelt was what used to be called a Knickerbocker, whose ancestors had been the original Dutch settlers of New Amsterdam, which the English renamed New York when they captured it in 1664. But he had a Scottish-American mother, Martha Bulloch, descended on both sides from military families. Roosevelt inherited their martial spirit. As a young man with money and time to spare, he had gone out from New York to the Wild West to seek adventure. It came as a godsend to him when in 1898 war broke out between the US and Spain, essentially as a result of the ambition Americans had long nursed of annexing Cuba, the last major Spanish colony in the New World. The decisive confrontation between the two armies took place at the port of Santiago, which was first besieged, then captured by assault.

At Santiago, Roosevelt made himself famous. He had arrived as the colonel of the Rough Riders, a regiment of cowboys. He was a picturesque figure, and brilliant at what are nowadays called sound-bites: he gave to American English, and then to the English language generally, the terms 'mollycoddle', 'muckraker', 'big stick', 'square deal' and 'weasel words'. Many readers of newspapers back in the US must have gained a vague impression that Roosevelt won the war single-handed, so ubiquitous were reports of his actions and his comments on them. Now he was president, at 43 the youngest man ever to hold the office. The US had become an imperial power with colonies (not called that) in Cuba, Puerto Rico, the Philippines, Hawaii and Panama. At home Roosevelt, to the dismay of fellow Republicans, spent much of his enormous energy trying to break the trusts, or industrial cartels and monopolies. This match was drawn.

The most Scottish figure to have become president was Woodrow Wilson. His grandfather James had been born in Scotland, and emigrated to America in 1807. His father became a professor of theology, and Moderator of the General Assembly of the American Presbyterian Church in 1879, the year in which young Woodrow graduated at Princeton. His own name recalled a hero of one historic current in Scots Presbyterianism, the Revd Robert Woodrow, who in the early eighteenth century had defended the Kirk against attempts at political control of it. Woodrow also published a history of its sufferings to remind the faithful of their glorious heritage and to encourage their resistance. So, as Wilson grew up in Virginia, these Scottish cultural influences on him remained unusually strong.

They made him a most unusual politician. He always seemed more at home in the library than on the hustings; he had a deep moral earnestness which fitted ill with the robust nature of American politics. Up to the age of 54, he seemed certain to live out his days as an academic. Twenty years before, he had become professor of jurisprudence at Princeton; a decade after that he was president of the university, a worthy successor to John Witherspoon, the signer of the Declaration of Independence. Wilson admired and praised his Scottish predecessor, who he said had turned Princeton into 'a seminary of statesmen'. Wilson was an active reformer in the same mould. But he also suffered a political handicap which would dog him through the rest of his career – an inability to carry lesser men with him, indeed a degree of indifference to whether he could or could not. He grew tired of academic life, and resigned to run for Governor of New Jersey in 1910. Again, he was an active reformer, now with the power to get things done.

Wilson's work as governor formed a springboard for the presidency. He was the Democratic candidate in 1912 and won – only the second man from his party to do so since the Civil War. Once more, he set the pace with a programme of progressive measures, dubbed by him the New Freedom; the most lasting of them was the establishment of the Federal Reserve in 1913. But all domestic problems were cast in the shade by the outbreak of the First World War the next year. The US remained at first neutral, though Wilson's natural sympathies lay with the Allied powers. In 1917, when both sides were approaching exhaustion, the Americans entered the war and decisively tipped the balance against Germany.

So far Wilson's presidency had been a brilliant success, but bitter disappointment followed. He made the mistake of going to Versailles to take part in person in negotiating the peace treaty and of committing himself too far to the ideals he wanted it to embody, noble as those ideals were: self-determination and democracy for the peoples of Europe. But Europe was not America and the ideals could not be secured by signing treaties. The guardian of the settlement was to be the League of Nations, forerunner of the present United Nations. On his return, Wilson proved unable to persuade the Senate to ratify the accession of the US to it. The strain of these setbacks taxed him to the limit. In 1919 he suffered a stroke from which he never fully recovered. He became a recluse in the White House and some historians believe his wife Edith carried out the presidential functions most of the time. He died broken, but the example of his stern Presbyterian morality gave him a deserved aura of tragic grandeur.

The rich contribution of the Scots and Scotch-Irish to the US presidency thinned somewhat in the course of the twentieth century. Of later Presidents, Lyndon B. Johnson was descended from Scots who went from Annandale to Virginia in the seventeenth century. The Scotch-Irish forebears of Richard M. Nixon arrived in America in 1731. But according to one estimate, 75 per cent of the forty-two men who have held the highest office could boast

Scots ancestry, if only remote in several cases. The influence on them of the land of their fathers was anyway bound to diminish over time in a nation which sought to make itself a melting-pot.

Yet the relationship between the old country and the new country remains lively enough to be refreshed in different forms, even by men of no, or no known, Scots lineage. The sole president to have visited Scotland while in office was Dwight D. Eisenhower, who stayed at Culzean Castle on the coast of Ayrshire in 1959. The castle, with its stunning views over the Firth of Clyde, was full of memories for him because it had been his personal residence while Supreme Commander of the Allied forces during the Second World War. The suite of rooms he lived in was later gifted to him. Then he could use Culzean as a retreat for his favourite pastimes of golfing, painting and walking; he returned on several occasions during his retirement. The two Presidents Bush have also enjoyed Scottish hospitality through their interests in oil, a major natural resource in both Scotland and the US. Some enterprising Scots have extended their international contacts through the industry. One of them is James Gammell, who met George Bush senior while he was still just a tycoon in Texas. The friendship extends to their sons, George W. Bush and Bill Gammell. The Gammels have a country estate in Glenisla, and in his youth the president-to-be liked to spend holidays with them striding across the braes of Angus. US Presidents may be sure they will always be welcome in Scotland, even if nowadays they seek out the golf rather than the philosophy.

4

FIGHTERS

The American nation was born in war. Through war it expanded and unified. By war, even though peaceful methods might be preferred, it maintains and asserts its position as the world's sole superpower. American society remains, by the standards of Europe's ancient nations, a violent one.

Scots pride themselves on their prowess in war. In the days of the independent nation before 1707, their boast was that they had held the same territory against all attacks for more than two thousand years. Theirs was then a feudal society, organised for war, so that at any time the king or the nobility could call out the people living on their land to fight for them. It is true that Scots seemed to spend the greater part of their time fighting each other rather than the English or any more distant enemies. And by the end of the seventeenth century they noticed how peoples elsewhere in Europe had turned from this primitive mode of existence to commerce, out of which they were prospering better than Scots could ever hope to do. This was one motive for the Union with England, so that Scotland could also achieve peaceful progress through trade with a more developed neighbouring country and with its colonies.

Even so, old habits died hard. One region of Scotland, the Highlands, remained backward. There a feudal form of society persisted, at least for a few decades after 1707. In the Jacobite rebellions of 1715 and 1745, the chiefs called out their clans in the old way to fight against the Government in London. The rebellions were crushed, and that Government made sure they would never happen again by setting out to destroy the military power of the chiefs and to turn them into commercial landlords. Once the Highlands were pacified, their reservoir of fighting men proved useful to an expanding imperial power. Highland regiments of the British army were first raised for the Seven Years War, known in the US as the French and Indian War, in 1756–63.

It marked the start of a grand tradition. By the nineteenth century, even Lowland regiments were being clad in kilts and tartans, sometimes in the face of their own objections: Lowlanders had been used to regarding Highlanders as barbarians. But through the exertions of Sir Walter Scott, especially the visit to Scotland of King George IV which he masterminded in 1822, Scots were acquiring a more unified vision of their nation. As clansmen armed to the teeth marched playing their pipes through Edinburgh, its sober citizens were moved enough to be convinced that a martial spirit formed part of their heritage too. At any rate the bitter internal strife of former times ought to be laid to rest. All Scots would from now on be able to draw as much on the romantic heroism of the Highlands as on the hard-headed practicality of the Lowlands. Scotland would be stronger, Scotland could remain Scotland, but this would be a loyal Scotland, playing a full part in the United Kingdom and British Empire. Of that idea the Scottish regiments remained a potent symbol for two centuries. Scots pride themselves on it yet and on the colourful traditions which go with it as visible expressions of nationhood. Among their neighbours, Scots still have a reputation for being too quick to pick a fight.

When Scots went to America, they carried something of this martial tradition with them. After 1707 many served as colonial governors, and they often had to fight to secure the frontier. There were small wars with the Indians and bigger ones with the French. They had from Quebec penetrated the region of the Great Lakes and by way of the Rivers Ohio and Mississippi linked up with their second settlement in Louisiana. At this stage it was by no means clear that the Thirteen Colonies ever would or could expand across the long chain of the Appalachian Mountains running from Georgia to New England. Transport by river was much easier than transport by land, and the French could more readily control the territory beyond. They claimed that territory as their own, a claim not disputed till the pressure of a growing population in the British colonies created a westward movement of settlers. It also brought conflict with France.

In 1752 a bustling, energetic merchant from Glasgow, Robert Dinwiddie, arrived as Governor of Virginia. On his private account he at once bought a share in the Ohio Company, recently set up to acquire western land; the other stockholders included George Washington's elder brothers. Then Dinwiddie put his governor's hat back on and granted the company 500,000 acres in the valley of the River Ohio. Though in theory the boundaries of Virginia ran as far as the Pacific Ocean, the land was hardly his to give. Indians lived there, but more to the point the French had built a chain of forts across the back country for the express purpose of keeping Virginian settlers out. Dinwiddie gave the French notice to remove themselves. Washington, aged 21, was commissioned to carry the bad news to them. When they took no notice, Dinwiddie set about organising an expedition to expel them. For this major undertaking, troops were summoned from the homeland under General Edward Braddock. They landed in the summer of 1755 at Alexandria on the River Potomac and marched towards Fort Duquesne, which stood on the present site of Pittsburgh; Washington went with them as a volunteer officer. The column ran into an ambush by a combined force of French and Indians. Braddock himself was killed. Washington took charge and managed to keep the column from being annihilated.

The future US president was the hero of the hour, his courage and coolness contrasting with the blunders of the bumbling British. Governor Dinwiddie had not covered himself in strategic glory but, luckily for him, the disaster he brought on was soon swallowed up in development of a wider conflict, the Seven Years War. It was a global struggle between Britain and France, with fighting in Europe and Asia as well as North America, from which the British would emerge triumphant in 1763, having crushed French power in Canada and India.

It was for this war that those first Highland regiments in the British army came to be raised. They proved decisive in the capture of Quebec in 1759. Many of the Scots soldiers had actually served in the French army while in exile from their own homeland after the failure of the last Jacobite rebellion, but then were pardoned and came home, before being recruited over again. As they landed in darkness on the banks of the St Lawrence River above the doomed city, they were able to fool the Québécois guards by answering their challenges in their own language. When dawn broke, the defenders found a British army already drawn up on the Plains of Abraham. The French bravely went out to fight, but were routed by a charge of Fraser's Highlanders howling their war-cries and swinging their claymores. Canada became British.

But that victory, which soon brought most of North America under the rule of King George III, only created imperial problems beyond the capacity of contemporary government to solve. One result was the American Revolution in which, as we have seen, most Scots stayed loyal to the king. Even so, those who took the opposite decision made a major contribution to the revolutionary side. Two of George Washington's generals were American Scots. One was Henry Knox, the fat bookseller from Boston who would later become the first US secretary for war. Born in 1750, he joined the Continental Army as soon as hostilities broke out. At first it had no equipment: the recruits were patriotic citizens usually without training or arms, now to be pitted against professional soldiers. Weapons were the first essential, and Knox brought himself to Washington's attention by solving this problem. Right at the outset of the war Fort Ticonderoga on Lake Champlain, the fortress guarding the main route south from Canada, had been surprised and taken by the Green Mountain Boys. It housed cannon and mortar of no use to the British now. Knox crossed over from Boston in the depth of the winter and had these heavy armaments dragged by horses a hundred miles over the ice of the hard-frozen roads, all the way to his city. It lay still in British hands, but besieged by American forces; the bloody Battle of Bunker's Hill the year before had not altered the stalemate. The Americans could only break it by bombarding Boston from the low hills round about. Knox had now made this possible. On 2 March 1776 his artillery opened fire on the city. Within three days, the British had to accept a compromise. The Americans peacefully occupied Boston, while Lord Howe and his royal troops were allowed to leave unharmed. Washington entered a city which had cast off British rule for ever. Knox commanded the American artillery for the rest of the war.

The second American Scot in Washington's entourage was William Alexander, a born New Yorker who claimed the British noble title of Lord Stirling. He was distantly related to his namesake, the William Alexander who in 1621 had received the grant of Nova Scotia from King James VI and I, and tried without success to establish a permanent colony there. This Alexander was created Earl of Stirling (and Viscount Canada) by King Charles I, but the direct male line of the family failed in 1760. The House of Lords refused to accept that the William Alexander from New York was the next heir, but he took no notice and called himself Lord Stirling anyway: who in America could stop him? In this pre-revolutionary world, blue blood was the key to a command in all armies, and Stirling wanted to follow a military career. Washington would find his Continental Army attracting officers of dubious nobility from Germany or France who could not reach more senior ranks at home; Stirling belonged to the same class.

Stirling proved to be an adequate but never a brilliant soldier. The action in which he took the most notable part was the Battle of Long Island on 27 August 1776. The British held to a strategy through most of the war of taking and securing the major ports on the Atlantic seaboard, easily provisioned from the homeland. Raiding and other expeditions could be undertaken in the interior, while the Americans would be denied supplies. Boston was lost early on, but the British then became all the more determined to seize New York. In the summer of 1776, three forces arrived respectively from Britain, from Nova Scotia and from Charleston, South Carolina, to establish a large base on Staten Island. From there the troops crossed to Long Island and prepared to attack the American defences on Brooklyn Heights. Stirling commanded a force protecting the southern approach to the fortifications. In these early engagements the British enjoyed a huge advantage because the American army had so little experience. When they attacked Stirling's position they easily routed his soldiers, and took him prisoner; he would later be exchanged for captured British officers. For the time being Howe, the British general, decided not to assault the heights directly. Even so, the Americans found themselves pinned down and could no longer keep the East River clear of enemy ships, so they had to withdraw to Manhattan. New York was indefensible, and fell on 15 September: a setback so severe that Washington considered resigning his command. The city would remain in British hands for the rest of the war, indeed till after the peace had been signed. The Union Flag would only be hauled down there on 25 November 1783. Stirling had meanwhile taken part in the confused campaigns which criss-crossed New Jersey, where the two sides fought each other to a standstill. The outcome of the war was eventually to be decided in Virginia.

The biggest contribution of Scots on the American side had come at sea rather than on land. The Royal Navy could usually count on controlling the North Atlantic, but this grew harder as other European countries entered the war after the British armies in the colonies failed to bring the rebellion to a quick end. Then there were French, Spanish and Dutch fleets to contend with, as well as the few ships the Americans had at their disposal. These could not fight a maritime war, but they could harass and annoy the British, or attack unarmed merchant ships in what were little more than acts of piracy.

Nobody in Britain had heard of any French, Spanish or Dutch admiral, but everyone had heard of John Paul Jones, the American naval commander. And Jones was a Scotsman, born John Paul, the son of a gardener at an estate on the southern coast of Scotland near Dumfries. His devotion to the American cause remains to this day a bit of a mystery, because he had scarcely visited the colonies before the war broke out. He was a seaman who sometimes got himself into trouble on his voyages to the West Indies, and an officer's commission from the Americans may have come just at the right time to save him from some financial or other problem; it was perhaps for the same sort of reason that he adopted the extra surname of Jones.

Jones made his reputation by daring raids round the coasts of his homeland. After 1778, there were several invasion scares in Britain, amid what was now a general European war. The appearance of foreign ships offshore often prompted panic among local people. Jones not only appeared but landed. For example, he directed his men to the home of the Earl of Selkirk, just a mile from his own birthplace, where the countess pluckily met them and handed over the family's silver. After threatening Leith, the port of Edinburgh, Jones sailed down the coast of Yorkshire. There, off Flamborough Head, he was intercepted by HMS *Serapis*. A famous engagement ensued on 23 September 1779. With two ships locked in battle at close quarters, the naval vessel ought to have had the advantage, but Jones refused to give up. When called on to surrender, he cried: 'I have not yet begun to fight.' And eventually he forced the British captain to strike his colours.

The American War of Independence ended in 1783, but by 1812 Britain and the US were again at war, in a conflict essentially forming a sideshow to the greater one in Europe. It was a needless, scrappy and inconclusive affair, which made only one reputation, that of Andrew Jackson. The fierce Scotch-Irishman had spent the years since US independence in Tennessee, which he helped to bring into the Union and served as a Congressman. He settled at Nashville, acquired the nearby Hermitage and was elected major-general of the state's militia, the base of his power. Between 1812 and 1814 he fought a sideshow of his own.

There were two other theatres in the war, in Canada, which was easily defended against American incursions, and in the Atlantic Ocean, which the Royal Navy dominated without too much trouble, as shown by the burning of Washington DC. But in the South a different situation prevailed. The present states of Mississippi and Alabama, together with the western half of Georgia, remained Indian country, held by what became known as the Five Civilised Tribes, the Creeks the most powerful of them. They had been British allies in the War of Independence and remained so now, hoping an imperial power could hinder the encroachment of American settlers on their land. The British did give them some, if hardly adequate, support. So did the Spaniards, who had regained Florida and the Gulf Coast in 1783, but also feared the Americans would not long leave them in possession of these territories. For Jackson, the War of 1812 was a struggle against the Indians and against the European powers behind them, Britain and Spain.

This part of the South was a lawless region, peopled by a mixture of white settlers, by different Indian tribes, usually divided into factions, and by black slaves or ex-slaves who had escaped or been freed by the British: a consistent policy which made a point against the Americans. Violence was anyway almost incessant. But the war proper can be said to have begun here when in August 1813 the Creeks overran Fort Mims, fifty miles from Mobile, massacring the whites and their Indian allies inside. Jackson was ordered by the US Government to march his militia south and exact revenge for this disaster.

Among Jackson's men were two other American Scots, Davy Crockett and Sam Houston, destined to become famous on the frontier. Jackson moved fast. By November he reached the Creek town of Tallushatchee, where he carried out a retaliatory massacre. Crockett would later write in his memoirs: 'We shot them like dogs.' A week later Jackson fought a pitched battle against the Creeks at Talladega and defeated them. His success attracted volunteers, and he soon had an army of 5,000. With this he turned against the main Creek fortress at Horseshoe Bend, not far from the present city of Montgomery, Alabama. It was a strong position: 1,000 warriors defended a headland in the Tallapoosa River almost surrounded by water behind a breastwork across its neck, eight feet high and with a double row of firing holes. The place could only be stormed. Houston was the first to breach the wall. The Creeks refused to surrender and were slaughtered. The Americans cut off the tips of their noses to keep a body count, and by the end they had 557, while another 300 were reckoned to have jumped in the river and drowned. This battle broke the power of the Creeks for ever. Jackson rampaged through their country in a reign of terror, and by April 1814 they surrendered. He forced them to cede to the US more than twenty million acres of land, half of all their territory, including most of Alabama and the part of Georgia they held. The rest of their nation was to be expelled beyond the Mississippi River during Jackson's presidency: he always settled old scores.

Jackson had meanwhile heard about the British capture of Washington and suspected the next attack would come in the South. He decided to counter by taking the Spanish outposts on the Gulf, Pensacola the main one. Spain and the US were not at war, so he had no authority for this unprovoked aggression – not something that bothered him in the least. Strategically he was right, for the British forces had indeed sailed round from Chesapeake Bay to the Gulf, under the command of the Scots admiral, Alexander Cochrane. He meant to land at Mobile and march on New Orleans, an American city since the Louisiana Purchase, freeing slaves and gathering Indian reinforcements as he went.

Jackson forced a change of plan, a direct attack on New Orleans. He was there, frantically gathering men and building defences. The British could have availed themselves of various tactics in the complex geography of river and swamp. But after their artillery failed to destroy the American positions they decided to try a frontal assault, on 8 January 1815. It was a catastrophe. Ten minutes of trying to advance against the American hail of fire proved enough for the British troops, who turned and ran leaving 800 dead behind them; Jackson had 61 casualties. The Battle of New Orleans was the only real American victory against the British in the War of 1812, which, ironically, had already come to an end. News was still on its way of the treaty of peace signed at Ghent in Belgium on Christmas Eve, 1814. It would arrive on 11 January: three days too late to stop Jackson becoming his nation's military hero. He later recorded that, before he had been orphaned many years before, his mother told him girls might be made to cry but boys were made to fight. That was what he did all his life, and his career sums up the spirit of the Scotch-Irish in America.

Britain and the US were never to go to war again. In effect the Treaty of Ghent, though it did not say so (it said very little) formed an agreement that the two countries would carve up North America between them. The US would abandon any serious ambition of absorbing Canada, while Britain would no longer hinder the Americans' westward movement by encouraging Indians, Spaniards (or soon Mexicans) to resist them. So the next armed conflict involving the US, in 1846, did not rerun the War of Independence; instead it was fought against fellow-Americans, those of the Republic of Mexico which had only thrown off its own colonial yoke a quarter of a century before.

Directed by President James Knox Polk, in many ways this war marked the high point of Scottish influence in US military history. One of his leading generals, Winfield Scott, was the grandson of a soldier at the Battle of Culloden in 1746 which had brought the last Jacobite rising in Scotland to an end. He served in Canada in the War of 1812 and during the 1830s oversaw the Cherokees on the Trail of Tears, their removal from their homeland in the Appalachian Mountains to what is now Oklahoma. By 1841 he was the supreme commander of the US army. In the Mexican War, he led the landing at Veracruz which was to strike straight at Mexico City, 250 miles inland. From the day of his disembarkation in March 1847 his troops had to struggle every step of the way along a road which, over that relatively short distance, rose from sea level to an altitude of 7,500 feet. It took them six months of often savage fighting. In September 1847 Scott's army entered Mexico City after the final weeks of hand-to-hand combat in its fortified suburbs. Military operations then came to an end; the US annexed Texas, New Mexico and California. Scott was still commander of the US army when the Civil War broke out in 1861. He was by now, however, well past his prime and President Abraham Lincoln retired him before the end of the year, after the feeble initial offensives by the armies of the Union.

The Civil War was the first event in the internal history of the US to arouse passions in Scotland. In England's ruling class a good deal of sympathy with the Confederacy showed itself, and there was occasional talk of extending official recognition to it by the British Government. Something of the same feeling may have existed in Scotland too, for instance, among the textile manufacturers who imported cotton from the South. But the majority of Scots wished the Union well. The ever fiercer American controversies over slavery had had a moral effect inside Scotland too: that moral effect was to judge slavery wrong. American Scots fought on both sides in the Civil War and right in the heart of Edinburgh is a monument to them all erected in 1893 on the initiative of the US consul; little is known of him but, with a name like Wallace Bruce, it is hard to believe he had no Scottish blood. The monument stands in the Old Calton Burying Ground, beside the tombs of the philosopher David Hume and other luminaries of the Enlightenment, and is adorned by a statue of Lincoln bestowing freedom on a slave. Six Scots killed in the war were re-interred nearby.

Lincoln had plenty to do with American Scots, and not always happily, during the four years of fighting. They figured, for example, among the Union's mediocre generals who failed, in the first year or two of hostilities, to achieve the decisive breakthrough which the superior resources of the northern states in men and material ought to have brought. Winfield Scott was succeeded as supreme commander of the US army by George B. McLellan, aged only 34, who never showed the energy which might have been expected of his comparative youth. The first battle of the war, at Bull Run a few miles from Washington, showed the southerners would be by no means easy to defeat. The Union's forces there, led by Irvin McDowell, could make no impression on the Confederates under Joseph E. Johnston.

On the other side the hero of that battle was Thomas 'Stonewall' Jackson, who inspired his troops to stand 'like a stone wall' against McDowell's assaults. He came of Scotch-Irish stock, with the virtues and the vices this implied. He was a strict Calvinist, religious almost to the point of mania, curt and blunt in speech, indifferent to his personal needs. His was the God of the Old Testament rather than the New. He actually proposed that neither side should take prisoners, that all captives falling into their enemies' hands should be killed at once. While on the march he would call a general halt, usually once a day, for his soldiers to say prayers. He felt powerful, presumably divine, intuitions: with no explanation to anyone, he would rouse his army at midnight and set it in motion. His career in the war was brilliant but brief. He spent 1862 on a sparkling campaign in the Shenandoah Valley, across the Blue Ridge of Virginia, clearing it of northern forces and ruling out its use as a corridor of invasion. Then he played a major part at the Battle of Fredericksburg, where the Union's army, trying to advance directly on the Confederate capital of Richmond, was slaughtered in frontal assaults on his positions. When it renewed its campaign in the spring of 1863, it advanced to Chancellorsville on the River Rappahannock, with 130,000 troops against 60,000 Confederates. In a stunning manoeuvre, these divided their forces and Jackson was entrusted with rolling up the Union's flank – which he did with tremendous dash, falling on the hapless northern boys as they bivouacked in relief that no real fighting had occurred that day. It was a triumph for Jackson. But at dusk he fell mortally wounded as he closed his trap, shot by a detachment of his own men who mistook him in the fading light for an enemy officer. The Confederacy was never able to replace him.

The South kept going on little more than such feats of arms, in which daring exploits by the cavalry prominently figured. Most daring of all was another Scottish-American general, James Ewell Brown Stuart, known to his men as Jeb and loved by them for his gallantry and humour. He enjoyed his war: he specialised in raids round the rear of the Union's armies, to wreak havoc, carry out reconnaissance, confuse the generals and divert their forces. One in July 1862 disconcerted the cautious McLellan even more than usual. Another helped the Confederates to win the Second Battle of Bull Run. A third took Stuart far into the North. He was then engaged at Fredericksburg and Chancellorsville, before going on to the decisive Battle of Gettysburg.

Gettysburg took place in southern Pennsylvania. With the Union fought to a standstill in Virginia, there was every incentive for the Confederates to invade northern territory. States like Maryland, slave states which had not seceded, might be induced to do so. It was even possible, given a sustained and successful campaign, that Washington could be captured. Any victory on the Union's soil would shatter its confidence. But Gettysburg put an end to such hopes. It was fought over three days, 1–3 July 1863. Stuart did little to help because this time he ranged so far, to within twenty miles of Washington, as to lose touch altogether with the rest of the Confederate army. The Battle of Gettysburg finished when, in frustration, hardened southern veterans were sent charging over an open field a mile wide towards the enemy's breastworks, much as the northerners had done at Fredericksburg; they, too, fell in their thousands. The Confederacy had shot its bolt. It would afterwards fight on slowly contracting lines till strangled. Stuart did not live to see that; he was killed during a minor action in 1864.

The final and fatal squeeze began in the West. Johnston had been transferred from Virginia to the Confederate command in this theatre. He more than met his match in Ulysses S. Grant. Grant, to all appearances a charmless, dull and silent fellow, had had a bad start to his military career. He fought in Mexico, in a war he regarded as wrong, and a few years later was forced to resign from the army because he drank too much. By the time the Civil War broke out he was shabby and discouraged, working as a clerk in his brothers' store at Galena, Illinois. But he joined up again and was lucky enough to be made colonel of a regiment of volunteers. In his capacity to handle these men his hitherto hidden military abilities at last shone through.

Grant made his name with the capture early in 1862 of Fort Donelson, which guarded central Tennessee. He attacked it with such vigour that its Confederate commander asked for terms. Grant replied: 'No terms except an unconditional and immediate surrender can be accepted.' At a time when the Union was failing everywhere else, this made him a hero. From then on he was known as Unconditional Surrender Grant. He went on to capture Nashville, capital of Tennessee, and Memphis, the state's largest city. His object now was to advance down the Mississippi River, so as to control the main artery for supplies in the region and to cut the Confederacy in two. New Orleans had already been captured by a naval assault, and soon along the whole length of the river only the fortress of Vicksburg was held by the Confederates. Grant besieged it, an immensely difficult enterprise because the fortress stood on a headland amid swamps and the Mississippi frequently flooded. Months were spent in various futile operations, while Grant took regular refuge in whisky. Any other general might have abandoned the siege. But he had an odd psychological complex about turning back. He seemed unable to retrace his steps, even when it would be the simplest thing to do. Johnston tried to come to the relief of Vicksburg, but was held off. It surrendered on 4 July 1863 just as, a thousand miles to the east, the shattered Confederate army started its retreat from Gettysburg.

The days of the Confederacy were numbered. Johnston reorganised his ragged forces in the Army of the Tennessee. It could do nothing to stop William Sherman's march to the sea through the heart of Georgia, laying the state waste from Atlanta to Savannah. 'War is hell,' he said, and certainly he made it so. Meanwhile Lincoln, despairing of all his other generals, put Grant in command of the Union's entire armed strength. In the spring of 1864 he arrived in Washington, for the first time in his life, and opened the terminal phase of the war.

Still, an initial series of bloody battles – the Wilderness, Spotsylvania Court House, Cold Harbour – amazed Grant with the energy and martial spirit of the Confederates; he had seen nothing like this in the West. He decided Richmond could not be stormed by frontal attack. Taking his army to the James River, he laid siege to the capital of the Confederacy from June 1864 to April 1865, gradually extending his lines westwards so as to cut off supplies and reinforcements, while Sherman hastened up through the Carolinas. The Confederates had to lengthen their lines round Richmond too, till they were weak at every point. In the decisive assault, on 2 April 1865, Grant broke through – and the war came effectively to an end. He was never a brilliant general; he just kept fighting till he won. American Scots had given more than their fair share of heroism and sacrifice in the reforging of the nation that the Civil War represented.

One and indivisible, its continental territory defined and secured, the US could begin its long ascent to global power. During the remainder of the nineteenth century it began to build an empire, though not called that, because Americans took a curiously self-righteous, not to say humbugging, attitude to the contemporary European imperialism. But, for all the world like Britain or Germany, the US rapidly extended its sway beyond its own boundaries, in part by attacking lesser rivals.

The Spanish–American War of 1898 represented as good an instance as any of a stronger power taking over by force from a weaker one. Theodore Roosevelt, of Scottish blood on his mother's side, played his part in the conquest of Cuba in just the same sort of swashbuckling spirit as any European imperialist in Africa or Asia. He waxed as loud in his triumphalism afterwards. The independence of Panama from Colombia in 1903, during his presidency, followed by the immediate cession of the Canal Zone to the US, was an example of his playing fast and loose with a territory and people who could by no means be regarded as bent under a colonial yoke. Three American warships lay in the harbour of Colon when the Panamanians staged their timid little revolution, and marines promptly landed to 'restore order'.

The ultimate aim of the US was, of course, to bring its possessions, or most of them, to self-government. But that was Britain's aim too, and in fact the US moved only a little ahead of the European powers during the final phase of decolonisation in the mid-twentieth century. Americans long remained wary of saying out loud that might was right.

In the annals of this lengthy phase of more or less formal US imperialism one Scottish-American name stands out, the name of MacArthur. The clan claims descent from King Arthur, the legendary ruler of Britain in the Dark Ages; later it was absorbed into Clan Campbell, which came to dominate the West of Scotland. It was from Glasgow that Arthur MacArthur emigrated to Massachusetts in 1825. His son, who had the same name, found his vocation when he joined the US army in the Civil War and rose to be a colonel by the age of twenty. He was wounded three times, mentioned ten times in despatches and decorated for his gallantry at the Battle of Missionary Ridge, while fighting under Grant in Tennessee. Years later in the Spanish–American War he saw combat in Cuba, where he became a friend of Roosevelt's, and the Philippines. After they were ceded to the US he became the military governor, introducing progressive legal and educational reforms. He was the father of General Douglas MacArthur.

The younger MacArthur seemed destined from the start for a distinguished military career. His father's connection with Roosevelt brought him to the White House while he was still in his twenties as an aide to the President. In the First World War he went to France, fought vigorously and was decorated several times. Afterwards he became superintendent of West Point, the American military academy. He spent more time in the Philippines and eventually, in 1930, was appointed chief of the general staff in Washington, where he developed warm relations with President Franklin D. Roosevelt. But the US was still in its isolationist phase and a senior general had little to attend to except plans for a future conflict of which the nature remained unclear – though Americans were already suspicious of Japanese ambitions in the Pacific and Far East. MacArthur actually retired from the US army in 1937, having done all he could do in peacetime. In fact his career had hardly begun.

MacArthur had already been recalled to overall command in Asia before the attack on Pearl Harbor in December 1941; clearly Roosevelt was expecting war with Japan. MacArthur set up his headquarters in the Philippines, which the Japanese at once invaded. Hard fighting followed, but the Americans were forced to evacuate the archipelago after a few months. 'I will return,' said MacArthur as he left. He went to Australia to take command of all Allied forces in the South-western Pacific. The conflict in this theatre became primarily naval and aerial, fought by bombers from aircraft carriers. Only after the Japanese navy had been decisively beaten at the Battle of Midway Island in June 1943 could the long fight back begin over the various territories occupied by the enemy. MacArthur conducted the campaign which recaptured New Guinea in the course of 1944 and by the next year he was back, as promised, in the Philippines, whence he sent his forces on to Okinawa. The defeat of Japan was now a matter of time, yet it needed the dropping of atomic bombs on Hiroshima and Nagasaki to bring the war to a swift end. MacArthur accepted the Japanese surrender on board USS *Missouri* on 2 September 1945.

MacArthur was appointed to direct the Allied occupation of Japan – in effect, ruler of the country. History may record that for all his military glory he did his finest work, because it was the most permanent and constructive, in this civilian sphere. He dealt with the Japanese in no vindictive spirit, though they had fought the war ruthlessly and few in the West would have protested at his taking revenge on them. But the prime need in a shattered nation was to reconcile it to its fate, and in particular to see that it renounced militarism. MacArthur deferred to the sensibilities of the people by keeping Emperor Hirohito on as head of state, when he could easily have been deposed or even executed. But from now on he would be a constitutional monarch, and Japan was endowed with the institutions which brought it into the family of democratic nations. That formed also the foundation of the huge economic success of the Japanese in the post-war period. MacArthur's achievement here was acknowledged as outstanding – so much so that fellow Americans believed he might also govern the US if he could govern Japan so well. But efforts to nominate him as the Republican candidate against President Harry Truman in the election of 1948 faltered when MacArthur did not find enough support in the primaries.

Even yet, his work for his country had not finished. Korea was one of the countries divided at the end of the Second World War into Communist and Western spheres of influence, both soon organised into separate republics. In 1950, North Korea invaded South Korea and overran most of it. This was the first big test of the new United Nations, which authorised its members to send contingents of their armies to resist the aggression. MacArthur was appointed their commander. The initial situation seemed desperate, but he broke out from the small area controlled by the UN and landed troops far behind the enemy lines, at Inchon, forcing the North Koreans to turn and meet his attack. Then he steadily drove them back to the Yalu River, which formed their boundary with Communist China. The question was now what the Chinese would do in the face of a potential threat to their own territory. If they were to unleash the huge Red Army, the whole nature of the conflict would change and might develop into a Third World War. At the same time, the Chinese would obviously aid the North Koreans while they could. MacArthur wanted in these circumstances to bomb targets in Manchuria, the province behind the Yalu. But Truman refused to authorise such a perilous move. It is normal for a general and his commander-in-chief to get into disputes about strategy, but the strong-minded MacArthur chose to make this one public, and the President relieved him of his command. MacArthur all the same received a hero's welcome when he returned to the US. He had in any event saved South Korea from Communism: a ceasefire in the war soon followed, leaving the boundary between the two Korean republics much as it had been before.

MacArthur was certainly a man who carried the old Scottish martial values to America, with his great fighting spirit which might tend in the heat of battle to become a little too rash, and have to be restrained.

5

WRITERS

There is more to independence than politics. The sager Scotsmen, such as Adam Smith, predicted during the American Revolution that even if the colonies were lost to Britain the accustomed relations between them would resume after the war – perhaps with still greater vitality, because both sides would then be free. And so it proved, especially in the sphere of economics and the trading links which most interested Smith. It meant that to some extent the US remained dependent on Britain, for example in manufactured goods, because at the time Britain had the more advanced, the first industrial, economy.

The point holds for culture as well. Till 1776, the British and Americans shared a common culture: they were schooled in much the same way, they read the same books, they played the same music, they sang the same songs, they built the same sort of buildings and painted the same sort of paintings. This, too, continued after the independence of the US, nurtured by a constant flow of new immigrants who, in the early decades of the Republic, still came largely from the British Isles. Whatever their motives for crossing the Atlantic Ocean, they brought their culture with them to reinforce the culture they found on the other side. This culture therefore kept much in common with that of the mother country. Not for perhaps half a century did Americans begin to find means of cultural self-expression which were truly independent, owed more to experience of the New World than to the example of the Old World, at the same time reaching a level of universal significance which made them worthy of attention elsewhere, and makes them worthy of attention today by anyone interested in western culture.

One problem in all this was that the culture of the English-speaking world remained quite an elitist culture. It was not so elitist as that of some European countries, especially France, but it was too elitist for Americans to feel quite comfortable with it, except perhaps in the lettered circles of Boston, New York or Philadelphia. English-speaking culture was dominated by London, compared with which those other cities felt like poor, provincial places, as their citizens sensed if they went to London. This was the capital of a great empire. It had a Court and an aristocracy setting the tone in fashion, manners and speech. They patronised museums and galleries and concert-halls and libraries. The city attracted writers and composers and artists from all over Britain and Europe. It was a huge cultural metropolis. Though Americans came from a lusty young country with nothing to be ashamed of, London made them feel inferior, above all culturally inferior.

But then, Scots felt exactly the same way. Their own capital of Edinburgh, a city both stately and picturesque, had once had a culture focused on the Court, but that disappeared to London along with King James in 1603. The Union of the Parliaments in 1707 then removed the immediate source of political patronage, on which creative thinkers and artists are often forced to rely. Edinburgh seemed to have lost its old glory. It, too, looked poor and provincial now. Scottish culture in fact remained vigorous, and grew if anything more vigorous. But there was a difficulty of validating it in the face of a metropolitan culture which assumed its own superiority and which was assumed by most observers to be indeed superior.

In other words, Scotland and America faced similar cultural dilemmas, especially in the period from 1707 to 1776 when they shared membership of the British Empire, but afterwards also. While they were divided by distance and many other things, some things they had in common. One of them was this complex though ultimately fruitful status of provincials in an oceanic empire which, through the consequent problems in relations with the metropolis, made both peoples define themselves better.

If we look at them in, say, the year of 1763, when the Treaty of Paris was signed at the end of the Seven Years War, we find both of them proud to be British and proud of the Britain which had just humbled France and other European powers in the first truly global struggle, winning military glory everywhere from Montreal to Manila. All the same, something in the awesome scale of this success made Scots and Americans a little uneasy, in particular abashed at the badges of their provinciality. They could not but be aware of how far away from the centre of affairs they were, how little their own concerns counted there, how hard it was to get through to the people who mattered – who might then, if at last reached, affect to be put off by the funny accents of Glasgow or Boston. There was an undercurrent of insecurity in the internal relationships of this empire, to offset its external triumphs. But the moral demands generated by the insecurity devolved on the provincials. The metropolis went on in its own sweet way, unheeding of the troubles it was laying up for itself. It fell to Scots and Americans themselves to deal with the dilemmas their situation caused. And in the circumstances they showed themselves capable of greater moral exertion than Englishmen.

Both Scots and Americans, for example, had to ask themselves some basic questions about how society is best constituted. Both their provinces felt conscious of standing on the edge of civilisation, and of the barbarism in the hills and forests beyond. Scotland had an internal frontier between Lowlands and Highlands, which only eighteen years before 1763 had been spectacularly breached by the Jacobite clans. In America after 1763, the British administration formalised the frontier between the area of white settlement and the territories of the Indian nations, in the so-called Proclamation Line, policed by colonial officials. So it seemed that Americans could look forward to living permanently next to ferocious and formidable neighbours. Nobody in London ever had to face a claymore or a tomahawk, and the fact that Scots and Americans did have to, or might have to, made them think rather differently about certain matters.

In Philadelphia on July 4, 1776, fifty-six men sign the Declaration of Independence, including twenty-one with Scottish blood and two born Scots, James Wilson and John Witherspoon.

'Signing the Declaration of Independence July 4 1776' by John Trumbull.
Yale University Art Gallery/Bridgeman Art Library

'I am American in my principles,' said the great Scottish philosopher, David Hume.

'David Hume (1711–76)' by Allan Ramsay.
Scottish National Portrait Gallery/Bridgeman Art Library

His waistline flattered by the portraitist, Henry Knox,
George Washington's general of artillery, rests a hand on one of the cannon
which blasted the British from America.

'Major General Henry Knox (1750–1806)'. Private collection/The Stapleton Collection/
Bridgeman Art Library

With the First World War over, President Woodrow Wilson arrives in Paris in December 1918 ready to stake all on his personal presence at the peace conference. He would lose.

© mirrorpix

The Scot stands on the burning deck, amid shattered masts
and fallen sails: the sort of tight corner from which John Paul Jones
liked to win his naval battles.

'John Paul Jones, Commodore in the service of the United States of America'
Private collection/Bridgeman Art Library

Several routes to the West were opened up by American Scots, in conditions less romantic than this evocation of the Oregon Trail by Albert Bierstadt.

'The Oregon Trail' by Albert Bierstadt. Private collection/Bridgeman Art Library

William McIntosh, son of a Scottish trader and an Indian princess, rose to be chief of the Creeks and introduced tartan fabric to the native costume.

John Carter Brown Library, Providence, Rhode Island

Davy Crockett, Scottish-American hero of the frontier,
'fresh from the backwoods, half-horse, half-alligator, a little touched
with the snapping turtle'.
'Colonel Davy Crockett (1786–1836)'. Library of Congress, Washington DC,
USA/Bridgeman Art Library

Of the 189 men who sacrificed themselves at the Alamo and won independence for Texas, fifty were American Scots.

'The Siege of the Alamo' by William H. Brooker. Library of Congress, Washington DC, USA/Bridgeman Art Library

The Ku Klux Klan, modelled on fake Scottish antecedents,
exerted a sinister influence in the South – and even in England,
where this picture was taken.

© mirrorpix

Andrew Carnegie, son of a weaver from Dunfermline, plays the Highland laird at
Skibo Castle after retirement from his tycoon's career in the US.

©mirrorpix

Publisher Malcolm Forbes, with daughter Moira,
receives an honorary degree at Aberdeen University, a few miles
from where his father was born.

© mirrorpix

All his rivals have found it hard to keep up with Rupert Murdoch, the
Scottish-Australian-American media mogul.

©mirrorpix

Katharine Hepburn glows in the tropical heat while
playing the female lead in *The African Queen*.
©mirrorpix

Robert Redford, here in *Butch Cassidy and the Sundance Kid*,
is not the only movie star born to an Edinburgh milkman.
© mirrorpix

Donald Trump and Marla Maples looking glamorous and wealthy.
© Getty Images

9.18 p.m. Sunday, July 20, 1969

**THE HISTORIC DAY
FOR WHICH THERE IS REALLY ONLY ONE HEADLINE..**

MAN ON THE MOON

From Arthur Smith at Mission Control in Houston

THEY'VE done it! AT 3.39 B.S.T. this morning, just five hours after lunar touch-down, astronauts Neil Armstrong and Edwin Aldrin opened the hatch of their spacecraft Eagle in the Sea of Tranquillity. And by 4 a.m. Armstrong was taking man's first steps on the Moon.

The astronauts, who had landed on the Moon at precisely 20 seconds before 9.18 B.S.T. last night, cut out a planned four-hour rest period and stepped out on the first real inter-planetary space spectacular.

The change in plan was fixed up in a dramatic early morning exchange of messages with Mission Control in Houston, Texas.

Armstrong said: "Our recommendation at this point is planning to start extra-vehicular activity at about 8 o'clock Houston time (2.15 B.S.T.), if you concur. We'll give you some time to think about it."

In two seconds flat, back flashed the answer from capsule communicator Charles Duke: "We thought about it. We will support it."

And with a flash of humour, he added: "You guys are getting prime TV time there."

Knock-out

Armstrong, referring to the £166,000 TV camera which was to record the Moon-walk, replied: "I hope that little TV set works, but we will see."

For the astronauts, the early walk solved a problem that could have been tricky.

After all the tremendous excitement of the landing, it is probable that if they had gone on with the planned rest period, they would have needed knock-out pills to cool them down enough to sleep.

And, in a chain reaction, they would possibly have had to take pep pills to shake off the effects of the first drug when the time eventually came to make their walk.

By going out early, they avoided all that and faced no risk that their judgment might be impaired by pills at a time when split-second reactions could be vital.

Finale

For President Nixon, the change of plans meant a quick up-timing of arrangements. Soon after the earlier walk was fixed, it was announced in Washington that he would speak to the Moon Men 55 minutes after they stepped on the lunar surface.

The walk was the grand finale to the greatest show in the universe, a show that began dramatically at 6.47 p.m. yesterday when Eagle, with Armstrong and Aldrin aboard. As it parted from the command module, Columbia, piloted by Mike Collins, third man on

4 am..Armstrong takes the first steps outside

the mission, Armstrong said exultantly: "Eagle undocked. Eagle has wings." The great adventure was go.

Then, for hours as millions watched on TV, the long, tense ritual of orbit and descent was played out, until just before 9.18 p.m. history was made as Eagle touched down on a pock-marked lunar plain.

"The Eagle has landed." Armstrong said. And within minutes he and Aldrin were sending back man's first close-up, ground-level view of the Moon.

Mystery

Meantime, as America triumphed, their space rival, Russia, stole into the picture. From Moscow it was announced that the mystery Russian Moon-probe Luna 15 had swooped into a new orbit within 10 miles of the lunar surface.

As speculation grew about a possible Russian scene-stealer landing by Luna-15, the mystery deepened when the spacecraft signals ceased after 9 p.m.

And early today there was a new theory—that the Russian craft might have smashed into a mountain on the far side of the Moon. From Moscow, there was no comment.

But nothing could steal the glory of Armstrong and Aldrin as they flew their fragile Eagle to a frightening, but safe, touchdown, bringing true

the centuries-old dream of men—to land in an alien world

From Houston, Texas, ground control told Eagle: "We're blue but we're breathing again."

Minutes after the landing Eagle was sending its signals back to Earth under the new proud call-sign Tranquillity Base.

Delicate

During the last few tense seconds of the descent to the lunar surface, reports flashed back and forth as Armstrong and Aldrin delicately jockeyed Eagle to a safe landing site—about four miles beyond the planned area because of rocks on the original site.

This was how it went:
From Control: "Eagle looking great. You're go."
From Eagle: "75 feet, looking good, 50 seconds, lights on. down 2½, forward, forward picking up some dust . . . just move to the right a little . . ."
Then, dramatically: "The Eagle has landed."

Disaster

Mission control flashed congratulations: "Guys, that was one beautiful job. There are a lot of smiling faces in this room, all over the world."

Armstrong replied: "There are two of them here. . ."

Behind the breezy cross-talk lay the relief of safe touchdown after what Armstrong revealed could have been

Continued on Back Page

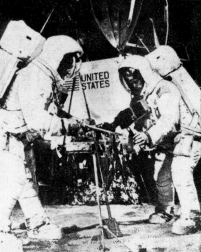

● THIS was how the astronauts prepared for the great Moon walk . . . by practising the whole operation inside a Moon simulator at Houston. On the last test run, when this picture was taken, Edwin Aldrin (left) used a scoop for collecting samples while Neil Armstrong tested a camera. Today they know if the rehearsal matched the reality.

MEN OF THE MOONSHOT—Pages 9, 10 and 11

Glasgow's *Daily Record* headlines the giant step for mankind.
It was soon discovered that both Neil Armstrong and Edwin Aldrin had Scottish blood.

© mirrorpix

One thing they thought about was culture and progress, what cultural conditions were conducive to progress and how this could be prevented from descending into chaos by stable institutions. The question was connected in turn with the distinctions in socio-political structure between England on the one hand and Scotland or America on the other. The main distinction lay between the dominance of a high aristocracy and its absence or non-existence. England was run by the landed class, into which even the merchants who might have competed with it bought themselves as soon as they grew rich enough. Scotland possessed an ancient nobility, but since 1707 most of it had gone to London. America by now housed great landowners, but no aristocracy as such. Both countries had to rest content with rulers from the minor gentry and professional class who could not vaunt themselves on blood or acres and did so instead on culture or politeness.

All this loosened the hold on the provincial mind of the traditions and habits which seemed so secure in England. It opened that provincial mind to new modes of thinking and to criticism of its cultural inheritance. While most people carried on in their accustomed ways, at the margin there was an effect on individuals' imagination and creativity in Scotland and America without which what we now call the Enlightenment in both countries could scarcely have occurred. Up to a point, amid the interchange fostered by political unity in the British Empire till 1776, this strengthened ties between them. The Founding Fathers of the US read the Scottish philosophers and employed their concepts, as we have seen. Of course, Scotland and America were also different from each other, not just from England, and the difference tore them apart politically. The relationship was not then destroyed, but became more subtle. One task for the US was now to forge a new cultural identity. That was the task Scots had faced since 1707, and Americans could learn something from their experience.

Perhaps surprisingly, the Enlightenment ceased to shape this relationship. The Enlightenment was an intellectual movement, in which great minds grappled with deep questions and sought new answers to them for the modern world. For that reason, its appeal to the people at large remained limited, because most of them were too caught up with their everyday affairs to bother with such things. About the Scottish Enlightenment in particular there was also something a little dry, even arid. Scots were themselves before long complaining that, while their thinkers might have generated a fresh outlook on life, they offered little sense of any meaning in it. Early on, the intense mental activity created a sort of emotional reaction.

James Macpherson was a Highlander who went as a young man in the 1760s to serve as a colonial official in Florida. He travelled to the back country and saw something of the Indians, though he does not appear to have been impressed by them as examples of the noble savage. He had gone to America to make his fortune, but failed. The way he did make it was, after he returned, by publishing *Ossian*. According to him, this was an epic poem of the primitive Celts dating back 2,000 years and celebrating their warriors' deeds in much the same way as Homer had done for the ancient Greeks. Macpherson claimed to have discovered old Gaelic bards in the Highlands who could still recite this poem, just as the *Iliad* and the *Odyssey* had once been recited: he was merely collecting and editing the fragments to present them to the public. He suffered denunciation as a fraud, but his efforts did make him famous all over Europe and America. Thomas Jefferson thought *Ossian* wonderful, and so did Napoleon Bonaparte. The poem struck some profound chord in an age of reason. It revealed, beneath the bland surface of civilisation, that there were elemental forces at work, that people even yet yearned to be sated by the passions of love and war. And it created an image of Scotland as a land where those passions could be evoked, a land of romance.

Macpherson remained an intellectual, however, and one who preferred to curry favour with the imperial elite in London. To make a wider appeal, romantic Scotland had to await a figure from a contrasting background, Robert Burns, son of a poor farmer in Ayrshire. Burns is even yet regarded as an authentic voice of the Scottish people, today perhaps more than ever before. His expression of pure lyrical feeling, arising from his loves, hopes, dreams and sufferings – most of this in the Scots language, which struck straight to the hearts of his first readers – is almost without parallel in the world's literature. His poems moved and move not only the Scots of the homeland but also those who have wandered far away, together with their descendants and many more who otherwise know nothing of Scotland. That includes Americans. Just two years after Burns brought out his work in the Kilmarnock edition of 1786, it was published in the US too. Numerous editions appeared there up to the turn of nineteenth century and beyond, Burns's use of his vernacular being apparently no barrier to understanding. His cult grew among the American people with hardly less vigour than among the Scots people. The Burns Supper in Boston marking the centenary of his birth in 1859 also attracted men of letters: Ralph Waldo Emerson, Henry Wadsworth Longfellow, James Russell Lowell and Oliver Wendell Holmes. The appeal of Burns to a varied public in a wholly different milieu from his own is at this distance in time a little hard to pin down. Probably it had something to do with the notion of the 'heaven-taught ploughman', the natural genius never bound by the rules of art who emerged from a simple, rural society, the sort of society most Americans still lived in. At the same time he strengthened the image of a romantic Scotland preserving and cherishing its heritage of poetry and song.

Even the popularity of Burns at the end of the eighteenth century was as nothing compared to that of Sir Walter Scott in the first decades of the nineteenth century. He came from a different background again. Essentially he was a man of Edinburgh, a lawyer at home among the literati of the Scottish capital. But he nurtured his roots in the countryside of the Borders where he at length built his own house of Abbotsford and lived like a laird (though a modern laird surrounded by mechanical contraptions and doing his writing by gas-light). Still, the greatness of Scott lies in the way he transcends social barriers, as well as the barriers of time and place, to create a gallery of characters rivalling that of William Shakespeare and Charles Dickens in range and in the conviction of the portrayals. And all of Scotland is there in that gallery, great Scots and humble Scots, good Scots and bad Scots, their heroic virtues as well as their despicable vices. Quite apart from his invention of the historical novel, with its variety, drama and colour, giving his enormous readership a sense of their own place in history, he remade Scotland, not only in image but also in actuality. It was Scott who masterminded the visit of King George IV to Edinburgh in 1822, the first time a reigning monarch had set foot in the country for almost two centuries. The Scotland that Scott then paraded before his sovereign was a new nation, a nation united because it had cast off its fatal divisions for a secure place in Union and Empire. While the devotion and sacrifice of earlier generations could be lauded in themselves, they must now yield to a recognition that the causes served by those earlier generations were things of the past. There was no purpose in ploughing up the exhausted soil of history all over again. In his writings, Scott joined the old and the new. He celebrated national tradition while rejoicing that it had, with whatever difficulty, carried the Scots to their present happy condition.

Scott is often remembered as a writer of novels about remote medieval times purveying an admiration of rather bogus values of nobility and chivalry; this impression is what accounts for his lesser appeal today. Yet the works which made him most famous in his own time were the Waverley novels, all set in the Scotland of what was for him a recent period, from the Union of 1707 down to the end of the Napoleonic Wars in 1815. They are about a people poised between past and present, and about a nation on the move. These novels often start with some formula recalling that the strange fictional events to be narrated in their pages are supposed to have taken place not so very long before. In effect the readers are invited to marvel at how fast things can change, and to reflect on the difference a short span of years can make to places and human types still to be seen around them. That sense of historical progress was easy to bring home to contemporary Scots, whose ancestors a century before had been burning witches, and who themselves now lived in a workshop of the world. This was one basic reason why they loved the novels.

But it is easy to imagine how the same sense of historical progress would have appealed to Americans, whose ancestors a century before had been pioneers in a wilderness and who themselves now lived in an optimistic young Republic founded as an example to mankind. At any rate, Scott's popularity in the US quite equalled that in any country of Europe, every new book being awaited with bated breath, guaranteed huge and immediate sales. Scott also had a positive effect on American writers and on the wider character of America's literary culture. His appeal helped to create a situation in which that culture could break free from its antecedents.

Ever since the Revolution, American critics had been calling for the creation of a national literature to reflect the new values of the young Republic. But it is not easy to write books reflecting new values if the literary models followed by writers are old, inherited from the civilisation of Europe. Scott showed Americans a way forward, because he had had to resolve the clash of new and old in his own work. It was Scott's Scottishness that allowed him to do this. Those Waverley novels which deal with an earlier period of history show Scotland as poor, backward, racked by religious and political fanaticism. The novels which deal with a later period take place against the background of a country which has enriched itself, which is advancing materially and marking up intellectual and literary achievements of the first order. Scottish writers were the ones who worked out this modern cultural identity.

They did so by ceasing to think of English or French (or Latin or Greek) models as the ones they were somehow obliged to follow in order to join the club of the culturally superior. They turned back to their own people, to its history and traditions and legends. They wrote about their own land, the mountains and glens, the straths and lochs, the picturesque burghs and the tranquil countryside. They described the home lives of its citizens, and the framework of habits and customs in which those lives were played out. Nobody did so better than Scott, with his urge to capture and preserve everything that was most strange and wonderful about Scotland. In all of this lay a clear message for American writers, who heeded it. From about 1820, they gained the confidence to start describing American manners, scenes and history, often taking Scott as their model and example. One critic, John Neal, set it out explicitly. What readers in the US should look for in their works of literature, he said, was 'a plain, real, hearty, North American story; a story, which, if we could have our way, should be altogether American – peculiarly and exclusively so, throughout; as much American to say all, in a word, as the Scotch novels are Scotch'.

The first American to make his living as a man of letters was Washington Irving. He came of a Scottish milieu which had changed little from being transplanted to the New World. Born in 1783 in New York, he was the son of a merchant from the Orkney Islands who settled there as an importer of goods from Britain and France and, unlike many others of his type, opted to stay on after the Revolution. The father did not, however, alter his accustomed way of life. A Presbyterian deacon and elder, he spent his evenings reading the Bible to his family and took them three times to church on Sundays. A strict upbringing did not cramp his three sons, all of whom took to literature and journalism in one way or another. This did not go down well in New York, a commercial city with as yet few cultural pretensions: the brothers were thought to be idlers. His father insisted that young Washington should train as a lawyer, but he preferred to write satires on his philistine fellow citizens. Soon he tired of them, and crossed the Atlantic to visit his relations in Scotland. There he made the acquaintance of Sir Walter Scott, of Francis Jeffrey, editor of the *Edinburgh Review*, and of John Murray, founder of the publishing house, while he practised to perfect his own literary style. The experience helped him to produce his mature works, the Hudson Valley stories, with the unforgettable character of Rip van Winkle, one of the original Dutch community in the region who falls asleep and wakes up twenty years later to find its tranquil way of life has been overturned by the American Revolution. For Irving the device, gently comic in effect, is really an expression of nostalgia, of regret over the results of progress. The stories deal with innocent love, with the beauties of nature and with moral decency, all meant to mark a contrast with the callous go-getting and hard bargaining of contemporary New York. Irving's readers took the point: they accused him of being un-American and (like Scott) a Tory at heart.

So Irving moved at best halfway towards producing the authentic American literature the critics were calling for. The comment of Neal's quoted above came in his review of a novel by James Fenimore Cooper, *The Spy*. Cooper was among the first to write American romances, and the one whose work has lasted best. Of course he did not, in a new country, have the same wealth of historical material as Scott had to draw on. Instead he found a motif which would enjoy a permanent popularity: the frontier. This was where he sought the settings and subjects, the habits and ways of life which could point a contrast with the humdrum existences of most of his readers and pose them the questions they ought to ask of themselves.

In Cooper's best novels, of which the most famous is *The Last of the Mohicans*, his big theme is the clash between the civilised and the primitive, between life on the frontier and life in more peaceful surroundings, between the white settlers and the Indian tribesmen, between land as property and nature as morality. Till the mid-eighteenth century, Scotland had had an internal frontier too, dividing the Highlands from the Lowlands, and Cooper's treatment of his chosen themes can be compared with Scott's treatment of that one. Neither author left his public secure in its prejudices: while the apparent message of their novels is that a well-ordered and rather conservative society forms the best matrix for its citizens to fulfil themselves, at the same time both hanker after a freer, more individual and independent existence. Scott's heroes in particular are often wishy-washy characters, and the reader will sense that his emotional interest lies rather in figures who on the face of it are less than morally exemplary. Scott cannot hide a sneaking admiration for the untamed Highlanders or the fearless Covenanters, a feeling which found parallels in Cooper's treatment of the Indians. The implication is that the Highland or Indian societies might have been in special ways better than their bloodless successors. Neither of those societies was merely anarchic. In their own fierce fashion, they had deep roots and strong bonds. In the modern world the roots have been torn up and the bonds have been broken. So human beings have now lost something which in its time gave their lives meaning. Even amid historical progress they are the poorer for it and perhaps we, the readers, are so too.

To claim that Scott marked a climax of the Scottish literary tradition has become controversial today, though this would have been accepted without question till fairly recent times. It may be a superficial reading, but his style of composition, his enlightened values and his Tory politics seem too remote from the Scotland of the twenty-first century. One of the problems is that nobody much followed him in the range and the depth of his universal interests. England had Charles Dickens and France had Honoré de Balzac or Emile Zola to fix their probing gaze on the advance of an industrial society, to bring out its tensions and to suggest how the human damage it caused might be healed. Scots witnessed social upheavals during the rest of the nineteenth century if anything still more shattering than those among the English and French, yet their literary response proved pitiful. It was as if Scots could not put into words what was happening to them. Instead they hid it from their eyes and buried their noses in drivelling tales of immaturity or sentimental laments for doomed ways of life. With Scott, the Scottish novel for the time being peters out – except in one respect.

An older Calvinist tradition, of which Scott himself had been wary, turned out to be unexpectedly resilient. The tradition had itself always displayed a deep suspicion of imaginative literature as something morally dubious because it dealt in untruth and because it aroused passions. Most Scots brought up in that tradition had apparently felt themselves debarred from writing plays or novels – at least till the Enlightenment loosened its hold on them. Then, while its hold remained strong, they felt freer to explore the flaws and ambiguities in Calvinism. This situation produced what is often reckoned to be the greatest of all Scottish novels, as a single achievement surpassing even anything by Scott, *The Private Memoirs and Confessions of a Justified Sinner*, published by James Hogg in 1824. Hogg often had a hard time in enlightened Edinburgh. He was known there as the Ettrick Shepherd, a reference to his humble social background and lack of education, for which – appalling as it seems today – he was often pilloried by his more cultured and polite contemporaries. Yet he showed his worth in this novel, which is remarkable for two reasons: its thrilling exploration of antinomianism, the (actually heretical) Calvinist doctrine that the elect of God can commit no sin, even murder, which will damn them, so that they constantly teeter on the brink of the diabolical; and its narrative structure, which contains two accounts of the same events, different in style and in telling details of the story, so that the question of what is truth imposes itself throughout. Nowhere can the reader understand better the idea of Scottish culture as dualism, the play of opposites yoked together in what the modern poet Hugh MacDiarmid was to call the Caledonian antisyzygy, always prey to instability and collapse, undermining whatever hard-won and short-lived balance or harmony may be possible.

It is a vexed question how much *The Justified Sinner* was known or read in America. Early editions of the work are held in the older libraries of the US but, compared to Scott, Hogg never seems to have gained more than a small following. Indeed, it is easy to see how those mentally unprepared by some knowledge of Scotland for his harrowing exposé of the national psyche might soon have been put off him. Yet there are clear parallels between him and the first American writers to win, in the mid-nineteenth century, the appreciation of Europeans for being authors of work as profound as any produced at the time in the Old World. They, too, for the most part sprang from a Calvinist milieu, in New England. Calvinism in this region was, to be sure, English rather than Scottish in origin, and there are historical differences between the two. But these writers posed the same terrible questions about election and damnation.

With suitable adjustment of background, it is not hard to imagine how Nathaniel Hawthorne's *The Scarlet Letter*, his first successful novel published in 1849, might have been set in Scotland. The theme of a fallen woman and her love child also occurs in Scott's *Heart of Midlothian*, for example, though Hawthorne is much harsher in condemning a Calvinist society for pursuing with such relentless rigour anyone who offends its morality. He shares Scott's interest in history, notably in the *House of the Seven Gables*, the chronicle of an old family in New England with fortunes founded on pious theft. But Hawthorne comes closer to Hogg in his liking for symbolism and allegory as tools for psychological exploration of good and evil, of individual responsibility and guilt for them, and of the flawed idealism which issues in misery. There is more than one aspect to crime and retribution, both authors insist, and those intent on enforcing moral laws may do greater wrong than they repress. Historical experience seems indeed to demonstrate that every Calvinist society has its darker side. Every one has erected standards of respectability and conformism for the godly which can crush the spirit of those who, on whatever grounds, fall short of them. This is sin, the sin of intellectual and moral pride. Both Hogg and Hawthorne knew all about it from their own lives, Hogg from his scorned efforts to achieve propriety and Hawthorne from the horrible awareness that his own reputable family had reached its social position by humbugging greed and by its part in persecuting the witches of Salem. Pride forms a central motif of their own work.

Though born in Boston, Edgar Allan Poe is not really to be counted among this school of writers from New England; his parents, who were itinerant actors, just happened to be in the city at the time of his birth, and both died within a couple of years. Still, he did have a closer connection to Scotland, because then he was fostered by John Allan, a Scottish tobacco merchant in Richmond, Virginia (from whom he took his second name). Allan did business on both sides of the Atlantic Ocean. He took young Edgar with him to Britain for several years, and this sojourn included visits to Scotland, where Allan still had family at Fenwick in Ayrshire. It cannot be said that the experience left much literal impression on Poe's adult work, in which Scottish references are rare. Till he gained fame not long before his death, he had to scratch a living as a literary critic in the newspapers and his opinion of the books from Scotland he reviewed was in general not high.

Yet Poe had one unacknowledged debt to the classic Scottish novels. Part of their appeal to readers had lain in their evocation of the supernatural. From an early age Scott was fascinated by ghostly legends and superstitions which, with a sort of reluctant scepticism, he later wove into his plots: this folklore formed part of the romance of Scotland which he wished to present to the public. Into *Redgauntlet*, for example, Scott inserted the diabolical Wandering Willie's tale. An enthralling short story of his, 'The

Two Drovers' – which, apart from anything else, acutely observes the differences between Scotland and England – sets off with the irresistible line, 'There is blood on your hands, and it is English blood', towards its gory conclusion. Hogg threw off the enlightened constraints which Scott had imposed on himself in use of the supernatural. War, women and witchcraft were, in the title of Hogg's longest novel, *The Three Perils of Man*: each of them mysterious, unknowable, at the least unpredictable. Confusion, terror and evil are the devices in his work for dissolving conventional values and identities. In other words he takes us much further on from the discretion of Scott into the eerie world of Poe, the recognised modern master of the supernatural.

Poe spent most of his life on the margins of American society, as a man of letters struggling with sexual and alcoholic excess, but Herman Melville was by the standards of the US an aristocrat: born to mercantile wealth, destined for landed and official security, if with alarming pitfalls along the way. He was something else too – in the words of MacDiarmid:

> Melville (a Scot) kent weel hoo Christ's
> Corrupted into creeds malign,
>   Begotten strife's pernicious brood
> That claims for patron Him Divine . . .

Melville was indeed of Scottish descent, and preserved the Scot's anguished relationship with a Calvinist God. One of His continual little jokes seems to be the constitution of respectable, conformist societies which alienate their most talented, creative members. So it was with Melville too. He felt that he was a great writer, as in truth he was, yet that his fellow Americans did not grant him his due. He never got over the way the affluence and comfort of his childhood had been blighted by his father's bankruptcy. His youthful travels on a shoestring, including a spell on a whaler in the Pacific Ocean, brought him instant literary success when he wrote up his adventures, but the complexity of his masterpiece, *Moby Dick*, put the public off and his reputation soon faded. For the last forty years of his life he published hardly anything.

In that masterpiece the alienation of the writer is almost stuffed down the throats of his readers: they are apparently meant to swallow, for example, the long series of so-called cetological chapters on the biology of the whale and the technicalities of whaling. What they are meant to digest is that this represents a satire on the rational, analytic, scientific mode of thinking which forms the framework of modern consciousness, and on its lamentable inadequacy as a way of comprehending brief lives cast in a mysterious universe. Creative imagination may start to deal with the mystery, or at least set us off on a quest for meaning. But this itself, as in Captain Ahab's pursuit of the great white whale, can be corrupted, can turn malign and pernicious, finally and self-destructively obsessed with strife and blood, all the more so when we claim divine sanction for it. Man is irrevocably fallen, in Calvinist doctrine, and his state does not alter if he manages to construct a successful society: its confidence and complacency can even make things worse. These were Melville's underlying themes. They were also themes which might have been addressed in Scottish literature after Hogg, had it been able to produce another novelist of anywhere near his or Melville's stature. As it is, we may reflect that literary connections may be due not so much to the direct influence of one writer on another as to the way that each of them personally responds to the problems posed them by a common, or closely related, culture.

Instead the greatest writer of Victorian Scotland was not a novelist, or at least hardly recognisable as such. Thomas Carlyle first won renown as a critic, later as a historian and biographer. Those of his works which fall into other categories were for the most part baffling allegories and satires, quite without the beginning, middle and end that readers still expected of a novel. Apart from anything else, before he reached the age of 40 he despaired of literary life in Scotland and moved to London, where he stayed for the rest of his days. His personality, his style and his moral outlook remained impressed with the marks of his austere Calvinist upbringing. Even so the world, including the Americans, probably thought of him from then on as an English rather than a Scottish writer, and as a philosopher first and foremost.

Before his move, however, Carlyle received in the summer of 1833 an American visitor at his home in a remote corner of Dumfriesshire. This was Ralph Waldo Emerson, who had read his essays in various journals and wanted to seek out their author while on a European tour. In those days it took a good deal of effort to reach Craigenputtoch, a house lonely even by the standards of an age when there were few roads and little public transport. The effort proved worthwhile, because the two men struck up an immediate rapport. For a whole day they could not stop talking, and Carlyle felt his oppressive isolation broken. 'It was like the visit of an angel', his wife Jane wrote, 'and though he stayed with us hardly twenty-four hours, yet when he left us I cried – I could not help it.' This was the start of a lifelong friendship, reinforced by occasional later meetings but maintained mostly by a fruitful correspondence.

Both Carlyle and Emerson felt in 1833 deeply dissatisfied with life. Carlyle had been struggling to succeed as a writer for about fifteen years and, while his efforts were not in vain, the results still fell well short of his expectations and needs. In particular, he simply could not earn enough – this was probably the main reason for his move to London less than a year later. Emerson had just thrown up the career as a Unitarian minister for which his education at Harvard was meant to prepare him. In New England, Unitarianism gradually replaced the older Puritanism which had prevailed there before the American Revolution. This happened largely on the initiative of the congregations; since there was no longer any religious establishment, as under the British, they could determine for themselves which doctrines to accept and which preachers to hear. Emerson, after serving a short time at the Old North Church in Boston, found himself in discord with his flock over the nature of the Eucharist. He decided Unitarian ideas were too tainted with modern rationalism for his liking. Now, on his travels, he was looking for something new.

Carlyle supplied it. From the start of his writing career, he had denounced the materialism of the age, visible above all in the emergence side by side of vast wealth and grinding poverty. The industrial revolution was mutilating humanity and forcing on it a rational, scientific outlook which drained the soul of emotional and intuitive nourishment. To counter this fatal development, people must look into themselves for what was of real importance, not outwards to the superficial values of a decadent age. And then they would see that all spiritual worth could only be found in the individual life. These were the views which Carlyle propounded with growing vehemence, and perhaps desperation, for the next half-century. At this early stage, there was a coincidence with Emerson's gentler outlook, arising from the collection of ideas which came to be known in the US as Transcendentalism. Emerson, too, together with the other young Americans round him, disapproved of materialism and the neglect of spiritual values, while also blaming religion for a growing failure to tap the deeper side of human nature. They were as concerned with ethical issues as Carlyle, but more romantic in inspiration, more inclined, for example, to seek a remedy for modern ills in healing nature. But for the time being there was enough common ground between Carlyle and Emerson for their exchange of ideas to acquire a durable literary value.

Later, Carlyle's opinion of the US, as of most things, grew more tendentious. He became dismissive of the idea, urged by the writers in New England, that Americans might redeem themselves from the sins of their confidence and complacency. Carlyle wrote to Emerson that America was 'mainly a new Commercial England, with a fuller pantry: little more or less. The same unquenchable, almost frightfully unresting spirit of endeavour, directed (woe is me!) to the making of money.' Over time, Carlyle acquired a hatred of democracy and a conviction that social ills could only be cured by the rule of titans like Oliver Cromwell or Frederick the Great, whose biographies he wrote. The American system was never going to breed such men, indeed had been designed to prevent their emergence. So Carlyle condemned the US for having produced 'no great thought' and 'no great noble thing'. All it had done was double its population every twenty years: 'They have begotten, with a rapidity beyond recorded example, Eighteen Millions of the greatest bores ever seen in the world before.' Finally Carlyle turned into a racist and wrote a tract called 'Occasional

Discourse on the Nigger Question', the title of which perhaps says enough about it. It was admired in the South up to the Civil War but it ensured, if Carlyle's other opinions had not already done so, that he would lose his influence in the US. There the intellectuals' horror of modernity anyway diminished, and Americans reconciled themselves to the fact that theirs was going to be a more materialistic, less aristocratic civilisation than Europe's. Its achievements would come within that framework, not through rejection of it.

The first major Scottish writer to see the US for himself was Robert Louis Stevenson. Love carried him across the Atlantic Ocean in 1879. He had met an American woman, Fanny Osbourne, earlier in France and could not live without her. When she went home to California, he at length followed. The journey, by an emigrants' ship to New York, then by train across the continent, was terrible. He being in poor health anyway, it almost killed him. It did kill some of the romantic attraction America had previously held for him, in its energy, movement, cheerful spirit and wide-eyed optimism. He had seen the ugly, wretched obverse of all that, something of life at the bottom of the heap in the US, and he did not find it attractive. When he got to Monterey, the old Spanish capital of California where Fanny was waiting for him, he mourned the passing of its historic character: 'It is not strong enough to resist the influence of the flaunting caravanserai, and the poor, quaint, penniless native gentlemen of Monterey must perish, like a lower race, before the millionaire vulgarians of the Big Bonanza.' He and Fanny married in San Francisco in 1880, but decided they did not want to stay. They returned to Europe and, after a further spell in California some years later, started wandering the South Seas, where they eventually settled on Samoa.

Stevenson's experience in a sense confirmed what Carlyle had dogmatically expounded: that America was now alien territory for the cultured Scot. A century before the two countries had shared a cultural condition of provincial dependence. America had cured this by complete cultural independence, while in Scotland the consequent problems were only posed in new forms.

6

TEACHERS

I n their respect for learning and education two provinces of the first British Empire, Scotland and America, had no reason to feel inferior to England. During the eighteenth century the ancient English universities, Oxford and Cambridge, went into decline. In the earlier age of the Renaissance and Reformation, they had shared in the cultural life of Europe and figured among its leaders. For reasons primarily political, this role was not sustained. England became a confessional state, where membership of the Established Church was required for full citizenship and participation in public affairs. Oxford and Cambridge applied tests which excluded all religious dissenters from the higher education they provided. In itself that cut them off from some of the liveliest intellectual circles in the country, from people who sent their sons to dissenting academies instead. At the same time the curriculum in the universities actually narrowed, at Oxford to concentrate on the classical languages, at Cambridge on mathematics. When in the later seventeenth century Sir Isaac Newton, a fellow of Trinity College, Cambridge, discovered the laws of gravity, he could not get his university to teach them: the first courses in Newtonian physics were offered in Scotland.

By the time of the American Revolution, the English universities had become finishing schools for the ruling class. They did contain some fine scholars, of course, but these were left to work for themselves, without wider effect on their institutions. Fellows of the colleges, many of them plump and idle clergymen, had no need to do anything much. Adam Smith, who won a scholarship to Balliol College, Oxford, noted how they received their wages regardless, whereas at his own university of Glasgow the professors had to earn their living by collecting fees from students and so sought to attract a large attendance to their lectures. As for the undergraduates at Oxford and Cambridge, there was little to stop them spending their time in hunting, gambling or whoring; those of noble blood, for example, could take their degrees without examination. In short, a profound intellectual slumber settled over these venerable seats of learning.

A quite different tradition developed in Scotland. At a time when England had only two universities, Scotland had five. Like Oxford and Cambridge, three were medieval foundations: St Andrews, Glasgow and King's College, Aberdeen. Two more, Edinburgh and Marischal College, Aberdeen, resulted from the revival of learning in the sixteenth century. After the Reformation, they gained a specific and vital function in the new, Protestant nation. It had been a grave objection to the Roman Church that many of its priests and monks were irreligious, ignorant or even illiterate. The Church of Scotland was to have a learned ministry, conversant with Scripture and capable of imparting its knowledge to the people. What was more, the people should be taught to read the Bible for themselves. The Scottish reformer, John Knox, laid it down in the Second Book of Discipline that every parish in Scotland was to have a school where children could be taught the rudiments of learning.

This national system was supervised by the Church of Scotland. Scholars still dispute how well it worked. Perhaps it never did in the more remote parts of a mountainous country. But in the Lowlands, especially in the burghs, it seems clear the commitment to education produced something rare in contemporary Europe, a largely literate population. That in turn created a broader constituency for the universities. If the clergy had to be learned, so did the schoolmasters and lawyers, then other professions as they developed. The Scottish universities retained the wide medieval curriculum, covering all the main branches of knowledge, so new ones could be readily absorbed into it.

Learning was pressed on the Scots people with a sort of benevolent authoritarianism. At the same time, they became eager to acquire it. Theirs was a poor nation, and one of the few things it had in surplus was trained minds. For the people, a trained mind was the key to any position in the small society of Scotland. If, as so often, it could not be used there, then it was a passport to opportunity in the world beyond.

In America matters were different again. In a new country education had to be started from scratch, and by the efforts of the people themselves. Since most were English, the traditions they inherited were English also. But the situation they faced looked more like that in Scotland. There were no idle rich among the early colonists, and the students had no need to acquire manners and polish: it was enough for them to be taught to read and write in a log cabin. When it came to higher education, the priority for the colonists was a learned clergy. Their eagerness to make sure they had one is attested by the fact that an American college, Harvard, was set up in 1636, just sixteen years after the Pilgrim Fathers landed; for its first session, it housed one professor and nine students. It was established at Cambridge, Massachusetts, and named after John Harvard, a graduate of Cambridge, England; he had just died and left his money and books for the foundation. In its early days it was run by graduates of Cambridge, a stronghold of the Puritans in the mother country before they were later rooted out. For that reason, among others, the developing English example in higher education would not prove of much use and Harvard went on in its own way as a seminary for Puritan preachers.

A novel pattern began to emerge more clearly from the second American academic foundation, William and Mary College at Williamsburg, Virginia. It was inaugurated in 1693, long after the first settlement at nearby Jamestown in 1607. Scholars surmise that this was because during the decades in between Virginia did not have too many children to teach. The early colonists suffered fearful mortality in what was for them an unhealthy climate, and only by waves of fresh immigrants, rather than by natural increase, could the population be replenished. But towards the end of the century it stabilised and grew. This, together with the colony's burgeoning wealth from the trade in tobacco, gave Virginians the confidence to look to the future and the education of their children.

Seeing that Virginians were in a great majority English, it comes as a surprise that the first president of William and Mary was a Scotsman, James Blair, a graduate of Marischal College, Aberdeen. The explanation lies in the facts that Blair was an Episcopalian clergyman and that the Church of Scotland, having won its definitive Presbyterian constitution in 1690, was expelling the Episcopalians in its ranks. Two hundred ministers lost their kirks and manses. Some took refuge in Virginia, where Episcopalianism was the established religion. The Church of England, which often had trouble finding colonial clergy, stood ready to offer them a living. Blair was one of the earliest to arrive. A resourceful and ambitious man, he had got himself appointed the representative of the Bishop of London, to whose diocese Virginia belonged. From that position, he made himself a force to be reckoned with in the colony's politics.

Blair's great project was to found a college in Virginia, and his efforts made him the natural choice for its first president, a post he would hold for fifty years till his death in 1743. He was a quarrelsome fellow, the bane of many a royal governor's life. Yet he shaped the whole early history of William and Mary. The college conducted worship for its students and this worship was English, or rather Anglican. But its learning was in many respects Scottish, in its breadth and in its organisation, with each entrant body of students formed into a class which a single tutor took through the entire course, as in the Scotland of the time (professorships for particular subjects only came later). Others complained that Blair appointed too many of his countrymen to these jobs, and one Englishman wrote of those who arrived 'from the Scotch universities, who usually come young, raw and undisciplined, tainted with Presbyterian principles, and no real friend to our Episcopal Government'. Still, it was in this way that the youthful Thomas Jefferson was to acquire a Scottish tutor, William Small, and imbibe from him the philosophy that would help to shape the American Revolution.

The wandering Scot, educated but poor and unable to earn a

living in his own country, before long became a familiar figure in American classrooms. William Smith was another Scottish Episcopalian who, disqualified from any academic career at home, emigrated from Aberdeen to New York in 1751 to become a tutor in a wealthy family. Much like Blair in Virginia, he was amazed that a thriving community should lack a college (after all, every city of any size in Scotland had one). Within a couple of years he drew up a proposal addressed to the legislature of New York, 'A General Idea of the College of Mirania'. This was the first work of educational theory published on American soil. It set out a plan of schooling in science and religion designed for the New World and for all classes of society. It was sententious in tone – 'What is law without morals?' Smith asked, before answering, 'It is better to follow nature than to be led.' And the New Yorkers appear to have regarded it as too utopian.

The scheme did, however, catch the attention of Benjamin Franklin who, among his many other activities, had just established a learned academy in Philadelphia. He, too, wished his city, the largest and most cultured in the colonies, to have a college. And Smith seemed the perfect person to design its curriculum. He did so on Scottish principles, so that a student could proceed from the general to the particular in all branches of knowledge. Smith served till his death in 1803 as provost of the college, which was to become the University of Pennsylvania.

This college also organised the first important medical school in America. It was the work of Benjamin Rush, a son of Philadelphia who followed a varied and colourful career owed to his Scottish education. He was not a Scot by blood – on the contrary, he was proud enough of his English ancestry to display at home the sword with which his grandfather had fought under Oliver Cromwell. But after his undergraduate training at Princeton he wanted to become a doctor and was advised that the best place to fulfil this ambition would be Edinburgh.

The Scottish capital housed at that time the best medical school in the world. It had come into being after 1700 through Scots returning from Leiden in Holland, where medicine was taught not from dusty old books, as had been the universal practice since the Middle Ages, but from live patients and their diseases. In Edinburgh's Royal Infirmary, the earliest modern hospital, Scottish physicians and surgeons had all the real cases they needed to set about improving their methods of diagnosis and treatment, and the dead bodies to dissect if they failed. Under this impetus, Scottish medical education expanded enormously in the course of the eighteenth century. By the end of it, the universities of Edinburgh, Glasgow and Aberdeen boasted a range of specialist professors who could count to their credit fundamental discoveries in their disciplines. Students came to them from all over Europe, from as far away as Russia – and from the colonies too. Between 1750 and 1780, about a hundred Americans enrolled in the Scottish universities, more than sixty of them to study medicine.

As young Rush found when he arrived in Edinburgh in 1767, the city had much more to offer than a formal education, in its convivial and at the same time intellectual social life. It was said that you could stand at the Cross of Edinburgh and, within a short time, shake fifty men of genius by the hand. From home Rush already knew Franklin, who had visited Scotland some years before and furnished him with letters of introduction. So he went to dinner with David Hume: 'his person was rather ungenteel and clumsy', Rush recorded, 'he spoke but little, but what he said was always pertinent and sensible.' Still, as a devout Christian, Rush felt shocked by the philosopher's religious scepticism, and once his circle of acquaintance widened he preferred to keep more orthodox company. He travelled across to Paisley to visit its minister, John Witherspoon. Rush had been told that his old college, Princeton, wanted Witherspoon as its president. He helped to persuade the Scot to accept this offer and so set him off on his own momentous American career.

The time Rush spent in Scotland equipped him for many roles after his return home. He at once became an influential and popular teacher. On the model of Edinburgh he recast the medical instruction in Philadelphia, encouraged by the president of the city's college, William Small, the tutor of Jefferson, who had now moved there and was introducing a more Scottish curriculum. When the Revolution came Rush joined up with George Washington's army as a medical officer. He was chosen a delegate from Pennsylvania to the Continental Congress and he signed the Declaration of Independence. He had visionary ideals for the young Republic: 'America has ever appeared to me to be the theatre on which human nature will reach its greatest civic, literary and religious honours. Now is the time to sow the seeds of each of them.' He set about realising some of those ideals in person.

Rush founded the first anti-slavery society in the US. He campaigned against the abuse of alcohol. He advocated humane treatment of the mentally ill. He saw the key to America's future in a system of non-elitist and non-denominational education, concentrating on science and spreading outwards from the original colonies with the movement of the people. He himself founded Dickinson College at Carlisle in western Pennsylvania. From a Princeton now headed by Witherspoon, Rush's fellow alumni, often Scots or Scotch-Irish, followed him in this aspect of his endeavours. Foundations such as Transylvania at Lexington, Kentucky, Miami at Oxford, Ohio, Jefferson at Canonsburg, Pennsylvania, Lafayette at Easton, Pennsylvania, and the University of North Carolina were the result of their efforts. The small college in some pleasant rustic nook with a liberal curriculum, different in its welcoming atmosphere from the anonymous universities of the big cities, remains an attractive feature of the US system to this day. In a sense, it was all due to the Scottish education of a young American.

It reminds us also that Witherspoon, apart from his revolutionary role and his wish to imbue a new country with Christian principles, exerted no less influence on its educational institutions. When he had first arrived at Princeton in 1768, he found a faltering Presbyterian seminary riven by theological dispute and desperately trying to maintain some stability and continuity. He had come with the aim of making it the leading college in the colonies, and one of the best in the British Empire.

The model Witherspoon sought to emulate was that of Edinburgh, which in the eighteenth century set an example in higher education to the rest of Britain and Europe. It should be added that Glasgow and Aberdeen followed not far behind, and in fact much of Edinburgh's modern curriculum had been borrowed from Glasgow. The high quality of instruction was to be found not only in the medical faculty, but across almost the whole range of contemporary knowledge, including new sciences such as chemistry and geology. Moral philosophy lay at the core of the curriculum, being compulsory for all students, but the sphere of moral philosophy was reckoned to include new liberal subjects as well, especially history and political economy, or economics, and what we now call the social sciences in general. The man who did most to raise Edinburgh to this eminence was its principal from 1763 to 1793, William Robertson. A clergyman of the Church of Scotland, he remained orthodox in his theology, yet was committed also to a progressive humanism. He did not believe that religion and science should be at odds. On the contrary they were together the keys to uncovering the unity of human knowledge, and the sources of improvement in human society.

Robertson and Witherspoon were enemies, however. It formed part of Robertson's outlook on life that the Church and university should be in no way disturbing to social order or to political authority. In other words he was a conservative and, needless to say, an opponent of the American Revolution. But the roots of his attitude should rather be sought in the history of Scotland, a subject he had written up himself, and its annals of religious war between rulers and ruled, ruinous to learning and progress. From his commanding position he appointed men who agreed with him to the jobs he had at his disposal in the Church and university: these men did not include Witherspoon or others of such radical stamp. Witherspoon spoke up, in the form of wounding satire, for those who were being passed over. He ridiculed the effete social pretensions of Robertson and his circle, accusing them of subservience to the powers-that-be. It is always satisfying to make the public laugh at an enemy, but this may harden his attitude without defeating him. What Witherspoon made certain was that he would never find further preferment in Scotland. His frustration was one thing that prompted him to emigrate to America. His memory of it led him there to the revolutionary, rather than the loyalist, side.

Witherspoon was an interesting because complicated character. He shared Robertson's intellectual, but not his political, outlook. And while he shook the dust of Scotland off his feet, he arrived at Princeton intent on turning an old-fashioned theological seminary into, in effect, a Scottish university. He could have accomplished little without his own tremendous energy. He not only ran the college as president, but also supervised its teaching of philosophy, history and rhetoric (or English). He gave the sermon in its chapel every Sunday. He delivered its public orations. He tutored students in French and Hebrew. He acted as headmaster of the college's preparatory school. At every level, he reorganised the curriculum so that young Americans, too, would gain the benefit of a Scottish education, focused on moral philosophy. Students in the western world got a good grounding in the classics in the eighteenth century, yet it was rare for them to make the acquaintance of modern authors. Witherspoon ensured they did at Princeton. Among those he set them to read were living Scots thinkers, including Adam Smith and even David Hume, though Hume was an atheist. Witherspoon took the view that, in order to refute a philosopher, you first had to find out just what he had said.

Princeton in this way formed the channel into America of Scottish ideas. The measure of Witherspoon's achievement is that Scottish philosophy became American philosophy too, or at least – since the US remained culturally dependent for some decades ahead – the main foreign philosophy by which young Americans were introduced to the central questions of the western tradition.

This Common Sense philosophy of Scotland became the leading British school for almost a century after Hume's death in 1776. Common Sense formed the staple diet in the classrooms of Scottish universities. And because higher education was so widespread it pervaded Scottish society, where visitors often remarked on how the people amused themselves with abstract debate. Its task was to clarify those first principles – of knowledge, of perception, of causality, of conscience – which allow people to reason on the evidence of their senses. Not only were the issues at stake of the highest importance to philosophers, they also proved ideal for the discipline of young minds. Common Sense was for the common man. If trained in it, he would be able to think about the

106

facts of his existence and about his morality. And he could acquire such training because the data it employed were gathered not from mental gymnastics or from deep reading in the thinkers of the past but from everyday experience of the world around him. There, the common man's ideas could be as good as those of any philosopher. In Scotland, the result came to be called the democratic intellect. It suited Scotland, a more egalitarian nation than England. It also suited America.

In a previous chapter we have already seen how Scottish philosophy offered a rich source of ideas to the Founding Fathers of the US – in fact the reference to 'self-evident truths' in the Declaration of Independence was probably borrowed from Reid by Thomas Jefferson. The whole revolutionary idea of founding a nation not on the rule of one man or class or clique but on a separation of powers and on a system of checks and balances ultimately derives its confidence in the people from a belief that, through all their inevitable discords, they will still see the 'self-evident truths' and that these will hold them together. The mechanism is complex, but there will be a general agreement on first principles to make it work.

In that case, education in these first principles is no less important, for the people as a whole, but especially for those destined to rise out of the people to make the mechanism work. This was why Witherspoon's achievement at Princeton, in turning it into a centre for the diffusion of Scottish ideas, proved to be of such inestimable value to the US. According to Woodrow Wilson, a later head of the college, Witherspoon made it a 'seminary of statesmen'. Wilson counted up its contributions to the young Republic: one president (James Madison), one vice-president (Aaron Burr), six members of the Continental Congress, nine members of the Cabinet, twenty-one senators, thirty-nine Congressmen, twelve governors of states, three justices of the Supreme Court, thirty-three other judges and thirteen presidents of colleges.

Clearly this Scottish influence extended beyond the American Revolution and the political separation of Scotland and the US in 1783. It remained strong in the educational sphere right through the nineteenth and into the twentieth century.

Scots continued to exploit the international prestige of their institutions and send out professors and teachers to parts of the world still modernising their schools and establishing systems of higher education: this was true not only of the US but also of the Americas generally, as of Africa, Asia and Australasia. Scots also found fresh means of communication among the citizens of this advancing world. Edinburgh and Glasgow were centres of publishing, the dependable staple of this risky business being textbooks for use in classrooms wherever the English language could be read. New standards for quality journalism – clever, irreverent and probing – were set by the *Edinburgh Review*, founded in 1802 by a circle of able but unemployed youngsters. The editor for its first thirty years, the lawyer Francis Jeffrey, visited America, talked to James Madison and James Monroe and, not least, married a girl from New York. With these exalted contacts in the US he boosted the *Review* there as a prime vehicle for literary criticism and political comment; it also took a positive view of American development.

So the Scottish influence ran much wider than Princeton, yet it was remarkable how that college remained the driving force behind it. Joseph Henry was a son of Scots immigrants who rose to be Princeton's professor of natural philosophy, or physics, though this proved to be just the start of a distinguished career. In 1846 he was appointed the first secretary and director of the Smithsonian Institution in Washington DC, just beginning its work after a long delay since the original endowment in 1829. That, under the will of John Smithson, a merchant in London, had provided only for the fortune he left to the US to be used for 'the increase and diffusion of knowledge among men'. So far this had created little more than the 'the nation's attic', a collection of antiquarian curiosities.

Henry vigorously set about turning the institution into an umbrella organisation for museums of every kind – today, from folklore and portraits to design and astrophysics – and into a centre for scholarship and research in its own right. As an ensemble it is by now the largest museum in the world. Henry can take the credit for having introduced and developed many of its activities, and laid down its policies, again on the Scottish principle that by proceeding from the general to the particular, then by comparison of the particulars, useful knowledge can be assured. Even the Smithsonian did not take up all his time. He invented the electro-magnetic telegraph and inaugurated the US National Weather Service: from which point, perhaps, stems an American obsession with the weather which matches the Scottish one, our climate being more changeable, theirs more extreme.

Princeton's links with Scotland remained close and the uni-versity again sought a Scottish president in 1868, exactly one hundred years after it had summoned Witherspoon. Its choice this time fell on James McCosh, professor of moral philosophy at Queen's College, Belfast, but born at Patna in Ayrshire. The college had been new when he went there in 1852. Irish higher education was till this time monopolised by Trinity College, Dublin, an institution like Oxford and Cambridge in its religious exclusiveness; that is to say, it admitted only Anglicans. The Presbyterians of Ulster had no college, and sent their brightest sons to Glasgow and Edinburgh, while for the Roman Catholic majority in the rest of Ireland there was nothing. The reign of Queen Victoria saw various attempts to remedy this lack, one of which was the foundation of Queen's, Belfast. Officially non-denominational, it soon took on the character of the Presbyterian population that supplied many of its students.

McCosh was the professor who did most to endow it with this character. He would have preferred to work in Scotland but, when he was a young academic looking for a job, the first to come up had been at Queen's, Belfast. He was already the author of a bestseller, *The Method of the Divine Government*, which set out to show that the intellectual progress of the Scottish Enlighten-ment gave no support to scepticism but, on the contrary, could be reconciled with Christianity. In the controversies of the age, especially whether Genesis gave an accurate account of the Creation, he continued to argue that advances in knowledge multiplied proofs of the wisdom of God: science and religion confirmed each other. This stance ought to have commended him to one of the Scottish universities, where orthodoxy in gen-eral held firm against a rising tide of agnosticism and atheism in society at large. But in this respect he was too liberal, and the chance never came for him to make his way back to Scotland from Ulster. At length he gave up his efforts to return and went to Princeton instead.

Scotland's loss was America's gain. Any one of the Scottish universities, which were now just starting to look like rather hidebound institutions, would have benefited from the burst of energy McCosh brought to Princeton, and he relished the freedom he found there. One student compared his arrival to 'an electric shock, instantaneous, paralysing to the opposition, and stimulating to all who were not paralysed'. In essence, McCosh made of Princeton a modern university. He appointed new professors in arts and sciences. He reorganised the curriculum so that the undergraduates could take specialised options in addition to their basic course. He started the first graduate work. He founded schools of science, philosophy and art. He erected new buildings, including a great library and a gymnasium, following the classical maxim of 'a healthy mind in a healthy body'. He had an almost postmodern concern with the undergraduate diet and encouraged the formation of dining clubs: a far cry from the sack of meal the Scottish student of old had carried to college, made into porridge and dumped in a drawer, from which a spoonful could be taken whenever he was hungry. Again, McCosh developed the grounds of his university into what would now be recognised as a campus: a word first used at Princeton. He later wrote: 'I remember that some critics found fault with me for laying out too much money on stone and lime; but I proceeded on system, and knew what I was doing. I viewed the edifices as means to an end, at best as outward expressions and symbols of an internal life.'

Like Witherspoon before him, McCosh found time amid these endless presidential duties to teach students himself. Charles Darwin's *Origin of Species* had been published a few years before and most American clergymen, like their fellows in Britain, rejected the theory of evolution. But McCosh accepted it. Evolution was a holistic concept, and God was a holism. Once the polemics over Darwin had died away, McCosh believed Christians would come to understand that evolution also formed part of the divine plan: to him, it served only 'to increase the mystery of the process of creation'. It could also be an educational stimulus, because it let his undergraduates bring into their studies the latest scientific advances and appreciate how they fitted with 'the good old solid course of study handed down from our fathers'.

Beneath all this we can discern a purpose of training young men at Princeton to emerge not just with expertise in particular subjects but also with a rounded character and a mature view of the world and their own place in it. McCosh engaged in a public controversy with Charles Eliot, president of Harvard, where students could choose, more or less as they liked, among two hundred courses. This made dilettantes of them, McCosh argued, with their knowledge 'scattered like the star dust out of which worlds are said to have been made'. But the Scottish philosophy of Common Sense, to which he remained faithful all his life, had as its ideal that type of man, trained to think from first principles about every branch of knowledge, which he aimed to produce at Princeton.

When we pass from James McCosh to Woodrow Wilson we pass from an unmistakable Scot, who found at Princeton an outlet for his talents no longer available at home, to an unmistakable American, who blended his Scottish heritage into the US mainstream. Of his university Wilson wrote: 'She has been made largely by Scotsmen and, being myself of pure Scots blood, it heartens me to emphasize the fact.' But whereas McCosh offered the rather charming example of an old-fashioned academic, giving of himself to every good cause though happiest with the life of the mind, Wilson is already the modern American college president, certainly not unintellectual but first and foremost a forceful political figure whose interests lie as much in money and power as in knowledge.

Wilson had himself been a student at Princeton and after he returned there, first as professor of jurisprudence then as president from 1902, he worked out plans which staggered the trustees who supervised the place, a body of worthy, conservative Presbyterians. In his first report to them, he proposed spending $12.5 million to transform Princeton into the outstanding university it is today. While this multiplied the existing budget twenty-five times they, somewhat bemused, let him go ahead. They would soon find that they had at the same time handed their authority to him.

No incoming president can forbear to reorganise the curriculum and Wilson at once set about this, to provide a unified course of general studies for undergraduates in their first two years and the choice of an academic 'major' for their last two. He tightened academic standards so severely that admissions to Princeton actually fell till 1907. But the strategy paid off: he was able to add an honours programme for the brightest and to embark on a great expansion of graduate studies. He did so in science especially but also in biblical criticism – a shock to those trustees who believed Holy Scripture to be literally true and therefore not open to criticism. He arranged the instruction in different subjects into departments under heads responsible to himself. Then he took from the trustees effective power over academic appointments.

Wilson went out on the first fund-raising campaign among Princeton's alumni and drummed up enough for fifty assistant professorships to be created, which doubled the teaching staff; he shocked the trustees again by appointing first a Jew, then a Roman Catholic. Wilson also approached Andrew Carnegie, the head of US Steel who had been born at Dunfermline in Scotland. Though Carnegie was a philanthropist on a grand scale, Wilson found him uninterested in endowing a school of government, as was hoped. All he would pay for was the excavation of a lake, where the students could row and not spend so much time playing football. The disappointed Wilson still accepted the offer, for he had cast his own cold eye on their social habits. He disapproved of the dining clubs McCosh had encouraged in order to take the students out of taverns in the village of Princeton, because he thought the clubs had become too snobbish: this would not aid a training for life in the American democracy. Wilson wanted to create colleges, on the pattern of Oxford and Cambridge, where undergraduates would live and work alongside some of their teachers. The proposal embroiled him in a huge controversy, again with the trustees and also, more crucially, with the generous alumni. It was the start of the acrimony which would persuade Wilson to leave academic for political life. He was not the last bold, energetic and far-sighted college president to run foul of institutional inertia. But, in retrospect at least, Princeton is glad to have had him.

This chapter has concentrated a good deal on Princeton because that was the American college with the deepest Scottish roots and the closest Scottish links. Through its distinguished alumni, that influence spread out over higher education in the US and made its contribution to a modern system which has, of course, drawn on many other traditions to assume its present shape. If Witherspoon had run in the eighteenth century what was to all intents and purposes a Scottish university, Wilson by the twentieth century ran one which was clearly American, responding to the needs and demands of its own society.

In many ways German ideas about higher education have in the end proved more attractive to Americans than British ideas. Till quite recent times British universities, whether Scottish or English, devoted most effort and resources to the teaching of undergraduates. The notion that the true glory of a university lies in its research, at the doctoral and higher levels, developed in the Germany of the nineteenth century. It met resistance in Britain as divorcing the life of the mind from the life of the world. But it was taken up with alacrity in the US, where today the undergraduate instruction can seem to the British visitor elementary, while the competitive demands on graduates raise them to a level of scholarly specialisation which may equally offend his more gentlemanly standards. Still, the results are plain to see: American research, as measured by the award of Nobel Prizes and the like, leads that of other countries in many disciplines.

The steady and ever more intense specialisation in the world of learning was itself fatal to the old Scottish academic system and its generalist principles. But deeper forces undermined it. A basic motive for the Scots' elaboration of the philosophy of Common Sense had been defence of the Christian religion against the barely concealed atheism of their countryman, Hume. At that time Scotland had been a Calvinist nation, and the work of its Church in education, welfare and the enforcement of moral standards was interwoven with its everyday life.

But in the later nineteenth century Scotland became, like

every western country, more secular and sceptical in outlook. This shift often started outside the Church and the universities, in an educated population which read books and reviews, went to public lectures, kept abreast of scientific advance and followed, for example, the debate about evolution with bated breath. In fact the relative decline of the Scottish universities which then set in can be traced to a reaction among extreme Evangelicals and their desperate attempts to keep or take control of academic chairs, often to the exclusion of better, if less orthodox, scholars. This still could not stop a general shaking of faith in God, or of faith in a universal Common Sense with which God was supposed to have endowed humanity so that it could perceive the solid reality of Creation. On the contrary the work of one son of Scotland, the great physicist James Clerk Maxwell, proved that the universe is not as our senses apprehend it but can only be grasped mathematically. The philosophy of Common Sense was then obsolete, and Scots lost their intellectual leadership.

That left the universities of Scotland leaderless too. They had built up a great tradition since the Enlightenment, but now it had run its course. The consequence over time was steady assimilation to a British or, as its critics say, an English system. Some of the old ways persist yet. Scottish students enter university having taken a wider range of subjects up to their leaving high school. They are often allowed, or even encouraged, to follow a wider range of undergraduate courses than is possible, for example, at Oxford and Cambridge. The Scottish universities long retained some autonomy because they were financed by a special grant from HM Treasury which, while not a generous organisation, never tried to interfere in academic matters. But after 1970 all British universities came under the centralised control of the Department of Education and Science in London, and an era of marked anglicisation in Scotland got under way.

The restoration of the Scottish Parliament in 1999 has not yet put that trend into reverse. There may be an unmistakable Scots accent to such studies as law and theology, and to a growing extent history and literature. Still, Britain has a unified system of higher education, in which staff and students move around without regard to the border between Scotland and England.

Within it the one real Scottish legacy is that it has now become a system for the masses, entered by more than fifty per cent of every age-group in Scotland, and only by a little less in England. In any event, the English idea of university as a finishing school for the ruling class is gone. Britain, like every other modern western country, has to educate the people to as high a level as it can afford.

It was the US that set the example here, in sending a similar proportion to university while England, at least, was still sending a small minority. Right round the globe, academic systems are becoming more like one another. America stands out nevertheless for a diversity unmatched anywhere else, from the civilised pursuit of learning in the Ivy League, to the degree factories of the big cities, to the little liberal arts colleges and to many more humble institutions which give self-improving citizens their chance in life. Notable also is the split between the public and private sectors, about half and half, whereas in European countries most universities are run by the state; in Britain, with a single exception in England, they all are.

Few questions are ever asked about the effect of this on academic freedom, the precondition of excellence. British academics grumble about the heavy hand laid on them by governmental bureaucracy, yet seldom reflect that its lifting – for instance, by a different economic organisation of the universities – might allow them the freedom and diversity which they lack, and which the Americans enjoy. That freedom and diversity have given the US the world's greatest universities, and these are private universities, where no professor ever has to worry whether officialdom approves of him. In Scotland at large, a more common complaint is that the universities have ceased to reflect the nation's character and aspirations. Again, it is hard to see how they might break out of provincial mediocrity while a centralist state controls them. America once learned its academic lesson from Scotland; Scotland has yet to learn that academic lesson from America.

7

EXPLORERS

The people of the US looked westwards right from the foundation of their country in 1776, but at first not into a continent they knew well. Within it, the Thirteen Colonies had occupied a confined position along the eastern seaboard. It was as much as the colonists could do to establish effective occupation of the strip of land, varying in width, between the shores of the Atlantic Ocean and the range of Appalachian Mountains which ran 2,000 miles all the way from Georgia to Maine. They were deterred from penetrating beyond the mountains first by the fact that on the other side stretched an apparently limitless and largely unexplored wilderness, then by the fact that it housed Indian nations seldom friendly to white men who might want to settle there.

In their suspicions the Indians were encouraged by the French who occupied Canada, then called New France, till the British captured Quebec in 1759 and were ceded the whole territory in 1763. The Thirteen Colonies already had a population of a million, while Canada contained just 50,000 Frenchmen. And from the Thirteen Colonies the Indians were rapidly vanishing, or were already gone, the victims usually of devastating epidemics of European diseases to which they had no resistance, but also of war and dispossession by ruthless and greedy settlers.

It must have seemed perfectly plausible when the French

spread hair-raising tales to the Indians that their extermination was the English colonists' ultimate aim. The French, on the other hand, had always shown by their behaviour that they wanted to live in harmony with the Indians, to trade with them and convert them to Christianity, of course, but not otherwise to disturb them in their traditional ways of life. When the first Americans crossed the mountains, the French often incited the Indians to attack and repel them. For a time it looked as if the French could remain, through their Indian allies, masters of the interior of North America.

From New France, by way of the St Lawrence River and the Great Lakes, it was possible to cross with little trouble to the headwaters of a tributary of the Ohio or Mississippi Rivers. Robert de la Salle did this and sailed down the Mississippi to the Gulf of Mexico in 1682. Then he claimed the whole basin of that mighty river for his king, Louis XIV, and called it Louisiane, rendered as Louisiana in English. Once New Orleans was established at its mouth in 1718, a journey of a few weeks, by water and by easy portage, along a chain of forts at St Louis, Detroit and so on, could take French soldiers or officials or missionaries all the way to Quebec. The Thirteen Colonies were hemmed in, or would be if they tried to expand. The French also began to explore westwards, till they approached the territory in the far West which the Spaniards claimed and at least pretended to rule from Mexico City. The realisation came first to Frenchmen that, by controlling the river-systems of North America, they could reach most parts of the continent. Canadians, the so-called voyageurs, travelled these systems by canoe and developed trade in furs with the Indians.

Americans knew only vaguely about all this, even after the French were expelled. As an imperial power, Britain remained just as intent on confining her own colonists within narrow bounds. The Government in London defined the so-called Proclamation Line in 1763. It contained eastern Georgia, most of South Carolina, but only about half of the later extent of North Carolina and Virginia, together with the south-eastern portion of Pennsylvania, New York state as far up as Albany and then, excluding Vermont, the present New England. All beyond was to be Indian country, according to British conceptions. The colonial superintendents (royal officials who monitored the frontier) encouraged the Iroquois, the Creeks and others to form confederacies occupying territory within marked boundaries, like any European nation. White settlers could not physically be stopped from crossing the Proclamation Line but its purpose was to make clear that the British army would not be bound to come and rescue them if they got into trouble: or, if it did, that the colonies would have to pay the costs. This was one of the bones of contention in 1776. To most Americans at that point their continent was still a closed book, and they would have to explore it just as if they were discovering it for the first time.

Even then they did not really have the opportunity till President Thomas Jefferson purchased Louisiana from France in 1803. Jefferson had an insatiable curiosity. One of his interests was the West, where he felt sure the future of the US lay as an agrarian republic, a nation of hardy, independent farmers. The year after the purchase he sent out into this newly acquired territory the expedition of Meriwether Lewis and William Clark. Lewis was Jefferson's private secretary and Clark was a redheaded Virginian of Scottish ancestry, a military officer with long experience of dealing with the Indians. Jefferson put a request to Congress for official finance of the expedition, since its aims would ultimately benefit all Americans. It was to find an overland route to the Pacific, to strengthen US claims to the Oregon Territory (which included also the present state of Washington and part of British Columbia) and to gather information about the native peoples, the terrain and the resources of the West.

The carefully selected members of the expedition – fifteen soldiers, who would also be accompanied by some slaves and Indian guides – underwent a rigorous training for the ordeals to come during the winter of 1803. In the following May they set out westwards from St Louis up the Missouri River. They spent the winter in Indian villages in what is now North Dakota. They faced the hardest part of their journey in 1805. They reached the forks of the Missouri, then followed the branch they now named after Jefferson as far as they could into the Rocky Mountains. With the help of the local Shoshone Indians, they crossed the high passes on horseback. Then they descended the Clearwater and the Snake Rivers, still through wild mountainous country, to the Columbia, which issues into the Pacific. They spent their second winter, a wet and miserable one, in a crude outpost they built on the coast.

Starting back in the spring of 1806, Lewis and Clark split their party, in order to explore as much of the territory as possible. Lewis went down the Marias River while Clark followed the Yellowstone River. They were reunited at the confluence of the Yellowstone and Missouri in August, and arrived back in St Louis on 23 September, to find themselves acclaimed as national heroes. Since the expedition was sent out under official auspices, it kept meticulous records. These were afterwards published, giving the first accounts of the unknown regions Lewis and Clark had traversed.

Famous as the exploit of Lewis and Clark became, they were not the first to cross the continent by land. That honour had already been claimed twenty years before by a Scotsman, Alexander Mackenzie, who travelled on what is now Canadian territory. In fact most of the exploration of North America would be carried out from Canada, often by Scots based there. The long-term aim in the US was settlement, and settlement would inevitably be a slow process. But in Canada the long-term aim remained, right up to the Confederation of 1867, to keep the West empty. This was because the country's wealth came from furs, or from other natural products; once the land was settled and farmed it could yield no furs. At the same time, the lucrative trade in furs gave an incentive for ever more of the wilderness to be opened up and for ever more remote Indian tribes to be brought into the trading system. This, together with the search for the Northwest Passage, a route by sea round the top of North America to the Pacific and the Orient, was what made exploration such an imperative in Canada.

The English had as far back as 1670 established the Hudson's Bay Company for trade in furs from the Arctic region north of New France, though it came over time to employ many Highland Scots. The company's trading expeditions began and ended in London, but the last port of call for its ships before they set sail on the wide Atlantic was Stromness in Orkney. The sea-faring Orcadians joined them there, while others flocked to do so from all over the northern counties of Scotland and from the Western Isles. Scots had also before the American Revolution achieved a certain degree of dominance over the trade in furs so far as it could be carried on from the Thirteen Colonies, from its centre at Albany in upper New York. Once New France fell these Scots moved to Montreal, because communications to the interior would be easier from there. The Revolution confirmed that this was where they should stay. They founded a rival to the Hudson's Bay Company, the North West Company. It was in the service of the Nor'Westers, to give them their usual nickname, that Mackenzie embarked on his momentous journeys.

Mackenzie was born at Stornoway in the Western Isles, probably in 1764. His parents emigrated with him as a boy to Albany, and they all followed the rest of the loyalist Scottish community to Montreal during the American War of Independence. When the North West Company was formed in 1787, Alexander became a partner in it. The next year, he and his brother Roderick were given commercial charge of the district of Athabaska, at what is now the northern edge of Saskatchewan. Their base, Fort Chipewyan, was dubbed the Athens of the North because in this howling wilderness they set up a library. The Mackenzie brothers were educated men of good family, a cut above the sort of traders usually to be found in such remote regions. They were equally typical of Scots who went out into the Empire in their tenacity, bravado and readiness to seize what pleasures they could from lives of hardship and danger. They thought little of walking 600 miles on snowshoes to pass Hogmanay with a friend, dining on roast beaver and boiled suet pudding, washed down with their favourite 'eggnog', rum laced with caviare. Here is the account of a dinner laid on by Mackenzie for another Nor'Wester, William McGillivray:

> We dined at four o'clock, and after taking a satisfactory amount of wine, perhaps a bottle each, the married men . . . retired, leaving about a dozen to drink their health. We now began in earnest and in true highland style, and by four o'clock

in the morning the whole of us had reached such a state of perfection that we could all give the war whoop as well as Mackenzie and McGillivray, we could all sing admirably, we could all drink like fishes, and we all thought we could dance on the table without disturbing a single decanter, glass or plate by which it was profusely covered.

The party ended like this:

Mackenzie now proposed to drink a toast to our memory and then give the war whoop over us fallen foes or friends all nevertheless on the floor, and on attempting to push the bottle to McGillivray at the opposite end of the table he slid off his chair and could not recover his seat, while McGillivray in extending himself over the table in the hope of seizing the bottle fell helplessly to the floor.

When Mackenzie was not enjoying himself with his friends or his books, he followed that imperative of exploration. First, in the summer of 1789, he ventured north of Lake Athabaska to a still larger body of water, the Great Slave Lake. He found, issuing from its western end, a great river, now known to be the twelfth largest in the world (it is named after him). Excitement in his expedition grew when the river at length turned north. He little suspected that it was a thousand miles long and that it would take him several weeks to reach its mouth. He and his companions sometimes journeyed sixteen hours at a stretch under the midnight sun through ever more desolate country. It was an anti-climax when they did get to the Arctic Sea, because Mackenzie had already realised that this could never be the route to the Orient he hoped to find: it was inhospitable enough in summer and would be frozen solid in winter. There was nothing for it but to turn back, though the Nor'Westers did at once set up a chain of trading posts along the Mackenzie River.

Mackenzie still dreamed of a short cut to the Orient, but now he knew it would have to go over the Rocky Mountains to the Pacific. After careful preparations he set out on a second expedition in 1793. This time he and his party went up the Peace River, which descends due east from the mountains into Lake

Athabaska, then up its tributary, the Parsnip River. He crossed the Continental Divide and to his surprise found the rivers on the other side flowing south. If he had descended the largest of them, the Fraser River (named after his brother Scot, Simon Fraser, who was to travel its whole course in 1808) Mackenzie would in fact have reached the Pacific at what is now Vancouver. But he believed this was going out of his way, and that he had to keep heading west. That meant striking out in the most arduous and perilous conditions across the several coastal ranges still separating his party from the ocean. At last by way of the Bella Coola River, which he descended in a borrowed dugout, he reached a tidal inlet of the Pacific. The inscription he carved on a rock is still there:

> Alex Mackenzie
> from Canada
> by land
> 22 July 1793

Throughout the expedition Mackenzie had been a tower of strength, meeting every test with restraint and courage, cheering his men on when they reached the brink of exhaustion and despair, finally bringing them all safe home. Yet his journals reveal an obsessive, highly strung character given to black depressions. It was true the second westward route he had discovered was, like the first, impossible for normal trading traffic. But at least others admired his achievement, even if he himself still felt disappointed. His published chronicle of the journey was a bestseller, and King George III awarded him a knighthood. Mackenzie now left the West and returned to Montreal for a few years, before going home to Scotland in 1808 and buying himself an estate at Avoch in Ross-shire, where he died in 1820. Round his grave in the churchyard the flags of all the Canadian provinces today stand sentinel.

During those last years in Canada, Mackenzie found himself embroiled in an ever more intense, and often violent, conflict between the country's two great trading companies as they competed for the resources of the West. In a sense he himself set it off, by defecting from the North West Company. The conflict was only resolved in 1821 by a merger, though under the name of the Hudson's Bay Company.

For forty years afterwards the merged company was controlled by another Scot, George Simpson, who ruled it with a rod of iron. He made it a largely Scottish outfit: he recruited two-thirds of its officers from his homeland. In his time its territory formed almost an independent state, one of the largest in the world, covering the whole of the Canadian West and Arctic, together with Oregon. Simpson continued the earlier policies of keeping settlers out, so as to maintain the trade in furs harvested by the Indians, and of pushing out the bounds of exploration. Some expeditions were sent forth by the company itself, some by other benefactors, some by the British Admiralty, where the First Lord was a Scotsman, Robert Dundas, Viscount Melville, with wide scientific interests. But it was primarily for naval purposes that he wanted the Arctic to be explored and a Northwest Passage to be found. For these arduous tasks he often relied on his brother Scots.

In 1818 Melville sent out an expedition under John Ross, who came from Stranraer in Galloway. At that time the likeliest route through the Arctic Archipelago seemed to be the wide Davis Strait, which runs between Greenland and Canada into Baffin Bay. Ross's flotilla sailed north as far as was possible while the waters remained open during the summer. But finally the land and the ice closed in. Ross named a Melville Bight on the coast of Greenland and then was forced to set off home again, but he had added greatly to knowledge of that region. With him on the voyage he took his nephew, James Ross. The next year James, only 19 years old, returned to the Arctic in company with an Englishman, William Parry.

Explorers had already identified the problem that their Arctic expeditions were bound to be long and gruelling, the more so as they had to bring all their supplies and equipment with them. Yet indigenous people, the Eskimos, inhabited these frozen wastes. By copying them, the explorers might be able to make life easier for themselves. Young Ross sought to discover how the Eskimos managed to exist in such extreme conditions, and to learn their techniques for hunting and shelter with whatever they had to hand. In several further expeditions, he managed to cut the unnecessary hardship to a minimum.

These expeditions continued the work of exploration, pushing westwards from Baffin Bay through 500 miles of the Lancaster Sound to Melville Sound and Melville Island, also named for the First Lord of the Admiralty. There the explorers were actually getting towards the western edge of the Arctic Archipelago, beyond which lay a stretch of the Arctic Sea open in summer and a passage to the Pacific through the Bering Strait, though Ross and Parry remained unaware of this. The most useful of their discoveries were important whaling grounds. In 1829 the two Rosses, uncle and nephew, set off on a second voyage together. Two years later they identified the Magnetic Pole in the middle of the Boothia Peninsula on the northern mainland of Canada. They knew they were there because they tried holding out several compasses but found the needles in every case immobilised. James Ross afterwards devoted most of his career to exploration of the Antarctic, where the Ross Sea and the Ross Ice Shelf are named after him.

Governor Simpson of the Hudson's Bay Company had helped to finance that expedition of 1829, but for later ones he chose a young Orcadian doctor, John Rae, whom he had appointed to his staff. Between 1846 and 1854, Rae led four parties on journeys through the Arctic which altogether covered 6,000 miles on foot and 6,000 miles by boat. On the first journey, in charge of a dozen men, he actually wintered on land in the polar regions, a feat unheard of. But he had learned his lesson from James Ross and he proved that a party of such size, living like the Eskimos, could indeed support itself in the icy wilderness. On his final journey, Rae ascertained that the lost expedition of Sir John Franklin dispatched from England had, by ignoring this lesson, starved to death.

Franklin had been one of the explorers originally selected by Lord Melville. He was sent in 1819 on an overland expedition from Hudson Bay far beyond the Arctic Circle to the mouth of the Coppermine River on the northern coast of Canada. Then he followed the coastline all the way back to his starting point: a journey of 5,500 miles from which the survivors returned in 1822. Despite the rigours he had suffered, like fellow explorers he fell under the spell of the Arctic. He returned again and again, mainly in efforts to map that coastline, because he reasoned this would reveal the Northwest Passage. By 1845 he was ready for the big effort to prove the existence of the passage by sailing through it. He set off with 129 men in two ships, the *Erebus* and the *Terror*. It was, of course, normal for Arctic expeditions to be out of touch with their bases for months at a time. But when, after three years, nothing at all had been heard from Franklin, people began to worry.

This marked the start of one of the high dramas of the Victorian era. Over the next decade, more than forty parties were dispatched into the Arctic to search for Franklin, many led by his old Scottish shipmates. John Ross, now 73 years old, came out of retirement to take charge of one. James Ross returned from the Antarctic to head another. Though the geographical knowledge gained through the searches was immense, no certain clues to Franklin's fate turned up till those found by John Rae in 1853–4 (for which he collected the reward on offer of £10,000, a mark of the immense public interest).

Francis McClintock in another expedition of 1857–9 discovered evidence confirming that tragedy had overtaken Franklin. This voyage, which was financed by Franklin's wife, found records left at Point Victory that the *Erebus* and the *Terror* had been caught by the ice as the winter closed in on an open stretch of water off the northern Canadian coast, between Victoria Island and King William Island. Franklin had died in 1847. Then his crews took the desperate and fatal decision to abandon ship, make for the mainland and set off on foot for civilisation. The nearest depot of the Hudson's Bay Company, York Factory, lay 1,000 miles away. The decision was insane, and to this day it is hard to say what prompted it. One theory supposes that lead in the containers of preserves from which the crews were living poisoned them without killing them, but made them incapable of rational judgement. However that may be, not a single man lived to tell the tale. Relics and documents of Franklin's expedition, including human corpses preserved by the cold, were still being found as late as 1960. He himself is known to have kept a diary, which may yet be unearthed.

It was during the search for Franklin that one of James Ross's captains, Robert McClure, finally did discover the Northwest Passage. He had approached the Arctic Archipelago from the Pacific, sailing through the Bering Strait, following the coast of Alaska and Canada then turning north past several islands to Melville Sound, which Ross and Parry had reached from the opposite direction more than thirty years before. This was in fact the western entrance to the passage.

McClure then found himself threatened by the fate that had befallen Franklin. In the winter of 1850–1 his ship was frozen in the ice. McClure took this in his stride and went out by sledge to map the surrounding areas. But when the spring came the ice did not retreat far enough to release his ship; nor in the spring after that. His expedition then faced the same fraught decision as Franklin's, whether to abandon ship and try to escape over-land. Luckily, McClure's men had their sledges and made fast enough progress to reach a point where they were likely to be rescued, as the Arctic was swarming with parties in search of Franklin. Unlike him, McClure had set out prepared to live like the Eskimos. The Royal Navy being the Royal Navy, he was actually disciplined for having come home without his ship. On the other hand, when his maps established that he had indeed discovered the Northwest Passage, he received a knighthood. Once discovered, at such huge cost in lives and money, the passage remained worthless for all practical purposes. Only the detection of vast oilfields in Alaska in the late twentieth century created the commercial possibility of using it to ship the oil to the eastern US. But the technical problems of building, without risk to the fragile Arctic environment, tankers which also have to be icebreakers are yet to be solved.

Meanwhile, back in his headquarters at Lachine near Montreal, Governor Simpson had early on assessed that the Northwest Passage would not earn any quick profits for the Hudson's Bay Company. Like Mackenzie before him, he was driven to the conclusion that a trading route to the Pacific must go through the Rocky Mountains, and it would have to be a better one than Mackenzie had been able to discover. Not content with directing this search from his desk, Simpson went to have a look for himself. In 1824–5 he made the first of several journeys to the West, travelling from Hudson's Bay to the Pacific in eighty-four days, twenty days faster than anyone before. It was almost like a royal progress: Simpson sat perched in a top hat and immaculate tail coat on his grand canoe, from which he would step ashore, on reaching a trading post or an Indian village, to the tunes of his own pipers.

The westward strategy imposed on him also taxed Simpson's political skills, for it brought him into competition with the Americans. He kept them at bay by maintaining outwardly cordial relations, while at the same time working to undermine their commercial position. A few years after the expedition of Lewis and Clark, in 1811, a ship belonging to John Jacob Astor, the son of an immigrant German butcher who had become the richest man in New York, sailed round Cape Horn and anchored at the mouth of the Columbia River, which forms a fine natural harbour. A settlement called Astoria was founded, from which a string of trading outposts along the river could be set up. The US thus staked its claim to the territory. According to Simpson, however, the basin of the Columbia belonged to him. The river flows along the present boundary of the states of Washington and Oregon but it rises far up in the mountains of what is now Alberta. This whole region had been explored and opened up by the fur traders of the Hudson's Bay Company.

For a time it looked as if, by his own exertions, Simpson might be able to make good his claim. His great gambit was alliance with the Russians who, after crossing the Bering Strait from Asia, had since 1741 held a chain of trading stations in Alaska. He went in person to St Petersburg in 1838, on what can only be called a state visit, and triumphantly concluded an accord leasing the Alaskan panhandle from Czar Alexander II in return for supplying provisions to his remote outposts. The two men, who between them controlled one-quarter of the land surface of the globe, agreed on further co-operation aimed at keeping the Americans away from the entire northern Pacific seaboard. The expansion of the Hudson's Bay Company did not stop there. It put down a marker for the future by setting up at San Francisco, in what was still Mexican territory to the south of its existing stations. Here, too, it financed exploration, looking for new products and trading routes. It employed a botanist, David Douglas, who tramped about in the interior of California collecting specimens.

Explorers have to be hard men, but Douglas is one of the most attractive figures in the history of the West. He came from a humble background, as the son of a stonemason at Scone Palace, the seat of the Earl of Mansfield in Perthshire. Douglas lived to be only 35, but in his short career won fame as a fearless explorer and at the same time gained the respect of the scientific community for his discoveries. His work as a botanist introduced more than 200 new species, including the Douglas fir named after him, into the forests and gardens of the Old World. Above all he was a lovable man, with a dauntless spirit, amazing stamina, voracious curiosity and an ability to make light of every hardship, a character capped with an enthusiasm so boyish as to amuse others. When at length he got to California, a companion wrote, after shooting down a huge condor circling over their camp:

> One morning a large specimen was brought into our square, and we had all a hearty laugh at the eagerness with which the Botanist [Douglas] pounced upon it. In a very short time he had it almost in his embraces fathoming its stretch of wings, which not being able to compass, a measure was brought, and he found it full nine feet from tip to tip. This satisfied him, and the bird was carefully transferred to his studio for the purpose of being stuffed. In all that pertained to nature and science, he was a perfect enthusiast.

The boy Douglas had never been good at school, but already had a lively enough interest in plants and flowers to find his first job as a gardener at Scone. He developed his knowledge and skills so fast that a few years later he was taken on at the Botanical Gardens in Glasgow, then at the Horticultural Society in London. The early nineteenth century has been called the heroic age of botany, which was being put on a scientific footing through an elaborate system of classification. European powers established political control over most of the globe, and their botanists could work without coming to harm. Rising industrial societies had an appetite for unknown plants, whether they were to be turned into textiles, used for brewing tea or given a new home in the herbaceous borders of suburban flower-beds. Scottish gardeners in particular took pride in bringing on exotic growths at the absolute extremity of their limits of cultivation: pineapples were planted in Perthshire, palm trees in Wester Ross. Douglas made his name out of responding to these new demands.

After an early trip to the US in 1824, Douglas found his way out to what would be the main theatre of his activity, the territory of the Hudson's Bay Company in western Canada. For the next ten years, with only a brief furlough in Scotland, he devoted his tireless energies to exploring this vast and little-known country, to collecting and classifying its flora and to recording the life of its Indian population.

He discovered the Douglas fir almost as soon as he landed at the mouth of the Columbia River in 1825. Some of its first seeds, which he then sent home, grew into trees still standing at Scone Palace, Dawyck Gardens and Drumlanrig Castle. The largest tree at present growing in the British Isles is a Douglas fir, called *Dughall Mor* or Big Dougal, which has reached over 203 feet high, in Reelig Glen at Beauly in Inverness-shire. Big Dougal still has a way to go before he matches his tallest Californian cousin, General Sherman, who boasts a height of 275 feet and a girth of 102 feet; some Douglas firs in their native habitat have topped 400 feet. This magnificent tree is not only beautiful but also useful as timber, and was more traded than any other in the twentieth century. A second discovery of Douglas's which has become even more familiar in his homeland is the sitka spruce. As he wrote at the time, it 'possesses one great advantage by growing to a very large size in apparently poor, thin, damp soils. This unquestionably has great claims on our consideration as it would thrive in such places in Britain where Pinus sylvestris [Scots pine] has no shelter.' These were prophetic words, for much of the Scottish Highlands, useless for any other agricultural purpose, has today been covered with plantations of sitka. Many complain that it makes the landscape boring and destroys the natural habitat, but it is now the mainstay of forestry in Britain and accounts for two-thirds of the country's production of timber.

Douglas's journals are invaluable besides as a source for the life of the Indians before this was destroyed, or changed beyond recognition, by the advent of the white man. He records curious customs and rites still of interest to anthropologists. He at first took a superior attitude to the Indians, but it gradually changed to admiration as he realised how kind and hospitable they could be when treated as equals. He walked altogether nearly 10,000 miles in the interior of North America, often alone or with only one or two companions. He often faced hardship and danger: 'Such objects as I am in quest of are not obtained without a share of labour, anxiety of mind and sometimes risk of personal safety,' he reflected in his matter-of-fact fashion. Only seldom did it get him down. He wrote in his journal one night:

> The fact is plainly this; all hungry and no means of cooking a little of our stock; travelled thirty three miles, drenched and bleached with rain or sleet, chilled with a piercing north wind; and then to finish the day experienced the cooling, comfortless consolation for lying down wet with no supper or fire. On such occasions I am very liable to become fretful.

Even so, Douglas recorded vivid and affectionate impressions of the unspoilt wilderness and of its natives' way of life. After surviving so many perils, he met his death by accident while on a trip to the island of Hawaii in 1834. After setting off alone on an expedition to climb the volcano of Kilauea, he was killed by a wild bull.

One of the little pleasures of life as a Scotsman is to come across compatriots in remote corners of the globe. The paths of Douglas and Governor Simpson happened to cross one day in 1826 at Norway House, a depot of the Hudson's Bay Company in what is now northern Manitoba. They had never met before but Simpson knew who Douglas was, for without the help he had authorised from the company the explorer would have been able to achieve little. Even the governor's imperious reserve melted somewhat when faced with Douglas's innocent zest. Simpson went so far as to offer him some linen, always useful in the wilderness; the men around gaped. 'I refused, at the same time extremely indebted to him,' Douglas blithely recorded.

It may well have been at Simpson's behest that Douglas went to Hawaii: it was a place the governor kept his shrewd eye on. In that same year of 1834 the Hudson's Bay Company founded an agency at Honolulu. Simpson called by there while he was on his way to St Petersburg, with friendly advice for the native king, Kamehameha III, about foiling the schemes to annex his islands of the French, the Russians and indeed the British. In 1848, Simpson sent Ranald MacDonald, the son of his secretary, on a secret voyage to Japan, six years before the celebrated visit of the American, Commander Matthew Perry (who was himself of partly Scottish ancestry). MacDonald was detained for some months at Nagasaki, where he learned Japanese and taught English to official interpreters. Unlike Perry, he did not succeed in persuading the authorities to enter into diplomatic relations with a foreign power.

This was the Hudson's Bay Company at its height: master of huge territories, immensely profitable, expanding through exploration. But within a few years the whole edifice collapsed. In 1846 the outbreak of war between the US and Mexico led to the victorious Americans' annexation of California, which was soon filled during the gold rush by hordes of settlers. It was high time for Britain and the US to resolve their differences on the Pacific coast; the Oregon Treaty set the border between their territories at the forty-ninth parallel, north of the Columbia River (which, however, the company would still be allowed to navigate). When British Columbia then became a Crown colony, the Hudson's Bay Company had no more control of the region.

The Confederation of Canada in 1867 sounded the death-knell for the company's strange, empty realm in the West. The new country, with five provinces on the Atlantic and one on the Pacific, would have to people the West in order to join them up: in fact, British Columbia made this a condition of its joining the Confederation. That meant the old ways of life in the West would have to come to an end. Governor Simpson had long seen the writing on the wall. He himself invested in railways and mining, activities bound to bring in settlers.

The change in direction left the company with hardened explorers on its books for whom new jobs would have to be found. But they were nothing if not adaptable. Rae, Simpson's favourite, found a fresh application for his intrepid talents in surveying the route for a telegraph line across the Rocky Mountains (he would later lay down a second telegraph line between Britain and the US by way of the Faroe Islands and Iceland). Others joined in the projects to link Canada from sea to sea, some requiring as much courage and resource as any journey of exploration in the wilderness.

The most prodigious project of all was the construction of the Canadian Pacific Railway. It was finished in 1885, four years later than planned, against formidable financial and physical odds. Success was owed to the efforts of two Scots who formerly worked for the Hudson's Bay Company. One was George Stephen, who had exchanged his dreary life as a draper's apprentice in Aberdeen for adventure in the New World. The other was his cousin Donald Smith, who hailed from Forres and served the company in Labrador and Manitoba. Stephen drew up the proposal for the railway and Smith put together the syndicate which financed it. Enormous technical difficulties had to be overcome to find a feasible route along the winding gorges and over the high passes of the Rocky Mountains, but the result was a triumph of Victorian engineering.

Smith himself drove in the last spike on the line at a place named Craigellachie, after a village near his birthplace. There is a famous photograph of him doing this, in his white beard and his tailcoat, while navvies muffled against the cold look on and a pine forest stretches away into the misty background. The physical completion of the railway by no means marked the end of its troubles. At first, there was not much traffic to go on it and bankruptcy soon threatened. A subsidy from the Canadian Government helped, but in the end the railway company had to be given lavish grants of land along the line, twenty-five million acres in all, which it could sell off to settlers and so generate its own traffic. For Stephen and Smith the outcome was happier: they grew immensely wealthy, graduated into the financial elite of Montreal and ended up in the House of Lords in London as Lord Mount Stephen and Lord Strathcona.

This may seem a strange fate for adventurers. But at least they died in their beds, which were presumably very comfortable beds – unlike so many of their brave fellow explorers who, thousands of miles from their Scottish homeland, found only a cold grave, or sometimes no grave at all, in the western wilderness or under the ice and snow of the Arctic.

8

FRONTIERSMEN

T he frontier is a central concept of US history and one basic to the American people's idea of themselves. The Manifest Destiny of which they spoke in the nineteenth century meant their westward movement from the Atlantic Ocean to the Pacific Ocean behind an ever advancing frontier which in its wake brought the blessings of democratic government, constitutional rights, rule of law and so on. A much broader cultural effect of the concept can be traced too. Special human virtues marked the pioneers who pushed the frontier onwards and started life afresh in the lands they opened up. These were virtues of sturdy self-reliance combined with a readiness to help neighbours and welcome strangers, so as to create a new society where freedom and equality became realities rather than theories. This new society could not be created without trouble: there was violence and rough justice among the settlers themselves, let alone expulsion from their lands or even extermination of the Indians who opposed them. Even so, a civilising process was set in motion, with the eventual result of the emergence in California or Colorado of communities as decent and peaceful as any in Maine or Maryland.

Obviously a lot of romantic myth-making has gone into the concept of the frontier, where everyday existence was no doubt in its way as dreary and humdrum as in a modern city. But the wave of humanity sweeping across the continent of North America framed values that flowed back over the regions settled earlier, so that even a modern New Yorker, who has never seen an Indian or even a cow, might imagine he partakes of the virtues needed to tame a wilderness.

Yet the concept of the frontier is being heavily modified in the kind of American history starting to be rewritten now. The US has emerged as the world's sole superpower – or, in older parlance, as a great imperial power – and not since ancient Rome has there been such a power without a rival (the British, French, German and Russian empires had to waste much of their energy and resources in competition with one another). It seems inevitable that American history will have to be recast in those terms, as a prehistory of imperialism on a global scale, rather than the largely self-contained account of a nation in the New World founded on principles meant to preserve it from the mistakes of nations in the Old World. All the same, it will take a long time for the myths which have inspired Americans to be diluted by the scribblings of academics.

Americans might be able to see in the Scots a useful example of how slowly time may work on something so deep and subtle as a national mentality or character. Scotland is surrounded on three and a half sides by water, yet the remaining stretch of its bounds is by far the most important. This is the frontier – or, as we prefer to say, the border – with England. That border has had if anything a stronger impact on Scottish history than the frontier has had on American history. The American frontier may in due course take its place as a mere phase in the history of a great imperial power. The effect of the Anglo-Scottish border can probably never be effaced so long as Scotland exists.

It has already been there a long time. The present territory of Scotland is much the same as that secured by King Robert Bruce in the Wars of Independence of the early fourteenth century, and indeed had been the same for a century or so before that. The sole major adjustment came with the definitive loss to Scotland in 1482 of Berwick, the main fortress on the eastern border. Yet anyone who goes to that picturesque, stone-built town today will hardly believe he is in England; though the people insist they are English, they speak like their neighbours in the Scottish county of Berwickshire, they spend Scottish banknotes in their shops and their football team plays in the Scottish league. For Scots, at least, England begins only once they cross the River Tweed, which washes Berwick's walls on the southern side.

Meanwhile, at the western end of the border the last and minor adjustment occurred in 1554, when the Debatable Lands were divided between Scotland and England by a straight line drawn between two rivers. Here it remains a real border. The language of the people changes right on the border, on the one side Scots, on the other side Cumbrian. The city of Carlisle a short way to the south already seems wholly English in character, with the mock-Tudor houses that Scots find so comical, the Anglican cathedral and the grim, workaday castle which looks as if it could at any moment resume its old role as garrison and refuge from cutthroat Scots marauders. Three centuries of Union between Scotland and England have hardly altered such superficial differences, let alone some deeper ones. The American frontier moved; the Anglo-Scottish border appears immovable.

And yet, of course, it is in another sense no border at all. When Scotland and England became one country in 1707, the border over which so much blood had been shed was relegated to a line on the map. Citizens of either nation could move back and forth across it in perfect freedom, and many have done so. The subject of English immigration to Scotland is not much written about, though it has at times been considerable, but the subject of Scottish immigration to England would make a book in itself. To Scots, moving out of the homeland has always been a more feasible, indeed desirable, option than it could ever have been to Englishmen, the sons of a much bigger and richer nation. For the reasons surveyed in previous chapters – the poverty and narrowness of Scotland, and the fact that all the same the country produced more trained minds than it could use – Scots early on grew accustomed to mobility.

The Union of 1707 merely made Scots a little more mobile. During the previous centuries of English enmity, they had sought their fortunes in Europe. In medieval times the *Scotus viator*, the wandering Scot, could be found anywhere from Riga to Rome. It

was remarkable, too, how readily Scots even then adapted themselves to their surroundings, whether as merchants in Poland, as
monks in the Holy Roman Empire, as soldiers in France. They
adapted themselves because they had to: they came from a small
country which could never impose its will on others or protect its
errant citizens. These habits of mind proved invaluable when
England was at last fully opened to them in 1707. For Scots this
meant that their sole frontier and their last frontier only became,
like all the others, no frontier at all. They would carry this attitude
to America.

There the Scots, or more especially the Scotch-Irish, often
moved straight to the frontier as soon as they landed. They were
latecomers to the Thirteen Colonies, and the more fertile parts of
New England or Virginia had already been settled. So the Scots
would set out at once from New York or Philadelphia towards
the Appalachian Mountains, and were often the first to cross
them into the region now covered by the states of Ohio,
Kentucky and Tennessee. Southwards lay territory in the possession of what came to be called the Five Civilised Tribes:
Creeks, Seminoles, Cherokees, Choctaws and Chickasaws. They
held all the land east of the Mississippi River and south of the
Tennessee River except for the narrow tract of English settlement along the coast of Georgia and the Carolinas.

These Indian nations were relatively coherent and well-organ-
ised. They were not technologically inferior to the early
colonists. They soon learned new military and commercial
methods from the whites. They were well able to defend their territory. They welcomed the establishment of trading towns at
Charleston and Savannah because through them European
goods became available. They did not welcome any attempt by
settlers to push far out from those towns. If that happened, the
Indians went to war and they waged war in (by European standards) a savage and ruthless manner, scalping, slaying, torturing
and kidnapping civilians without regard to age or sex. As a
result, the frontier in this region hardly moved for 100 years
from the first settlements in the 1670s, because the whites were
terrified of the Indians.

Here was a real frontier, and it took the Scots to cross it. The first of them to arrive in the region were captive Jacobite soldiers transported after the failure of the rebellion of 1715. They kept in touch with friends and family at home and formed the nucleus for a small but significant presence of Highlanders in later years. When the colony of Georgia was being formed in the 1730s, its agents went to Argyll and Inverness-shire to recruit settlers. Among those who returned with them, prompted by encouraging reports from kinsmen already in America, was a group of adventurous youngsters from Clan MacGillivray, whose territory lay on the eastern shore of Loch Ness. In Georgia, about fifty miles south of Savannah, they founded a township called Darien, after the lost Scottish colony in Central America. It did not prosper, partly because the conditions were so different from anything the clansmen knew and partly because they were harassed by the Spaniards occupying Florida. Unable or unwilling to go home again, they had to find other means of earning their living.

Among them was Lachlan MacGillivray, who had been only sixteen years old when he arrived. Unlike earlier settlers, he and his companions got on well with the Indians. They competed in feats of athletic prowess, such as tossing the caber or throwing the hammer or the ball-games that the Indians played. And once they learned something of each other's languages, both sides found they had a fund of often fantastic stories to tell, especially of how spirits and fairies and other supernatural beings intervened in the affairs of men. Apart from anything else, the two races were equally proud of their martial values and fighting qualities, above all of the fierce mutual loyalty which bound chieftains and warriors together both on the field of battle and in times of peace.

MacGillivray decided he could make his fortune among the Indians. He set out to do so through trade. As an intrepid Highlander, he had no fear of the frontier. He went far up-country, 500 miles or more from the ports on the Atlantic coast. He would take with him a train of packhorses loaded with what the Indians most wanted, rum and gunpowder and textiles. They had not known alcohol before the Europeans appeared, but soon discovered an insatiable and dangerous appetite for it. The gunpowder they used in their hunting and their wars. Their taste in textiles was exotic, and images of them surviving from this period show them dressed up rather like raffish Balkan brigands, in multicoloured breeches and waistcoats or even turbans, not in the warpaint and feathers we might expect.

From the hinterland MacGillivray brought back beaver-skins, to make the earliest form of waterproof headgear available in Europe, deer-hides, which were prized for their soft and supple leather, and others among the abundant products of nature. Out of this traffic he became a rich man. He bought himself an estate near Savannah. But his favourite residence lay at a place called Little Tallassee on the River Coosa in central Alabama, among the Creek Indians. He intrigued them by planting there a grove of apple trees, hitherto unknown to them, bearing fruit which they soon adopted as a tasty supplement to their diet.

The time approached for MacGillivray to take a wife. He might have chosen one in Savannah or Charleston, or even back in Scotland. But she would have had to tolerate life in the wilderness or else long absences on his part, and this did not seem proper for a lady of the status he felt entitled to seek. He was able to solve his problem because he also appeared an eligible bachelor to the Indians. Women occupied an honoured place in their society, one much more equal with men than in white society. The Creeks were ruled by their chiefs, but these chiefs succeeded each other through the female, not the male line. That is to say, they derived their succession through their mothers, not their fathers. The Creeks were divided into seven clans, of which the strongest and most prestigious was the Wind Clan. The clan had a princess called Sehoy of an age suitable for marriage with MacGillivray. In 1750 the pair of them were wed.

By his choice of wife MacGillivray became one of the most powerful men in this region of North America, respected and wealthy enough to be consulted by both the British and the Indians. Like other ex-Jacobites in the colonies, he turned ultra-loyalist to the Hanoverian Crown. He was a trusted counsellor to royal governors of the southern colonies and helped to make a success of their policies for consolidating their rule and keeping the frontier at peace. The Indians listened to him too as an oracle of sage advice who, through his connections by blood with them, had their best interests at heart. MacGillivray played a vital role in holding the Creeks and other Indian nations in alliance with Britain during the wars against the French in America and then during the Revolution. He returned to Scotland rather than live in the independent US, to die near the place where he had been born in Inverness-shire. But his influence persisted because his own children by Sehoy became through their matrilinear descent eligible for the highest rank in the Creek nation.

MacGillivray's son Alexander belonged fully to two worlds. He belonged to the culture of the Creeks, in which he was brought up in Alabama. He belonged also to the culture of the American Scots. He knew their songs and their stories and he enjoyed their convivial ways. He was well educated too: his father sent him to be taught by a kinsman who was a Presbyterian minister in Charleston, and later he would correspond on scholarly matters with William Robertson, principal of the University of Edinburgh and a central figure in the Enlightenment, who was writing a history of America. Above all, Alexander MacGillivray was a subtle and sagacious politician who came forward just when the Creeks needed him most.

The American Revolution was a catastrophe for the Indian nations. It removed the protection of an imperial power, Britain, which had been on the whole sympathetic to them, despite the opportunism of its policies. Basically the British did not want war on the American frontier, and they secured this object by a combination of friendship for the Indians and restraint on the white colonists. Now all such restraint was removed. The US showed an expansionist spirit from the foundation of the Republic. The Indians had little chance of finding anyone to listen to them in its democratic government. It soon admitted new states – first Kentucky and Tennessee, then others to the north – which were still being settled by a process of clearing the Indians off their lands. The floodgates of the westward movement were opened. Only the Five Civilised Tribes, in what are now the states of Georgia, Alabama and Mississippi, were powerful enough to withstand it, but the prospects for them did not look good in the long run either.

The custom among the Creeks was for the leaders of the seven clans to meet from time to time and elect one of themselves as a paramount chief for the whole nation. In 1783 they elected MacGillivray, just as Britain finally recognised the independence of the Thirteen Colonies and withdrew from America. In the treaty of peace, the status of the Indians was left ambiguous. The British appeared to be handing all the territory east of the River Mississippi over to American sovereignty, but whether they had any right to do this on behalf of the Indians remained unclear. At any rate the Americans did not yet control the Indian lands, least of all those of the Five Civilised Tribes.

MacGillivray saw it was vital for the perilous ambiguities in this situation to be resolved. Unless Indian rights were set down in black and white, there could only be endless conflict and opportunities for American aggression. So, at the head of a party of Creek chiefs, MacGillivray set off to argue his case to the only man with the authority to impose a settlement, President George Washington. They met in New York, the temporary capital of the US, in 1790. The result was a treaty to guarantee the Creeks' rights within their existing territory in return for accepting a vague American protectorate which in practice meant little. MacGillivray was honoured with the rank of a US brigadier-general and given a pension.

MacGillivray did not allow these last trifles to colour his realistic judgement. In fact he had no intention of being protected by the Americans, for he saw what that would mean. He continued to cultivate relations with other powers having an interest in Creek independence, with Spain, France and Britain, which he could play off against the US. It was a classic exercise in diplomacy, worthy of any European minister. It worked well, but only for a short while till MacGillivray's premature death in 1793. Even so the framework he erected held for another twenty or thirty years and allowed the Creeks a respite enjoyed by no other Indian nation, till the inexorable tide of white settlement swept over them.

During those decades the fate of the Creeks lay largely in the hands of Scots who had crossed the frontier along with the McGillivrays, father and son. Concepts of kinship among the two peoples were not dissimilar. One was matrilinear and the other patrilinear, but both recognised the family as something extended rather than nuclear, so that distant cousins could be as close to one another as parents to children. Both peoples were also indifferent to race. Just as Scots married Indian brides, so they and their offspring were accepted as members of the tribe, though many had more Scottish than Creek blood. Their sons continued to belong to two worlds. As boys they would be taught to hunt and to fight, and be instructed in the customs of the nation, just like their full-blooded Creek playmates. As young men, they might be sent for an education to Scotland, or at least to a Presbyterian academy in Philadelphia or Charleston.

In Scotland, the MacGillivrays belonged to the confederal Clan Chattan, of which the chiefs were the MacIntoshes of Moy. Sons of these MacIntoshes also went to America and one of them, William, became the leader of the Creek party which in later years favoured accommodation with the US; he was assassinated in 1825 by enraged tribesmen after he signed a treaty surrendering a large tract of their lands. At the same time, the leaders of the party which wanted to carry on an armed struggle for Creek independence were Lachlan MacGillivray's step-grandson William Weatherford (descended on the male side from a Lowland trader), and his grandson-in-law, Peter McQueen; their relationships sound complicated in English but become clear in the Creek genealogies, where they pass through three generations of formidable princesses each called Sehoy.

Weatherford looked like a Scotsman, with pale skin and red hair, but he dressed like an Indian brave, bare to the waist, with buckskin breeches and moccasins. It was he that submitted to Andrew Jackson after the Battle of Horseshoe Bend in 1814, the decisive engagement in the cruel war the American general waged on the Creeks. Weatherford did so to spare his fellow chiefs the humiliation of handing him over, as Jackson had demanded. He simply rode to the US army's camp and walked up to the commander's tent. Jackson was unsure how to react, and Weatherford said to him:

I am in your power – do with me as you please. I am a soldier.

> I have done the white people all the harm I could. I have fought them, and fought them bravely. If I had an army, I would yet fight, and contend to the last. But I have none. My people are all gone. I can do no more than weep over the misfortunes of my nation.

Even the hardbitten Jackson felt moved by such courage, though it in no way deflected him from his purpose of destroying the Creeks' power so that they could be expelled from their lands and exiled beyond the Mississippi. This eventually happened in the 1830s. But the fact that the Creeks had after US independence a final half-century on the lands that belonged to them can be ascribed in great measure to the Scots who came to live among them on the further side of the American frontier.

Of this the Creeks offer the most remarkable and best documented example, but it was by no means unique. Peter McQueen had a nephew, William, usually known by his Indian name of Osceola. The pair of them took refuge from Jackson among the Seminoles, who lived in Florida. The difference between Creeks and Seminoles was geographic rather than linguistic or ethnic. In the early eighteenth century the Seminoles had migrated south from the Creek country, but in their new home absorbed refugees from other nations as well as large numbers of runaway slaves, so as to form a new tribal identity – Osceola himself was to marry a black woman.

Florida still belonged to Spain, but the Americans had their eyes on it; Jackson prosecuted his campaign there just as if it had already been part of the US. The Spaniards saw the writing on the wall, and in 1819 offered for $5 million to sell Florida to the Americans. As they then prepared the territory for admission to the Union, they pursued the same policy as elsewhere in the region, of compelling the Indians to leave for the West. The Seminole chiefs agreed to do so in 1832. It was Osceola that led a rebellion of the young braves against this surrender, sparking off a series of Seminole Wars that lasted five years and cost the US the lives of hundreds of troops. At last, in 1837, Osceola let it be known that he would parley for peace. He was told to come to the fortress of St Augustine under a white flag. There, before

BOLD, INDEPENDENT, UNCONQUER'D AND FREE'

any negotiations could proceed he was simply taken prisoner, along with his family and followers, and sent in custody to Charleston. He shortly died in jail, a victim of white perfidy. Today he is a symbol of American mistreatment of the Indians.

For the Indians to co-operate with the Americans seldom helped them either. Probably the most advanced, though not the most powerful, of the Five Civilised Tribes were the Cherokees. They lived among the lovely mountains and valleys of the western Carolinas, eastern Tennessee and northern Georgia. They were, at least compared to the hot-blooded Creeks, a peaceable people. They early on realised that US power was irresistible and set about doing what they supposed the Americans wanted them to do, that is, gradually to take on the ways of the whites so that both races could live in harmony. They continued on this course, in growing desperation, even as it became clear that the real aim of the whites was to dispossess them.

In 1818, after being bamboozled into a humiliating cession of land, the Cherokees organised a regular government. They retained their paramount chief, called Pathkiller, as titular head of the nation. Under him was an elected national council. It supervised a judicial system of eight circuits, each with a judge and a marshal. The marshal, who was accompanied on his rounds by light horsemen to execute his decisions and perhaps to protect his life, also collected, on commission, the taxes. The main one was a poll tax of fifty cents on each head of family and single men under sixty. The taxes were deposited in the Cherokee treasury at Fortville, Georgia. Not far away, at a place called New Echota, the nation erected a capital to support the dignity of its government. It was soon introducing enlightened measures, such as an alphabet for the Cherokee language so that formal education could be started.

The real power in this government lay with the president of the national council. He was John Ross, born the son of a trader in Tennessee, seven-eighths Scottish in blood, but with a matrilinear descent from a well-born Cherokee great-grandmother which qualified him for his rank in his nation. He governed it for thirty-eight years. At the outset, perhaps, he nourished at the back of his mind a notion that the Cherokees might eventually form a state of the Union. But the Americans had other ideas. They piled on the pressure to make the nation move west. Ross resisted to the utmost, allying himself with the Creeks, ordering illegal settlers to be driven off his Cherokee land, appealing to the US Supreme Court. He postponed but did not avert his people's doom. It was at length he who in 1838–9 found himself forced to lead them on their Trail of Tears to Oklahoma.

Scottish adaptability is legendary. While in the pages of Rudyard Kipling or John Buchan we can read legends of Scotsmen who turned themselves into Asian khans or gods on Pacific islands, in real life there was nothing more striking than this affinity of the Scots and Native Americans. The parallels in their martial values, oral culture and social structure do not perhaps fully account for it. Somehow, the generosity and freedom in both peoples made a mutual appeal to them across the racial barrier (which they, of course, did not acknowledge).

Most remarkable of all was that, for a short time, the affinity appeared to point the way towards an alternative model of American development. The model which prevailed in the US during the early nineteenth century was of racial supremacy, including simple displacement, or even extermination, of Indian populations and cultures by white population and culture. What the Scots achieved was a mestizo culture, where an incoming group integrated with the indigenous people so that a fresh amalgam contained something of both. This resembled the Latin model in South America. It is a model not without problems of its own but ones clearly not to be solved by racial supremacy, an idea which the ever more complex mixture of blood in succeeding generations rendered absurd. If that mestizo model had been followed in the Old South, then the whites could have learned to live with their Indian neighbours on a basis of equality – and in time, too, perhaps might have found it in themselves to emancipate the enslaved population of blacks in the region. This was a road not taken, yet it is difficult to believe it would have been as hard a road as the history of war, suffering and oppression which the South actually chose.

Scots, being so adaptable, are apt to cast off at once any model which no longer works and put it completely out of their minds. Here, the sharply drawn American frontier cut across the fluid and porous Scottish idea of a frontier. All at once people had to choose, or were forced by their immediate circumstances into a choice which decided the fate of their families for generations. Among Lachlan MacGillivray's by now numerous progeny, for example, were those who defined themselves, and were defined by others, as Creeks. They would share the bitter destiny of that nation.

Others could choose to be whites. The Creek warrior Weatherford had a half-brother David Tait, also a son of the redoubtable princess, Sehoy III, but by her first husband, James Tait, a Scots colonel in the British army during the American War of Independence. David was one scion of this amazing clan sent to Scotland for his education. On his return, he entered into an inheritance which turned him into a gentleman of the Old South, a slave-owning planter. He had only daughters surviving him, but for a nephew he procured a place at West Point and a military career, while a grandson served as an American diplomat. Another member of their burgeoning kin who came down on the white side was George Troup, Governor of Georgia. He veered so far from his origins as to obtain the last cessions of Creek land in that state. Later, as a US Senator, he vindicated a state's right to conduct its own relations with foreign powers or peoples and, when he died in 1856, was still defending this, one of the most extreme positions taken up by southerners before the Civil War. Thus was the transition from Scot to American completed.

Meanwhile, with their own model of a frontier expunged, the Scots' fighting qualities allowed them to man forward positions on the American frontier. It was the scene of countless fabled exploits, but none has left a deeper impression on the American consciousness than the defence of the Alamo at San Antonio, Texas, in 1836. That defence was carried out by just 189 men against the armed might of the Mexican general, Antonio Lopez de Santa Anna. Of them, at least fifty are reckoned to have been American Scots, notably their commander, Jim Bowie, reputed inventor of the Bowie knife. Four had been born in Scotland, including one who served as piper to the garrison of the Alamo, John McGregor.

Texas was still at the time in the possession of Mexico, but it had long been infiltrated by American settlers; Bowie was typical of them, having left his native Kentucky to go into business in New Orleans and then, wandering westwards, having got a grant of land from the Mexican governor and married his daughter. A mestizo culture might have been formed here too, but Americans, even American Scots, were becoming conscious of their distinct nationality. The time came when, forming a clear majority of the local population, they wished to cease being Mexican provincials and form a democratic government of their own.

Their struggle attracted support from many of the legendary figures of the West. Of the American Scots among them, the most famous was Davy Crockett, whom we last saw fighting under Andrew Jackson against the Creeks in 1814. He was now 50 years old and, despite the career in public life he had meanwhile enjoyed, still at heart a country boy from Tennessee. After his youthful spell of soldiering he had been elected to the legislature of the state. When a friend suggested as a joke that he should go on to run for the US House of Representatives he took the idea seriously and served three terms there. He had had no formal education, but made up for this with his appearance and style of speaking, both unmistakably of the frontier. As he himself announced to a startled Washington DC in one of his tall tales: 'I'm David Crockett, fresh from the backwoods, half-horse, half-alligator, a little touched with the snapping turtle; can wade the Mississippi, leap the Ohio, ride a streak of lightning, slip without a scratch down a honey locust, can whip my weight in wildcats.' Having become a national character, he resented being thrown out by his ungrateful constituents in the election of 1835. This was why he went to Texas and found himself at the Alamo in 1836.

The Alamo was an old missionary station, dating from 1718, which had been turned into a fortress. At the outset of their uprising against Mexico, the Texans took it over. It lay in the path of Santa Anna as he approached with his force of several thousand men to suppress the rebellion. For one reason and another, the Alamo received hardly any reinforcements. But when Santa Anna demanded its surrender, the men inside refused. A siege went on from 24 February to 6 March. At last the Mexicans broke in and hand-to-hand combat followed, with the Texans pitted against enormous odds. At the end of it, every one of them was dead or dying.

This heroic resistance inspired all the other Texans, though it also brought sharp criticism of their military commander, Sam Houston, who had avoided battle with Santa Anna. Houston was another American Scot. Born in Tennessee, he had lived much of his early life among the Cherokees and been adopted by them into the tribe. He too fought under Jackson against the Creeks at the Battle of Horseshoe Bend in 1814, suffering serious wounds. His soldiering also proved for him a springboard to a political career and at length, in 1827, he was elected Governor of Tennessee. Then, two years later, came the death of his wife. It devastated him: he at once resigned and rode out to the West, rejoined his beloved Cherokees and for several years took refuge in drink. By 1836 he was recovering. He was a member of the convention that declared Texas independent of Mexico, and then took command of the new republic's troops.

Houston's strategy of retreating till he could strike a decisive blow was in the end vindicated. He brilliantly redeemed himself at the Battle of San Jacinto in April, when by a surprise attack, with his soldiers shouting 'Remember the Alamo!', he decisively defeated the Mexicans and captured Santa Anna himself. The independence of Texas was won and Houston, suddenly a popular hero, became its president. The republic lasted barely a decade. In 1845 it was admitted to the Union, with Houston as its governor – the only man ever to have served as governor of two different states. He remained its outstanding public figure up to the Civil War, when he had to resign because he opposed the secession of Texas from the US.

The annexation of Texas brought on the Mexican War, in which another legendary American Scot made his name on the frontier. Kit Carson came from Kentucky, but while he was still an infant his family moved to Missouri and from there, with no education, he ran away at the age of 16 and finished up at Taos, New Mexico. He earned his living as a teamster, cook, guide and hunter for parties of explorers, a sort of professional frontiersman.

He helped with cartographical surveys of California, which made his experience invaluable when the Americans set about seizing this second Mexican province in 1846. After the US army captured Los Angeles, Carson was sent overland with despatches and met a military force under General Stephen Kearny coming in the other direction. Since the general was unsure of the route, he ordered Carson to guide them back to California. Once there, the force was surrounded by Mexicans, but Carson made his way through the enemy lines and summoned the reinforcements from San Diego which saved them from capture. After the Mexican War he returned to ranching at Taos. During the Civil War he raised a regiment of New Mexican volunteers which fought against Indians supporting the Confederacy. Despite still being illiterate, he was later made a brigadier-general.

By now the classic age of the American frontier was passing, and by about 1890 it had come to an end. The US left this phase of history behind and embarked on its era of overseas expansion. Legend, literature and especially films have kept the memory alive. But the remarkable thing is that Americans today can still see for themselves something of what the frontier was like, because the most beautiful landscapes have been saved from development and kept in their natural state.

This achievement is largely due to another American Scot, John Muir, father and philosopher of the US national parks, founder of the Sierra Club (the first environmental pressure group) and a fine writer who rejoiced in the wholesomeness of nature: 'When we try to pick out anything by itself we find it hitched to everything else in the Universe.' Muir is a hero to modern America as the transmitter to the present generation of the optimism which an undiscovered country aroused in earlier ones: 'Go climb the mountains and get their good tidings. Nature's peace will flow into you as sunshine into trees. The winds will blow their own freshness into you and the storms their energy, while cares will drop off like autumn leaves.'

One of Muir's best-loved books, *My Boyhood and Youth*, tells how he was born in 1838 and brought up at Dunbar in East Lothian. His father Daniel was a typical Scotsman of the time, a stern parent and something of a religious fanatic who all the same believed in liberty and equality for everyone. It was his adherence to an Evangelical sect and desire to own land as a way out of his restricted place in local society that led him to uproot his family and take them to America. They might have gone to the West, but on the advice of other Scots already there they settled in Wisconsin. A new life did nothing to soften Daniel Muir's outlook. When they arrived on their farm he had to burn the brushwood to clear the land for the plough, and he would tell his son:

> Now John, just think what an awful thing it would be to be thrown into that fire – and then think of hellfire, that is so many times hotter. Into that fire all bad boys, with sinners of every sort who disobey God, will be cast as we are casting branches into this brush fire, and although suffering so much, their suffering will never end, because neither the fire nor the sinners can die.

The farm turned out to be a perfect place for a future naturalist like young John, then 11 years old, who found 'every wild lesson a love lesson, not whipped but charmed into us. Oh, that glorious Wisconsin wilderness.' After attending university, he intended to follow a career producing agricultural machinery but, nearly blinded in an industrial accident, he decided to devote himself to nature instead. He went to California and walked up into Yosemite in the Sierra Nevada. He was an expert natural scientist and his exploration of the roots of glaciers 14,000 feet up on Mount Whitney convinced him that this range had been shaped by ice, not by volcanic upheaval as the current theory had it. Overwhelmed by the beauty of these marvellous landscapes, he made it his life's work to conserve them.

With the fortune he eventually earned from developing the cultivation of wine and fruit in California, he spent his later years campaigning for the US federal government to create the national parks. There, in a moment of history, visitors of the present day can feel the same sort of thrill as the earliest witnesses of the unspoilt wilderness felt. They, too, reach a frontier – which turns out, in the Scottish fashion, to be no frontier at all.

9

CANADIANS

C anada is the closest part of the New World to Scotland, and this seems true not only in the geographical but also in some wider sense. The easternmost province of Nova Scotia is, after all, named for Scotland, the rocky coasts resemble those of the mother country and the Gaelic language is still spoken there: almost as if Scots and Nova Scotians lived only tens rather than thousands of miles apart. In the interior of the continent the visitor may be struck time and again by a Scottish air about this place or that – the Cantons de l'Est of Quebec, Glengarry County in Ontario or the tranquil landscapes on the northern side of Lake Erie where a leading economist of the twentieth century, John Kenneth Galbraith, grew up, later describing in his memoir, *The Scotch*, how the character of the people still bore the mark of the country they had left two or three generations before. Even Toronto, a typical modern city of North America, conceals behind its spectacular waterfront other quarters with a gloomier, Presbyterian visage, as if frowning at the frivolous azure skyscrapers which now overshadow them.

What is it that here damps the exuberant optimism of the US? Perhaps it is the more looming presence of nature, compared at least with the longer-settled regions to the south, where the environment has been tamed and turned to human service, rivers straightened, mountains provided with roads to the summit, deserts obliged to bloom. Canada remains in essence a strip of territory, at most points no more than 200 or 300 miles wide, running from the Atlantic Ocean to the Pacific Ocean, and beyond that lies a wilderness, not even an enticing wilderness. Scots may get some inkling of it, on a tiny comparative scale, from the so-called Flow Country of Sutherland and Caithness, which looks much like northern Canada, an expanse of hill or rock or bog, wet and green yet otherwise uninvitingly infinite in appearance. It will never be tamed, because there is just not enough in the land to reward the effort of doing so; it might as well be sea for all the use it is. And that is just its benign aspect, in summer under the midnight sun. In winter, it simply forbids the presence of man.

All this evokes in Scots their innate sense of being on the edge of things, at the furthest extreme of a comfortable or normal life, in a place where the thin crust of civilisation can casually be broken. It is a humbling feeling, and one that readily gives way to shudders of religious awe before the powers of a blind and heedless universe. But perhaps this is the very reason why Scots feel at home in Canada, and why so many have emigrated there when they could have chosen some more consoling destination. There can be scarcely a Scottish family which has no kin in Canada. Such figures as are available bear this out. In 1971, at the last census for which the category was recorded, two million Canadians declared themselves to be of Scottish origin, one in ten of the whole population, forming the third largest national group after the English and the French. This statistical presence was soon deleted by a stroke of the bureaucratic pen, however. Bilingualism became the official policy of the Canadian state, which then found it necessary to reduce the ethnic variety of the country to two founding nations: the Scots, and even the Irish, were redefined as British.

Statistics are one thing, realities another. What cannot be deleted is the huge contribution Scots have made to Canada: it would be no idle boast to say that the existence of the country is owed to them. After its conquest from France, following the fall of Quebec in 1759, it was often referred to in official documents simply as another part of British North America. And it was not impossible that Canada might have joined the Thirteen Colonies in seizing its independence. Absorption of Canada was certainly on the agenda of the Founding Fathers of the US. Military expeditions set out from New England. But they met with no popular response.

Still, the question whether Canada should remain separate was not to be laid to rest for another century. In the US Congress, any budding politician could cheaply win a chauvinist reputation by calling for the annexation of these remaining colonies. Meanwhile, in the early nineteenth century, heavy immigration from Britain into Upper Canada, now Ontario, created an English-speaking population which did not feel the US to be especially alien. If success had attended the rebellion of Canadian Radicals in 1837, it probably would have brought about a union of the two countries.

This pro-American sentiment was not confined to angry young men. The growth of Montreal into a great commercial emporium was the work of Scots and in Victorian times it became a largely Scottish city, making its fortune from exports of fur and timber. Its merchants, many of whom hailed from Glasgow, foresaw a future for themselves of controlling the trade of the interior of North America through the Great Lakes and the St Lawrence River. To them it seemed self-evidently desirable that the border between Canada and the US should vanish. Right up to the end of the century, well after the Confederation of Canada in 1867, there were people still arguing that the country should give up hope of ever becoming fully independent and throw in its lot with the US, playing there the same sort of role as Scotland played to England in the United Kingdom, a source of bright ideas, good sense and sound morality.

Defying this version of the Manifest Destiny, Canada remained itself and has since matured into one of the world's most decent and most respected democracies, which has also played an important mediating role in international affairs. It is one of the best friends of the US, as it is one of the best friends of Britain, the three nations having stood by one another in all the great global conflicts of the twentieth century. The most vocal complaint from Canadians comes over the more or less complete dominance of their industry by American interests, which an economic history of mild protectionism has quite failed to counter. This has its drawbacks for policy-making, though there are compensations in the prevalence of North American consumer culture and its high standard of living. Even so, they do not seem to make up for a certain insipidity, a lack of passion and commitment by Canadians to their own country.

So what exactly is the point of Canada's independence? While Canadians can see a distinction between themselves and Americans, it is not always immediately obvious to outsiders (or to Americans, come to that). Scots suffer a similar problem with visitors who, for some strange reason, think their country is more or less the same as England – needless to say, this includes most English visitors. Scots do, however, have things not to be found anywhere to the south, their mountains and lochs, their stormy seas and spectacular skies, their un-English architecture of sleepy burghs and silent castles, their history long unshared with England, their culture of music, dance, song, lament, of elegiac poetry and depressing novels together with an intellectual bent for abstraction, all of which find expression in the language of the people though more especially in what Robert Louis Stevenson called 'an accent of the mind'. Yet again, if Scotland can unite with its larger neighbour, why not Canada? There the cities, the highways, the billboards, the neat farms, the wide plains and the lofty mountains look just like those across the border. The history is short, the culture uncertain, the language identical. It might be easy to conclude that Canadian independence is a chimera, which could yet disappear before our eyes.

If that is wrong, Scots are largely responsible. We have seen earlier how much of the Scottish Enlightenment went into the making of the American Revolution, a view now accepted by many scholars in the US. Some see this influence as extending into its later history. In his recent book on the Enlightenment, Arthur Herman wrote: 'Americans built their world around the principles of Adam Smith and Thomas Reid, of individual interest governed by common sense and a limited need for government.' An implication here seems to be that the US of the present day forms the finest ultimate practical expression of the Scottish Enlightenment. Though enlightened thought has often failed to provide us with moral or intellectual systems founded on reason and nature to replace those founded on authority and religion, in the reality of modern America it yet finds a vindication.

It has to be said, however, that the Scottish philosophers of the eighteenth century felt a reluctance to follow their theories through to any too rigorous logical conclusion, unless tempered by experience, custom and our instinctive knowledge of human nature. That was as true of politics as of anything else. Thomas Jefferson's Declaration of Independence grounds itself on 'life, liberty and the pursuit of happiness'. These are noble aims, to be sure, but absolutes and perhaps dangerous ones – at least they were according to those many Scots who opposed the American Revolution. The equivalent Canadian declaration, admittedly written in London rather than by the Canadians themselves, comes in the preamble to the British North America Act which set up the Confederation of 1867. Its aims, the preamble says, are 'peace, order and good government' – aims doubtless perceived as absent in a US which had just emerged from the Civil War. They were in any event more congenial to the Scots who built Canada.

And Canada did have to be built. It was a conscious construction from ill-matched building blocks: the Maritime Provinces looking out on the Atlantic; Quebec even yet not reconciled to alien rule; Ontario, loyal and British; the as yet empty Plains; British Columbia, a shaky appendage 2,000 miles from the other areas of settlement. And most of these regions had closer economic links to the American territory south of them than to one another. The exception was Quebec, brooding in isolation as a relic of old France. In a sense it made Canada necessary because La Belle Province could never become a US state. What mattered to it was its French identity, hard enough to maintain under the British and sure to be swamped as an islet in the English-speaking ocean of any united North America. The conservative Québécois had made their choice almost a century before, when in the War of Independence the Americans bid for their support by marching on Montreal. Canada could then have been conquered again. But the people decided that, to remain as French as they could, they would have to settle for rule by the royalist British rather than by the revolutionary Americans.

Scots had helped them to make that choice, because they had experience of building and maintaining a nation inside an empire. The period just after the British conquest was perilous for the Québécois. They lay at the mercy of the victors, who came from a militantly Protestant nation where Roman Catholics were routinely deprived of civil rights. Britain imposed harsh penal laws on the Catholic Irish; why not on these faraway French?

But the first military and then civil Governor of Canada was James Murray of Elibank, of an enlightened Scottish family whose sons whiled away the frequent tedium of life in the army with writings on law, history and political economy. In Quebec, Murray befriended the fearful and forlorn French seigneurs, owners of the land, and came to admire their efforts to civilise the wilderness. They feared they would be dispossessed and forbidden to practise their religion. Murray protected and reassured them, while stressing to his superiors that this should become the settled policy in such a valuable addition to British territory. His actions aroused indignation in the more bigoted circles at home. He was recalled and charged with showing too much partiality to the French Canadians, though Parliament vindicated him. In the end it passed the Quebec Act in 1774 which provided, as he wished, for the established institutions of the colony, its Church and its law, to be maintained: interesting that Church and law were two things guaranteed to Scotland in 1707 in the Union with England. Murray made life tolerable for a people under alien rule, and his policy paid off during the American War of Independence.

This sympathy for the French was a consistent thread of the Scots' conduct in Canada. It survived the Napoleonic Wars, when France and Britain were pitted against each other in two decades of global struggle. Even after the peace in 1815, the governors sent out from London tended to regard the Québécois as potential traitors and sometimes did not treat them well, though in fact they had regarded the French Revolution with horror. At the same time, with more and more British immigrants the general Canadian population was growing so fast as to make a change in the system of government inevitable. The provinces had assemblies, but these were mere talking-shops with no control over the more or less absolute powers of the governors. The time was coming when some form of self-government would have to be granted, all the same. That meant the French would be governing themselves too: and who could say what old grudges might not then surface?

Doing nothing ceased to be an option in 1837, after the Canadian Radicals rebelled, to be joined by some of the French and supported by American volunteers. The leader of the uprising had been born in Dundee, William Lyon Mackenzie. Denied his chances at home, this young man did well after his emigration, rising to be editor of a newspaper and Mayor of Toronto. He thought that he owed his success to the freedom of the New World, and that many others could flourish like him if the hold of the imperial power was loosed. In particular, he felt furious that there had been no extension to Canada of the Reform Act passed for the United Kingdom in 1832. The British then took the first step to full democracy (though not a very big one), while Canadians still lay under the yoke of a colonial administration. The rebellion failed and Mackenzie fled to a long exile in the US, but he had shown the Government in London that it could no more expect blind obedience from Canada in 1837 than from the Thirteen Colonies in 1776. If there was not to be a second revolution in British North America, action became necessary.

Over the next few years reforms were cautiously introduced to Canada, culminating when James Bruce, Earl of Elgin, became governor-general in 1847. Elgin was one those able Victorian Scots who might have reached high office at home but instead spent his whole career in the British Empire. He served otherwise in Jamaica, China and Japan, and would die exhausted after a few months as Viceroy of India in 1863. He arrived in Canada with a mandate to bring in responsible government, that is, to choose ministers drawn from and supported by a new Canadian Parliament; previous governors had been able to appoint whoever they liked to public office. He was to be a constitutional monarch rather than an executive president. Elections gave a majority to French Canadians and English-speaking reformers. Elgin invited to dinner the rabble-rousing leader of Quebec, Louis Joseph Papineau, and talked to this former rebel in his own language: 'I found him a very well-bred, intelligent man.' But he assessed that Papineau was really too extreme for his own people, who would settle down under a fairer political arrangement. Elgin took the risk of constructing an administration out of the majority in Parliament, and it worked.

The one problem Elgin had was with the Tories, people who had made a point of backing without question all previous British governors and been rewarded with official patronage in return, using this to build up a true-blue, anti-French party among the voters. Some of these, feeling betrayed in their imperial allegiance, started a riot when Elgin was attending Parliament in Montreal in 1849. A howling mob pursued his carriage through the streets and hurled stones at it; he was lucky to escape without injury. Then they burned down the Parliament. It was an alarming moment, but Elgin kept his head and the trouble fizzled out. He had fulfilled his purpose, which was to establish that a country which always had been diverse, and always would be, must be ruled not through a loyal clique but by the consent of its people and with none of its minorities, above all not the French, excluded.

The way then stood open for full self-government, what would later be called dominion status, achieved with the Confederation of 1867. Its architect was one of the Tories originally opposed to Elgin: John Macdonald, who had been born at Dornoch and come with his family to Canada as a child. He was a politician motivated not by high principle but by common sense, a suave and handsome man who charmed rather than browbeat his way forward. Commitment to the British connection lay deep in him, but he saw now that it had to be sustained by other means than emotional appeal to the most loyal. Canada must be a conscious construction, in other words.

So far, disaffection in the country had tended to take on an anti-British colour, whether from the unforgiving French or from English-speaking Radicals who hankered after American democracy. Macdonald stressed that Canadian interests faced risk not so much from imperial authority as from the US. The answer was unity and a concerted effort to develop the West before the Americans seized it. This could be, and has been, defined as negative nationalism: Canadians, British or French, were to think of themselves as above all different from Americans and build a more ordered, stable society than the liberal experiment going on across the border. Negative or not, Canadians would grow ever more aware of it. Their concept of nationhood today, such as it is, they owe largely to Macdonald's foresight and hard work.

Construction of the Confederation took years and entailed many changes to Macdonald's original plans, which he sensibly conceded. In appeasing Quebec, the law and the Church figured again. As a prelude, Canadian civil law was codified in a manner congenial to the French mind, assuring the future influence of clever Québécois lawyers. Then, in the negotiations proper, the point was granted that within the provinces the real power should lie not with a lieutenant-governor appointed by the central government but with the provincial assemblies and ministers. Above all, education was to be their responsibility, which in Quebec guaranteed Catholic education. Macdonald even held out the prospect that Manitoba might become a second French-speaking province in line with the wishes of its small population at the time, composed largely of half-breed voyageurs, the trappers and traders employed by the Hudson's Bay Company. In fact they were soon to be swamped by British immigrants, but they retain a communal identity to this day. Altogether, Macdonald's settlement was sufficiently flexible and generous. For the French it worked well enough to create in them an acquiescence, if not something more, which would have been incredible not so long before. Wilfrid Laurier, the first Québécois to become Prime Minister of Canada, was leader of the opposition at the outbreak of the First World War in 1914, when doubts again arose whether the French could be relied on. But he declared: 'When Great Britain is at war, we are at war.'

Yet the nation-building project has remained unfinished, even to the present day, because the French remain so different from other Canadians. At the heart of the problem lie the feelings of a people cast up by fate on a shore far from their original home which they had made their own but which could not be theirs in the sense that an alien majority might one day overwhelm them and efface all memory of their labour and sacrifice. Scots found fault with the French too, yet never lost the admiration they first felt for the brave pioneers of New France on encountering them after the conquest. It was still being echoed by John Buchan, the Scottish man of letters and politician who became Governor-General of Canada in 1935 and who died in harness there in 1940. A character in his last, great and posthumous Canadian novel, *Sick Heart River*, praises 'this fine European stock planted out in a new country and toughened by two centuries of hardship and war. They keep their close family life and their religion intact and don't give a cent for what we call progress. Yet all the time they have a pretty serious fight with nature, so there is nothing soft in them.'

How are we to explain the Scottish sympathy for a people so different in temperament, language and religion? We may suggest that the Scots knew all the same how the French felt. The Scots, too, belonged to a small nation facing a constant, uphill struggle to preserve itself. They were conscious as well that the toil, with the often heroic qualities it brought out, could sooner or later go for nothing. It was possible their nation would yet disappear, borne down by forces which only had might rather than right on their side. Then everything precious to them, the rich ties to places and people that made a Scottish life worth living, would be forgotten. Scots had long fought on with this unbearable thought in their heads, but finally come to terms with it in another way. They made their peace with the Auld Enemy, and by Union with England set their country on a different historical course. Not that this gave them peace of mind: there had still been losses, often bitter, but from then on there were gains to set against the losses, and the balance of benefits to Scotland from the British Empire seemed clear. Even so, Scots perceived how other peoples placed much like themselves – the Irish, the French Canadians, the Boers in South Africa – could come to a contrary assessment of their own condition. Scots would not perhaps agree, but they would understand. They saw

the opposite sides of the argument because they were themselves neither fully nation nor fully province but both, neither
fully coloniser nor fully colonised but both. And perhaps, with
their insights, they could help others towards the choices best
for them.

Choices remain open because nations change. We tend to
think of them as constants, but in fact they do change: it probably
never occurred to Laurier that, only half a century after his declaration of imperial loyalty, many Québécois would start to
demand the independence of La Belle Province, just as Buchan
never thought that modern Scottish nationalism, the beginnings
of which he witnessed and did not wholly disapprove of, was
more than a pipe-dream. Nations change because they are composed of people confined in their own time and place, not bound
by their past if they need not be, though indeed in an old country
the past will always form a more powerful presence.

But in a new country the change can take place within a lifetime, or within a couple of generations. The most powerful
Canadian politician in the first half of the twentieth century, three
times prime minister, was William Mackenzie King, grandson of
the William Lyon Mackenzie who had led the Radical rebellion of
1837. His daughter, King's mother, brought her son up to think
that Mackenzie was the victim of great injustice: after returning
from exile in the US, he re-entered Canadian politics but lan-
guished in obscurity even though the country was by now
espousing his democratic principles. For King the history of his
family helped to explain how imperial loyalties loosened: 'My
father would speak of the Mother Country because his parents
had been born in Scotland . . . My mother would have thought in
a similar way, but the next and third generation did not think of
Britain or Scotland as the mother country.'

So, while the French clung fiercely to their identity, since
they had nowhere else to go, to Scots their identity was just one
thing that enriched a new life in a new land. In the early period
of emigration, to be sure, some came because they believed that
in Canada they could carry on with an existence growing
impossible at home under economic and other hostile pressures:
the voluntary removal after 1800 of the people of Glengarry in

Inverness-shire to Glengarry in Ontario offers the most famous example of that.

But the idea that they and others could create a little Scotland beyond the seas was a delusion. It did not take into account the greatest contrast between an old country and a young country. In an old country, the ties that bind, of history, of family, of habits, are so strong as to produce a steady bias in favour of what already exists – things can change, but only slowly. In a young country the constraints vanish: there is no history, the family may be thousands of miles away and habits have to be adapted to those of neighbours arriving from elsewhere if all are to settle down happily together. The result will be a novel ethos owing little – except perhaps a few consoling symbols, such as the kilt worn on St Andrew's Day – to the old country left behind. This was especially true in times before we could fly in a few hours from Scotland to Canada or back again, and emigrants had to make a choice that for most was deliberate and unconditional.

People on both sides often find this hard to grasp. It has been known for North American Scots to return to their ancestral homeland and don Highland dress to walk streets full of crowds rushing for the office or shopping with the kids. The mother country is not as they imagine it to be, and these well-meaning visitors feel surprised and hurt when they are mocked as clownish rather than clannish. While many Scotsmen will wear the kilt to a wedding or a formal dinner, only tourist guides and hotel doormen wear it every day; normal, workaday Scotland has to follow its own imperatives, with little time for historical consciousness, least of all for the fake historical consciousness of foreigners.

Let us not suppose, however, that native Scots are immune to it, or incapable of misconceiving the nature of their own diaspora, if that happens to concern them. In 1990 the literary critic David Craig, a Scot teaching at the University of Lancaster in England, published a book called *On the Crofters' Trail*. Oral history is fashionable nowadays to supplement the written record and Craig had the brilliant idea, which had occurred to nobody before, of going to Canada to collect popular memories of the Highland Clearances. Or rather, it would have been a brilliant idea if he could have found any. He could not. 'The people we met were proud to have been

part of the migration rather than troubled that it had ever been necessary,' he admitted in puzzlement. They insisted to him that their
forefathers had not been cleared, but had come of their own free
will and made the most of things: 'I now began to work out a theory of why clearance material was more elusive than that of more
voluntary emigration . . . From that point on we suspected that the
hardest thing to find in Canada would be memoirs of veritable
eviction.'

And so it proved. Amid allusions likening the Highlanders to
the Jews of the Holocaust, Craig was reduced to fulmination to
authenticate his thesis that willing migrants had been cleared:
'Apologists for clearance sometimes emphasise that hundreds on
Barra and South Uist "petitioned" to leave. So why the brutal
compulsions at the last minute? Conditions as well as estate heav-
ies (and the occasional minister) were *driving* them out.' No wonder that the ambition and mobility of the colonist escaped him: 'I
had not expected . . . that the Scottish settlers would have moved
on, most of them, so soon, having used Cape Breton as a stepping
stone to the American Middle West, the Canadian prairies, British
Columbia.' Craig had failed to spot a basic difference between an
old country and a new country: social solidarity in the one gives
way to fragmentation and dilution in the other, till the new country is able to come to a definition of itself. It is good that this
should be so, for a new country cannot live in the past. Nor
indeed will its people usually want to, because by the very fact of
coming to a new country, whether voluntarily or not, they have
made a break with the past.

The one thing which may hinder this process is if the immigrants have gathered at a particular place in such numbers that,
for a while, they can carry on as if they had never left home.
That was true of Scots in some areas of Canada. When Buchan
toured the country as governor-general in the 1930s, he was
often struck by how Scottish it could be. On Prince Edward
Island, repeatedly addressed in the Gaelic he did not know, he
wrote: 'I felt during my visit as if I had suddenly been transported to a Scottish parish.'

But he saw how in this alien environment a new nationality
was unlikely to duplicate an old one. The problem for him was

to help in forming a fresh allegiance: the people were 'very loyal to Britain and very loyal to their own province but not so loyal to Canada as a whole . . . Each province tends to regard itself as a separate unit and to look at a policy on the narrowest grounds, without consideration of Canada as a whole.' The remaining likeness to Scotland might suggest a remedy – in his own country, Highland and Lowland races had fused so that Scots had multiple loyalties. 'A man can never have too many loyalties,' he told the people of Prince Edward Island. It should therefore be a matter of pride that Canada housed such diverse cultures. If the country could gain more confidence, more sense of itself, that was something to unite the provinces rather than drive them apart.

During a speech in Montreal in 1937, Buchan said Canada was by now 'a sovereign nation and cannot take her attitude to the world docilely from Britain, or from the United States, or from anybody else. A Canadian's first loyalty is not to the British Commonwealth of Nations, but to Canada and to Canada's King.' At the time this sounded a note of nationalism radical almost to the point of subversion: and from the Governor-General too! But Buchan was right about what Canada had to do. Doing it, however, proved harder and took longer than he expected. Since his time, while the French have reasserted themselves, Canadian Scots have only seen themselves become less and less Scottish.

This is true even of the Maritime Provinces which in the 1930s still reminded Buchan so much of Scotland. The sense of loss is beautifully conveyed by one of their finest writers, indeed one of the best living writers in the English-speaking world, Alastair MacLeod. He is a reserved and taciturn man from Cape Breton Island who earns his living as an academic in Ontario. What he cannot bring himself to say seems to come out with all the more force in his written words.

MacLeod has a story about typical Nova Scotian migrant workers who are forced to seek a livelihood far away. The province once had a coal-mining industry that was manned by Gaels drawn in from the countryside. Mining fosters close-knit communities too, and did not damage the integrity of their culture. But now the seams are exhausted, and all the miners can do is take their skills wherever else in the world these may be of use. They know their way of life will pass away with them: 'It is unlikely we will be replaced in the shaft's bottom by members of our own flesh and bone. For such replacement, like our Gaelic, seems to be of the past and largely over.' When they go to work in South Africa they carry sprigs of Canadian spruce, as their 'Highland ancestors, for centuries, fashioned crude badges of heather or of whortleberries to accompany them on the battle-fields of the world. Perhaps so that in the closeness of their work with death they might find nearness to their homes and an inten-sified realisation of themselves.' The emotions are in a sense wast-ed, because unable to break a cycle which inexorably repeats itself, without obvious meaning, in changing times and circumstances: the ancestors' leaving of Scotland is annually re-enacted in the descendants' leaving of Nova Scotia.

Another writer from the same background, Hugh MacLennan, finds something a little more positive in all this. He remarks that his people owed the same passionate loyalty as their ancestors to the hills of home. 'The knowledge that I am three-quarters Scotch, and Highland at that, seems like a kind of doom from which I am too Scotch even to think of praying for deliverance.' But 'I belong to the last Canadian generation raised with a Highland nostalgia.' The conclusion that the links have now been broken is set out in his book, *Scotchman's Return*, published after a visit to the land of his fathers: 'Am I wrong, or is it true that it is only now, after so many years of not knowing who we are or wanted to be, that we Canadians of Scotch descent are truly at home in the north of North America?' That may be so, but in Canada as a whole the random assemblage of peoples has not yet formed the firm framework of a new nation-ality from which it can move forward. No potent sense of nationhood has arisen either to overlay the older communal loy-alties or to replace those fading away.

Still, nobody knew better than Scots that nation building is never an easy thing, and that conscious construction does not guarantee a stable edifice. The greatest nations grow by processes that remain mysterious, though helped by the right choices. In the twentieth century the US burgeoned and wantoned from the fertile soil of the principles set down by the Founding Fathers. Yet during that century the idea of America changed too. At the beginning immigrants were instructed in the English language, in the US Constitution and in the general system of values of their new country: America was a melting pot where the people, whatever their origins, would be one and indivisible. By the end of the century it defined itself as a multicultural society, on the somewhat superficial assumption that people can come from Mexico or Ethiopia or China bringing their way of life with them in their baggage.

Time will tell if the concept of multiculturalism has any substance but the certainty is that all immigrants to the US are at once plunged into the American economy, the locus of the melting pot today. This is why they have come, of course, ready to risk the harsh penalties of failure for the chance of success. The economy is, more than any other, an open and liberal one, and in that sense can be claimed as a child of Adam Smith and the Scottish Enlightenment. There has been a particular contrast with Canada or Europe in that the US, while following economic policies as all countries do, stops short of trying to steer development in one direction or another. If manufacturing dies out in New England, or if dot.com companies collapse in California, no administration in Washington DC says this must not happen and spends taxpayers' money to stop it happening. New Englanders or Californians simply have to find something else to work at, and, in the light of experience, this has been the best thing for them, whatever the short-term pain, and for the whole US. It is what has made the American economy so infinitely flexible and innovative, the industrial powerhouse of the world.

For most of its history, Canada followed a different path. In an economic as well as a political sense, Canada did not just grow but was deliberately developed, often through public enterprise, controlled and if necessary financed from the top. That happened from the outset under the Hudson's Bay Company, run by Scots, which enforced a policy of keeping the country empty while appropriating its natural resources, without any reference to the few inhabitants the West then had. Once the Confederation of 1867 imposed a different set of priorities the company's interests were swept aside, though generously compensated. The task now was to create a political entity that would rival the US in stretching from sea to sea, and in particular to stop the Americans taking over the whole Pacific seaboard. The key to this lay in the grand project of the Canadian Pacific Railway, which again was conceived and executed by Scots, relying on huge subsidies to bring to a triumphant conclusion what more timid people reckoned to be an impossibility.

The mistake would be to believe that the freewheeling economy of the US represents a Scottish idea while the steered economy of Canada does not. Adam Smith himself, when he published *The Wealth of Nations* in 1776, listed there the essential duties of government. After defence of the realm and the administration of justice, he included the construction of public works such as roads and bridges; if he had lived a century later, he might have added railways as well. Scottish thinking always tempered theory by experience, just as it judged experience in the light of theory. There is an ever-present danger that the one or the other can be carried too far and lead into futility; in which case, it is time to draw back and consider how to restore a balance.

For example, it has today begun to come home to Scots that during the latter part of the twentieth century the heavy-handed intervention by the state in every area of their national life may have squeezed out of them the spirit of enterprise for which they, too, were once famous. The restored Scottish Parliament wants to do something about that, in the first instance by even more frenetic intervention. If this does not work, a more thoroughgoing change of mind will be inescapable.

The Scottish legacy to Canada has produced a better result. Canadian economics traditionally rested on protectionism, which it owed to Macdonald and the so-called National Policy he introduced in 1879. His initial target was imports from Britain. His wish to impose tariffs on them aroused outrage in London, where it was assumed that the Empire should be run for the benefit of the mother country. He retorted that if the British wanted Canada to become a nation, and not fall into the hands of the US, then they would have to put up with whatever measures were needed to promote its own development. And he won his point. Later the US replaced Britain as the greater perceived threat to Canadian economic independence, and the same policy was applied to American goods. Till recently, household brands available in Detroit, Michigan, could not be bought just across the river in Windsor, Ontario. But since 1997 the North American Free Trade Association, including Canada, the US and Mexico, has made a common market of the whole continent; with it, Canadian protectionism came to end. It had outlived its usefulness. It was tending to make Canadian companies less efficient rather than protecting the economy as a whole from American penetration, and so defeating its own purpose. Canada decided that an economic policy which might have had its reasons in Victorian times was played out, and allowed experience to temper it.

It would not be far-fetched to regard this as a Scottish outcome, from the sort of choice of evils that form the reality for the less powerful peoples unable in their own circumstances to determine their place in the world. In 1707 the Scots gave up political independence for economic opportunities which, while from then on available, were by no means guaranteed. Canadians have now abandoned national control over much of their economy in return for potential continental benefits. The political consequences of this remain unclear. They are something of a gamble: if Canada is to survive, the economy will not help. Scots may be able to reassure their Canadian cousins that the future, if not always comfortable, will at least be interesting. An uncertain, challenging, taxing fate can make a nation too.

10

SOUTHERNERS

M ark Twain always said Sir Walter Scott had caused the American Civil War. In his own time, Scott seems to have been most popular for his medieval subjects, treated with a relish for romance and chivalry which is cloying to modern taste. Twain thought he had an ill effect on his many thousands of readers in the southern states of the US, giving them a misguided sense of their own identity and beliefs. Southerners would name their children and plantations after people and places in the novels, and stage mock-medieval tournaments in imitation of the one described in *Ivanhoe*. They wallowed in a cult of immaculate womanhood and of gallant manhood. In Scott they found an aristocratic ideal which justified to them a society where the elite lived at its ease on the sweat of slaves. They despised the egalitarianism and the commercialism of the North. Their make-believe world, in Twain's view, led to a rejection of progress as represented by what America was actually becoming. If that is true, then it arose from a misunderstanding of Scott; while he did more than anyone else to create the image of romantic Scotland, this was also a romanticism set in the context of realism.

Perhaps in old Virginia the southern self-image bore some faint resemblance to the truth. A tourist today has only to visit George Washington's Mount Vernon or Thomas Jefferson's Monticello or James Madison's Montpelier to sense the spaciousness of life in these great houses of the colonial gentry. But America promptly moved on from the Revolution. Half a century afterwards the influence of the class of men who had made it was vanishing, submerged in the democratic populism of the hard-bitten Andrew Jackson, who represented the frontier.

Jackson was also a Southerner, from Tennessee, yet with nothing in the least aristocratic about him. The lands he conquered for the US during the War of 1812, in Georgia, Alabama and Mississippi, were still Indian country and only ceased to lie on the frontier through the ruthless expulsion of their native peoples. Other southern states, Florida and Texas, were not admitted to the Union till 1845, yet a mere sixteen years later they were out of it again, when they seceded and joined the Confederacy. So for Southerners to delude themselves that they had anything much in common with the historic realms of Europe was a nonsense, as Twain rightly pointed out. The planters who lounged on the porches of their mansions surveying their plantations and their toiling blacks belonged, for the most part, to a society which had only just been hacked out of the wilderness, often by brutal violence.

It was not even as if these planters, in sheer numbers, represented much of the South. Their economic system had a great weakness: it made no money, or at best just broke even. Free labour is actually cheaper than slave labour because a worker on the open market has only to be paid his wage whereas a slave, while unpaid, has still to be housed and fed from the cradle to the grave, in sickness and in health. In *The Wealth of Nations*, Adam Smith had argued against slavery on the grounds that a man without a wage will have no interest in his work, and will work less. It seems unlikely that anyone in the history of American slavery ever got a good day's work, day after day, out of an unwilling slave. George Washington tried and gave it up as hopeless, though he was a stern and implacable master. Sham sickness was the usual pretence he met with; his letters to his overseers are full of hints for detecting black malingerers.

But the facts are clear. In 1820, cotton sold at sixteen cents a pound, while the average price of a young, healthy field-slave at Charleston was about $1,000. By 1860, just before South

Carolina led the secession of the southern states, it cost $1,700 to buy such a slave while the price of a pound of cotton had slumped to eleven cents. At that point, the South was staring bankrupcty in the face. It had become impossible to make money out of growing cotton except where the soil was abnormally fertile: hence the constant pressure from Southerners to create new slave states in the West, even to annex Cuba or Mexico. Many of the great planters did not earn so much as one per cent on their investment in land and slaves, and most lived on credit. The whole region of slavery from Virginia to Texas was weighed under with mortgages and debts.

This, abolitionists gloated, showed why the South remained backward compared to the North, because the Northerners invested their money in industry and railways: Southerners would be better off by emancipating their slaves of their own free will. But economic laws tend to work their own effect despite every effort to defy them, and in fact the system of plantations run on slavery had reached or passed its limits. Just 30,000 families in the entire South owned any slaves at all, and larger owners did not number 10,000. Still, however, they formed the ruling class of the region and determined its politics.

That, though, poses the question why this elite was able to call forth such incredible sacrifice from the rest of the white population, only nine million (and more than three million of them black slaves) against the twenty-three million of the North, during four years of terrible war. They kept it up right to the end, even after all was lost: we may recall how astonished General Ulysses S. Grant felt at the ardour and courage of the Confederate troops when in 1864 he arrived from the West to take command of the Union's army before Richmond.

These were the common soldiers of the South, country boys who had left their homesteads, horses and ploughs to bear arms in a cause hard to regard, with hindsight, as just. Clearly it must have seemed so to them, but then they would not have seen themselves as fighting for a few sumptuous planters. They were fighting for a way of life, an agrarian civilisation. It perhaps would have made no difference to their devotion to the cause if they had known that beneath the surface the South was assigning itself the subordinate place in a transatlantic economy. Had it survived, the Confederacy would have been a cotton-field for Britain, for the textile factories of Scotland and England, from which it would have imported its manufactures without the tariffs which the Northerners wanted for protection of their infant industries. It would have remained a country of small, peasant farmers, without much money but with stalwart self-respect. This was the social and moral ideal of Thomas Jefferson. It was an older America doomed to be borne down by the new.

Poor but proud: it was a Scottish ideal too. Scots and Scotch-Irish had formed only a minority of the South's original settlers but they remained an important minority which was not later swamped, as in other regions of the US, by fresh waves of immigrants with no roots in the British Isles. In the South people of Scots blood continued to make up a larger share of the population than elsewhere; some scholars estimate up to one-third. In any case they had always left a mark here out of all proportion to their numbers.

Those early Scots immigrants who after landing had gone straight to the back country, clearing the forest and building a log cabin, then standing ready to fight or even die for what they had won, wove a gaudy strand into the emerging tapestry of American culture. If their uncouth habits ruffled more civilised folk, they added to the gaiety of the nation with their colourful customs. In the old days they used to be called hillbillies, but crackers has emerged as a preferred expression in our politically correct times. It is an interesting term. The word crack, which may be Gaelic in origin, is an everyday colloquialism in Scotland and Ireland, meaning animated conversation, quite likely fuelled by alcohol. 'We stayed in the pub till closing time, and the crack was great,' would be a way of recalling a good night out in Glasgow or Dublin. Or, 'gie's your crack,' you might say to a friend to learn the latest news and gossip. The word crossed the Atlantic Ocean, and the activity turned into the human type, the cracker, the sort of fellow that works all day and drinks all night – perhaps thanks to Elijah Craig who back in 1789 distilled the first whiskey in Bourbon County, Kentucky. The cracker leaves off his crack only to chase a woman or to fight his mates.

This was the model of manliness among all those Andersons, Buchanans and Campbells who scattered across the southern states, living in tiny communities sometimes grandly named after the cities of the old country. Kentucky contains an Aberdeen, a Dundee and a Glasgow, while both North and South Carolina have an Edinburgh, as do (misspelled as Edinburg) Virginia and Texas. Also in the hills of Virginia is probably the sole genuine Gaelic place-name in the US, only slightly anglicised: Fincastle, from *Fionn Chaisteal*, white fort. Of course most of the settlers in the South spoke English, and an English which rapidly developed away from any British standard. It kept the rhotacism of Scots, the curled pronunciation of the letter r, and still uttered the suffix -ing as a sort of nasal grunt. But a twang soon distorted other sounds of the language. The vocabulary changed in line with rustic life in the New World, replacing shop with store, corn with grain, maize with corn, treacle with molasses and pig-breeding with hog-raising. On the other hand the Appalachian dialect retained an intimate, homely quality from Scots which could be coarsely humorous and ironic while showing a lack of embarrassment about physical functions. Passing strangers were hailed as 'honey', and children cosseted as 'little shits'. The crackers had a picturesque way with local landmarks. They named a Gallows Branch and a Cutthroat Gap and a Shitbritches Creek in North Carolina. In Virginia they named a Tickle Cunt Branch and a Fucking Creek.

These sterling qualities equipped the people of the South to fight the Civil War bravely and stubbornly. It was another question whether they were also the right ones to gain sympathy and support from the outside world, of which the Confederacy stood in great need. With Scotland it had economic links, created by exports of cotton for the textile industries, and this may have exerted some influence on local opinion, especially in Glasgow. But the workers, and the political establishment of the dominant Scottish Liberal party, almost always supported the North. In their eyes the central question was not Scotland's commercial self-interest but slavery. Though most ordinary people of the Confederacy did not own slaves, and were only defending home and hearth against invaders, this could never be enough in Scottish eyes to wash away the moral stain of slavery on their society.

When Southerners heard that sort of talk from Yankees they cried hypocrisy, pointing to the degraded lives of workers in the grimy sweatshops of New York or Boston, while in the streets outside the old and the sick were left to fend for themselves. The same criticism could have been levelled with equal if not greater effect at Victorian Glasgow. And some of Glasgow was built on the proceeds of the slave trade. During the early eighteenth century the trade had been mainly conducted out of London and Bristol. There are a few records of slaving ships at Scottish ports, even small ones such as Kirkcudbright and Dumfries, but evidently this traffic did not add up to much. As so often, the real money was made by expatriate Scots.

Among them were Richard Oswald and Alexander Grant, who hailed respectively from Glasgow and Inverness-shire. But both crossed the Atlantic and then returned to work in London. From there they bought in 1748 a disused, ruined fort on an island off Sierra Leone to serve as a base for the slave trade between Africa and America. It was largely manned by brother Scots who, as soon as they finished repairing the buildings, naturally laid out a golf course for their hours of leisure. The island, unfortunately, was not big enough for the course to have more than one hole.

Still, the island's commerce made Oswald and Grant rich men. For Oswald, his wealth led into high political circles, and he was appointed the chief negotiator for the Treaty of Versailles which ended the Revolutionary War and gave the Thirteen Colonies their independence in 1783; his opposite number on the American side was his old friend, from previous visits to London, Benjamin Franklin. Like many expatriate Scots, Oswald at length returned to his homeland. With his fortune he bought at Auchincruive in Ayrshire an estate with a big house (now the West of Scotland Agricultural College). And he equipped his family to play a continuing part in the public life of the region. His grandson James became MP for Glasgow and is commemorated by a statue on the north-eastern corner of George Square, 'erected by a few friends', where he wears an amazingly tall lum hat.

At the start, no moral stigma attached to the Oswalds for the money they made from the slave trade. In the eighteenth century, slavery seemed to Scots just to be one of the facts of life, doubtless an unfortunate one, but no more capable of being eliminated from human society than unemployment or crime. No book they might have read told them anything different. Slavery had existed since ancient times, and Greek or Roman philosophers took it for granted. The Bible said that bond and free were one in Jesus Christ, but not that slaves should actually be liberated. So, as we saw above in the opinion of Adam Smith, the first Scottish criticism of slavery came not on moral but on economic grounds. If there were no arguments in favour of its efficiency as a way of organising labour then, but only then, ought a presumption in favour of human liberty to prevail.

This seemed also to be the argument which carried weight in the first legal victory against slavery in Scotland. It took place in 1775 in the case of Joseph Knight, a black slave brought home by his master to Perthshire. Knight met a local girl he wanted to marry. For this he had to save up, so he asked for a wage and was refused. Knight went to law against his master and at the end of a long and complex case the Court of Session in Edinburgh declared that every slave landing in Scotland became by that fact a free man or woman. In other words, Scots abolished slavery on their own soil. There may have been as many as a couple of hundred slaves living in Scotland at the time, all belonging to expatriates who had worked in the Empire, and all now emancipated. Like Knight, they usually settled down in their new country, found a Scots wife or husband and got on with the rest of their lives. In a generation or two, this tiny black community was intermarried so far as to disappear into the general body of the Scottish people. So, while we may regret it that Scots did not condemn slavery in distant lands with enough moral vigour, it is worth recalling that at home they showed no racial prejudice (wives and children of mixed race brought back from India underwent the same experience of assimilation).

Still, it was not what Scots did at home but what they saw abroad that in the end made the difference to their attitudes to slavery. James Ramsay was a clergyman on the West Indian island of St Kitts. Life there appalled him. He wanted to take Christianity to the slaves too, but found them in a state so degraded that they could not respond to him. In 1784, after his return, he published one of the first abolitionist books in Britain and shocked the whole country with his description of the blacks' hardships and suffering. In the same year, the minister of Inveraray in Argyll got his son, Zachary Macaulay, a job on a plantation in Jamaica. He was only sixteen years old, the youngest of twelve children with no other prospects, and he feared he would appear ungrateful if he complained to his father about the horrors of slavery. So instead he wrote to one of the family's friends, telling this kindly clergyman he would never recognise the lad he once knew, 'were you to view me in a field of canes, amidst perhaps a hundred of the sable race, cursing and bawling, while the noise of the whip resounding on their shoulders, and the cries of the poor wretches, would make you imagine some unlucky accident had carried you to the doleful shades'. Macaulay eventually came back to take a lead in the abolitionist movement at home. It got the slave trade banned in 1808, and all slavery ended in the British Empire in 1833. But of course these efforts could have no effect in America after the independence of the US.

Macaulay and the other abolitionists achieved their aims through winning the battle for public opinion. The nineteenth century saw a rising tide of indignation against slavery in Scotland, fuelled also by the increasingly bitter debate in the US. Even so, other interests could cut across the morality of the matter. They might be purely economic as in the case of the Gladstones, a family which migrated from Leith to Liverpool and made a vast fortune out of the slave trade, among other activities. John, the father of William Gladstone, the future prime minister, claimed the blacks were better off in servitude: 'The manumitted Negroes are idle, indolent and slothful, and too often become profligate though they possessed good characters whilst they remained slaves.' For his own mad reasons, Thomas Carlyle took an ever shriller racist line on such social problems as those in the West Indies after the liberation of the slaves. He stopped little short of calling for them to be reduced to slavery again.

Even for Christians the issues were not always clear-cut. The greatest domestic Scottish crisis of Victorian times came with the

Disruption of 1843 when, after a long dispute over political control of the established Church of Scotland, it split in two. Those members unwilling to tolerate parliamentary interference walked out to form the Free Church of Scotland, which contained about a third of the ministers and a yet larger share of the congregations of the Auld Kirk. The Free Church was ambitious and dynamic, in effect a rebellion of the rising middle class against the powers-that-be. It set out to rival its parent body by building a place of worship and a school in every Scottish parish. For this much money was needed. While the Free Church raised astonishing amounts of cash from its own members, it also sent campaigners to the US to appeal to fundamentalist Christians likely to support its aims. Then as now, many fundamentalists could be found in the Bible Belt of the southern states, and some were slave owners. The Free Church's delegation returned home in 1845 pleased with themselves after collecting a large sum. They were greeted with cries of 'Send the money back!' American abolitionists had meanwhile been in touch with their Scottish sympathisers and alerted them to the taint on the gold about to go into the coffers of the Free Church.

Here was a choice of evils for Thomas Chalmers, the leader of the Free Church and a man who enjoyed immense respect at home and abroad. He did not approve of slavery, yet he had no doubt that the construction of the Free Church and of a visible presence for it in every corner of the country was a work of God. He received personal appeals from Americans, to which he gave this convoluted reply:

> Distinction ought to be made between the character of a system, and the character of the persons whom circumstances have implicated therewith. . . . We hope that our Free Church will never deviate to the right or to the left from the path of undoubted principle. But we hope, on the other hand, she will not be frightened from her propriety, or forced by clamour of any sort, to outrun her own convictions, so as to adopt, at the bidding of other parties, a new and factitious principle of administration, for which she can see no authority in Scripture, and of which she can gather no traces in the history of practice of the Churches in Apostolic times.

Chalmers could not be faulted. The Bible condemns sins of many kinds, some of which are hardly recognised as sins today. Yet it has nothing to say about slavery except to mention, in passing and without censure, the existence of slavery in the ancient world. American abolitionists claimed slavery was absolutely unchristian, and called for slaveowners to be expelled from the Churches. By contrast there were Presbyterian theologians in the southern states, Robert Dabney and James Thornwell, who defended slavery as compatible with Christianity. It was their arguments that Chalmers adopted. The Free Church kept the money.

In Victorian times most Scots still sought their morality in the Bible. And in the American Civil War, as in many other wars, both sides claimed God was with them. So the moral issues behind it did not appear at that time quite so clear as they do with hindsight now. Scots who happened to get caught up in the fighting in any event usually had to make their choices and take their chances according to their own circumstances.

Some made a deliberate decision to become involved, for instance, if they wanted to fight slavery. John Fraser from Cromarty was a fiery little professor of mathematics at Jefferson College in Pennsylvania who found a better outlet for his aggressions by joining up with the US army. John McArthur, from Renfrewshire, helped to organise a volunteer Highland regiment in Chicago. William Duff became a staff officer to General Grant, then went on after the war to serve as US consul in Glasgow before retiring to his home town of Elgin.

On the other hand, Scotland still produced soldiers of fortune, mercenaries of the kind who for centuries had been ready to sell their swords to the highest bidder. These – men such as Bennett Burley, Peter McGlashan and Henry McIver – usually found the Confederacy more exciting to fight for, and after it was defeated went off without complaint to other wars in Mexico and Latin America. There were two immigrant brothers, James Campbell working as a drayman in Charleston, and Alexander, a stonemason in New York. When the war broke out both joined up, but on opposite sides. In 1862 federal forces were sailed south in an attempt to capture Charleston, a major port, and the brothers Campbell found themselves on the same battlefield. Luckily they never came face to face, though they said afterwards that they would have done their duty if they had.

More often the war overtook all unawares those Scots who happened to be in the South for one reason or another. William Watson was from Skelmorlie on the Firth of Clyde and carried his skills as a mechanical engineer first to the West Indies and then to Louisiana, where he worked in a timber yard at Baton Rouge. He did not believe in slavery because he had found that the Caribbean blacks worked well as free men, and he did not think it a good idea for the US to divide into two nations. But he liked to spend his leisure volunteering, a favourite pastime of Victorian youth: that is to say, playing at soldiers, putting on a uniform to drill and march and practise shooting. When secession came in 1861, Watson's fellow volunteers seized the federal arsenal at Baton Rouge, and he just went along with his pals. Then they joined up with the Confederate army, and again he went along. A futile and uncomfortable winter spent defending Arkansas was enough to put him off the war. He managed to get to New Orleans, where the British consul arranged for his passage back to Scotland.

Again, Robert Smith belonged to a wealthy family of textile manufacturers in the West of Scotland. In the 1850s he was sent as its agent to Jackson, Mississippi, where he purchased the cotton to supply the factories at home. He settled down and became a pillar of the community. Though a foreigner, he too felt impelled to join up with the Confederate army when war broke out and before long rose to the rank of colonel in a regiment engaged in the complex campaign for control of a vital sector round the confluences of the Tennessee, Ohio and Mississippi Rivers. He was killed at the Battle of Munfordsville in 1862. He had known another Mississippian, Jefferson Davis, President of the Confederacy. When, after the war, Davis was released from his captivity in 1869, he recuperated by going on holiday to Britain, including a trip to Scotland. There he stayed with the Smiths at their house on Dowanhill, at that time still in the countryside to the west of Glasgow.

Confederate courage had not prevailed against the industrial might of the North, yet the southern states could only be conquered inch by inch. Their defeat was all the same total in the end. The US underwent a bloody but absolute rebirth, in which the whole for the first time became greater than its parts and the foundation for future imperial power was laid. Though President Abraham Lincoln meant to be magnanimous in victory, he lay dead, the victim of an assassin's bullet, only a few days after the battlefields fell silent. His successor Andrew Johnson would have continued his generous policies but lacked the necessary authority, and at length suffered impeachment for his pains. Counsels of unwisdom now held sway in the restored Union. It had been a bitter war, and too many of the victors wanted revenge on the vanquished. The era of Reconstruction was at first an era of exploitation when carpetbaggers, the crooks and rascals of the North, flocked to the South for loot and pillage. It was a surprise that any pickings remained, because the Confederacy had been devastated. Cities such as Richmond and Atlanta lay in ruins, while the economic structure, from railways to factories, was hopelessly run down through lack of materials to maintain it in four years of war, where not deliberately wrecked during the passage of invading armies. And the southern states now contained three million liberated slaves unused to fending for themselves who were supposed to find a place as American citizens amid five million hostile whites. It would take a long time for the region to recover.

No wonder that period left an indelible mark on southern consciousness. The Southerners had already felt different before the war, if in the factitious way so suspect to Mark Twain. The era of Reconstruction was not make-believe, however, but reality. And the reality proved painful and humiliating for a people who had felt proud of their values, not to say superior to the Yankees who now strutted as their conquerors. If anything, the victory of the North set the Southerners more apart from the rest of the US, even while it eliminated any threat to the existence of the Republic as such. And though by the end of the twentieth century the differences were at last dissolving, they are still strongly sensed, and can be sensed by any visitor too, in much of the old South.

The kernel of that contrast lies between the naive optimism of the general American outlook on life (which can, of course, turn into humbugging self-righteousness) and the experience of tragedy which long lay like a pall over the South. In the classical definition, tragedy arises out of a flawed heroism laid low by blind but cruel fate. The old southern society had its flaw in the institution of slavery, yet was robust enough to make its sons eager to fight for it; still, they could in the end do nothing against the wealth and might of the Union.

Such tragedy, though novel to Americans, was familiar to Europeans, indeed integral to the nationhood of many among them. Much of European history is marked by the building of empires. The continent's great nations often conquered, oppressed or even tried to destroy its small nations. In either the resigned acquiescence or the desperate resistance of those small nations lay an awareness that they could well disappear one day. They found out through bitter experience that history is not always a matter of onward and upward progress. On the contrary, fine and noble things can vanish as if they had never been, borne down by base and shameful things. Whole peoples have drawn either a fatalistic inspiration or at least a grim resolve from just such an awareness of the precarious and provisional nature of their existence. They have each had to come to terms with it as best they can. These peoples include the Poles, the Finns, the Serbs, the Sicilians, the Catalans, the Basques, the Dutch, the Irish and the Scots. They, whatever the rights and wrongs of the American Civil War, could have understood the feelings of Southerners and their stubborn attachment to their own identity. European experience is more like the experience of the South than it is like the experience of the rest of the US.

The best parallel between the South and Scotland in particular is to be found in their cultural situation since the end of the American Civil War in 1865. At first sight, the comparison hardly holds up. Whereas the South lay at that point prostrate under the conqueror's heel, Scotland felt broadly content with its place in the world, especially with its part in the British Empire, where Scots not merely ruled alien peoples but also brought out their potential for progress. Yet these contrasted positions, as between the South and Scotland, did not in the long run truly fit their cultural dilemmas. Once the Southerners began to recover, and once history knocked out of the Scots some of their cocksure Victorian confidence, both peoples found themselves caught up in a struggle to maintain their identity against the overwhelming political and economic power of neighbours inside the same country – and without the option of fighting for their identity, even as a last resort.

In other words, both Scotland and the South have had to endure existence as sections or regions or provinces (it is difficult to find the right word) of a larger political entity which defines its general culture without reference to them. The outcome has been an edgy, restless, hesitant relationship between the cultures of nation and region (or whatever we call it). In this unending argument, concepts such as union and independence are not dry political abstractions but are vitally tangled up with individuals' ideas of their own selves, of the places they live in, of the people who belong there, of their traditions and culture, of others' right to rule over them. A counterpart is the incessant questioning whether they are the same as or different from their neighbours, whether they are first and foremost Scots or British, Southerners or Americans, and in what measure both.

Scots have ready to hand a range of symbols to flaunt when they want to feel Scottish – many of which also owe their potency to Sir Walter Scott and his reinvention of Scotland. There are kilts and tartans, saltires and lions rampant (though some Scots are just as ready to brandish the Union Jack when it suits). The American South has by comparison a dearth of symbols. There is the Confederate flag, also a saltire, with a star-spangled blue-and-white cross of St Andrew against a red field, now often deemed politically incorrect. Many small towns have their well-tended memorials to the dead of the Civil War, and sometimes more imposing statues of southern heroes. Still, the South presents otherwise much the same aspect as the rest of America does to the visitor. Unlike in Scotland, he will not be so constantly reminded by ordinary sights and sounds of the streets that the South is where he is.

Given that the Confederacy has left an ambivalent legacy, it is interesting that some Southerners nowadays grasp at Scottish symbols to make their cultural identity more explicit – for instance, a Confederate tartan has been invented. There is some justification for this in the fact that Southerners do have quite a lot of Scots blood in their veins, as their names attest and as some of their folk-music and folk-songs recall. But that hardly accounts for the enormous upsurge in popularity of Highland games held at such places as Grandfather Mountain, North Carolina, or at Stone Mountain, Georgia (these overlooked by gigantic effigies of Confederate leaders carved into a cliff). At the average Highland games in rural Scotland, a few hundred people might turn up; at the American equivalents there are crowds of 50,000.

Such occasions now look back on a long enough history for them to have started contriving spurious traditions of their own. The sport of competing to toss a sack of grain as high as possible with a pitchfork, which I once saw played in all seriousness by men in kilts at Stone Mountain, is unknown in Scotland. Under the pine trees nearby were stands set up by Clan Smith and Clan Brown to sell tartan trinkets. Elsewhere, it seems, members of the different clan societies will form a St Andrew's cross on the field and toss torches on a bonfire in the middle, announcing their names and the glens or isles of their ancestry. Not all have even a remote romantic attachment to a vaguely Scottish ethnic identity. Celeste Ray, an anthropologist from Tennessee who has written about this sort of thing for the amazed Scots of Scotland, reports that these clansmen include Afro-Americans, Native Americans in tartan and Mexicans in kilts and sombreros. She comments: 'Heritage is a rhapsody on history. We strike the chords we wish to hear.' In other words, the games are more about America than about Scotland.

This particular association of the South and Scotland in fact goes back further than we might think. It dates from the terrible time after the American Civil War, though it long remained underground. The Ku Klux Klan was founded at Pulaski, Tennessee, on 24 December, 1865. Its name is in part garbled Greek, from *kyklos*, a circle, but the allusion to clans was added because the inaugural members were 'all of Scotch descent', according to one of them, John Lester. The Klan became the focus of resistance to the northern occupiers of the South and to the apparatus of Reconstruction. Members of the Klan dressed themselves as ghouls, with tall, conical masks and flowing robes; when they rode out on their errands of terror they carried a skull on their saddles. In this guise they were meant to represent the Confederate dead, seeking revenge for past and present wrongs. After the Yankee soldiers had gone home again, the Klan turned its rage on the freed blacks and those whites thought to favour them. It was a secret society bonded by elaborate rituals, employing violence to achieve its aims, above all the maintenance of white supremacy.

Since the Klan was a secret society, it is not easy to know what went on when members gathered. In any case, they seem always to have formed a looser and more intermittent organisation than was imagined by their victims or by the federal authorities. The initial surge passed with the worst abuses of Reconstruction. A revival took place in the early twentieth century, in the familiar racist form, but probably also then prompted by more general anxieties in the US over enormous waves of immigration from eastern and southern Europe which seemed bound to change, as they did, the character of the country as basically white, Anglo-Saxon and Protestant. One cultural product of the era was a classic film, D. W. Griffith's *Birth of a Nation*. And Griffith had among his sources a novel by a writer from North Carolina, Thomas Dixon.

Dixon's book, *The Clansman*, published in 1905, was meant to celebrate the South's Scottish heritage. But he believed this to be represented in his own time by the Ku Klux Klan and so put the action of the novel in a context which would scarcely have occurred to any genuine Scots clansman. In the preface the author says: 'How the young South, led by the reincarnated souls of the Clansmen of Old Scotland, went forth under this cover and against overwhelming odds, daring exile, imprisonment, and a felon's death, and saved the life of a people, forms one of the most dramatic chapters in the history of the Aryan race.' The main female character has to endure the ordeals of Reconstruction, but summons up the necessary courage when 'the heritage of centuries of heroic blood from the martyrs of old Scotland began to flash its inspiration from the past'. At one point she finds herself a supplicant to President Andrew Johnson: 'Mr President, you are a native Carolinian – you are of Scotch Covenanter blood. You are of my own people of the great past, whose tears and sufferings are our common glory and birthright.' There is much else in this repulsively ludicrous vein, but such was the fevered atmosphere at the time of the book's publication that it did have one real effect in adding a further ritual to the repertory of the Klan. Another character declares: 'In olden times when the Chieftain of our people summoned the clan on an errand of life and death, the Fiery Cross, extinguished in sacrificial blood, was sent by swift courier from village to village.' The fiery cross features in Sir Walter Scott's 'Lady of the Lake', and may have been an invention of his; in any event, it became part of the Klan's mumbo-jumbo.

This association of a make-believe Scotland with a make-believe South has been hard to shake off. Not much is heard of the Ku Klux Klan nowadays but organisations espousing similar aims spring up from time to time. One is the League of the South, founded in 1994, which has adopted the Scots form of the saltire, with the cross of St Andrew, as a symbol of the region's Celtic heritage, to the embarrassment of Scottish Nationalists. An upsurge of American interest in Scotland and Scottish traditions is especially pronounced in the South, though not confined to that region. In many ways it seems harmless enough. Restive and mobile Americans are constantly lectured that they live in a multicultural society where it is important for them to have roots. And Scottish roots, bogus or not, appear preferable to many others: someone of Scots ancestry is, almost by definition, a WASP – even though many Roman Catholics have emigrated from Scotland and many would argue that Scots are Celts rather than Anglo-Saxons. Yet without doubt, in the South, there is a sinister underside to this innocence.

Contrasted with Canada, which has similar problems of defining itself against a dominant culture, the South appears to have received from Scotland an influence not altogether benign, in fact rather malign in certain respects. It lies in make-believe.

Canadians do not on the whole cherish flagrant cults of Scottishness. Kilts have recently become fashionable there as in other countries, but most Canadian Scots of the past would never have been seen in one. They led modest, frugal, hard-working lives which made an enormous contribution to the country, but on the whole by blending themselves into the new society which had to be formed on this alien soil. They left their mark, yet not one that advertised itself with the flaunting of a lion rampant. This has been the general reality of Scots going out into the world. They do not set up little Scotlands beyond the seas. After bringing their Scottish influence with them, they merge into the background.

The make-believe in the South was less healthy. Yet the example of make-believe had been set in Scotland too. Both Scots and Southerners have become best known to other peoples through potently romanticised portrayals of their histories. From Sir Walter Scott onwards (and in part through a misunderstanding of him), native authors wrote up Scotland, its past, its people, its landscapes and legends, as incarnations of romance. In the same way, after the Civil War the writers of the South created a nostalgic if deceptive image of the way things had been before that catastrophe. It is interesting how the modern world's dream-factory of Hollywood has found this material equally productive, in *Gone with the Wind* and in *Braveheart*. Yet Scots or Southerners delighted at the international impact of these films might reflect that they are also complicit in a distortion of their culture through the corruption of history by mythology and of truth by legend. Art translated into ideology is often a little dangerous, never more so than when it induces feelings of victimhood and self-pity or the urge to blame others for past and present misfortune. It is hard to see how the future will improve through indulging such feelings. Neither Scotland nor the South has had an easy or comfortable history, and the images of tragic heroism they generate are by no means misplaced. But their value is cultural rather than political: better if they do not offer a refuge from reality.

11

CAPITALISTS

T he first big business in Scotland was American business. It arose out of that transatlantic trade in tobacco which, as we saw in an earlier chapter, helped to cause economic then political revolution in Virginia and created the resources for industrial revolution in Glasgow. For Scotland capital was the key. This had been a land without capital before the Union with England in 1707 and for some time afterwards. People still thought of capital as consisting in gold and silver. A nation which could accumulate gold and silver was rich; a nation which could not was poor. Scotland could not. Scottish coins were seldom struck, and the circulating currency amounted largely to a random collection of money which happened to have arrived from abroad for one reason and another; much of it anyway vanished with the futile expeditions to Darien in 1698–1700.

That was a familiar tale, however. Scots supplied little that could be sold abroad except a limited range of agricultural produce. In good years when they had a surplus to export, gold and silver came into the country. In bad years when the crops failed – a not infrequent event given the treacherous climate – gold and silver left again because grain had to be imported to stop the Scots starving. But most did not miss the money they seldom saw. They had no need of it because they laboured solely to feed themselves and their families. If they had to make a payment, for example the rent to their landlords, they could make it in kind, that is, out of crops they grew – so and so many bolls of meal for a year's tenancy. Even professionals such as ministers and schoolmasters were often remunerated in this way, receiving food to the value of their notional salaries.

Scotland was locked into a primitive and poverty-stricken economy. Desperation to break out of it formed the main motive for the madcap venture to Darien and for the Union of 1707. England and Holland were moving far ahead of Scotland with agricultural improvements that raised the productivity of land and labour, and with the establishment of the first manufacturing industries. But all this required capital investment at a time when Scotland had no capital. Even the Union did not of itself solve the problem, though it provided opportunities for doing so.

Scots were anyway already trying to think how they might get along without the gold and silver which seemed unlikely ever to come their way. John Law went as a young man from Edinburgh to London and made his living as a gambler. He had other vices. He was forced to flee after a duel in which he killed the husband of a woman he had seduced. He went to Amsterdam, the financial centre of Europe, and saw how business was carried on there. He returned to Scotland in the dismal years after Darien to offer his countrymen a way forward.

To their astonishment, Law told them wealth did not consist in gold and silver but in the brains and hands of the people: in his career at the gambling tables, his own brains and hands had often filched the gold and silver of less skilful players. Where brains and hands were set to work, gold and silver would follow. If capital was needed it could be raised as credit, by borrowing on the strength of existing assets – which in Scotland was mostly the land. Still, Law's notions seemed too much of a gamble to his more cautious countrymen. He presented an economic plan to the Parliament in Edinburgh which gathered dust. Because he was against the Union, he left for France in 1707 and found a more receptive audience there. By 1719 he rose to be the French Minister of Finance, graced with the title of Duke of Arkansas because he had launched the Mississippi Scheme by which the vast resources of the New World were to be developed on credit, or on money he raised from optimistic investors. Despite his brilliance, however, he had never got round to defining how credit might be controlled, and soon the scheme collapsed. Thousands of irate Frenchmen lost their investments. Law was forced to flee once again, this time to Venice, where he died in poverty. But he bequeathed an important legacy to the future.

The French, though they had their fingers burned by him, never forgot Law's grandiose ideas for public spending. Nor were his brother Scots to forget his ideas on how a poor country could get rich. Later in the century, David Hume and Adam Smith read the writings he left behind him, while Smith learned about trade from the merchants of his home town of Glasgow. The two Scottish philosophers saw the force of Law's argument that wealth lay in human industry and ingenuity, not in gold and silver. They went further than he did by reasoning that individual liberty was the best way to encourage ingenuity and industry, and free trade the best way to win the rewards available from them. This was why Hume and Smith objected to the colonial system imposed on America. It required Americans to export their agricultural produce to Britain and forbade them to make any manufactured goods of their own, these being sent instead from the mother country. Hume and Smith forecast that a system of such one-sided economic restrictions would bring political trouble, and they were right. It became one of the major causes of the American Revolution. Yet afterwards Glasgow's trade with America flourished as never before. The restrictions had not been needed to sustain the trade – and they had caused war. In the end nobody was better off because of the colonial system.

The War of American Independence taught Scots another useful lesson, that in capitalism you must not get into a rut. The cosy privileges of the colonial system had been deceptive because reality was bound to catch up with them one day. And then their beneficiaries, lulled into a false sense of security, might be too slow to switch to more reliable ways of earning a living. Luckily, that was not what now happened in Glasgow. In the years just before 1776, imports of tobacco and their re-export to various European destinations had reached a peak. Then they came to a stop. It says much for the enterprise of Glaswegians in those days that, without a blink, they redeployed their capital. Textiles already had a modest presence in the city's economy. They now offered the most promising of the opportunities available. Money poured into them. One result was rapid technological advance which soon changed the structure of the industry. Individual weavers working at home (and cultivating radical politics in their spare time) gave way to a downtrodden proletariat trudging into a grim factory at dawn to toil at some tedious operation till it was time to trudge home again in the twilight, too tired to do anything but eat and and go to bed. The human effects of early capitalism horrified observers of it.

One of Glasgow's biggest businessmen was David Dale, who started as a weaver's apprentice himself before he went on to make a fortune in banking. In 1786, in partnership with the English inventor of the spinning jenny, Richard Arkwright, Dale built a textile mill at New Lanark, a few miles up the River Clyde, just below waterfalls to power the machinery. He was a religious man who wanted to be a model employer. He decided his workers should be limited to shifts of eleven hours, instead of the normal seventeen. He provided them with food, clothes and housing, in modest but elegant tenements still standing today amid woods on the same pretty stretch of river, designated a World Heritage Site. Now it is perhaps hard to discern here one of the seedbeds of capitalism, so idyllic is the scene. But in its day New Lanark employed 2,000 hands, more than any other factory in Europe or America, most of them women and children recruited from local orphanages, others including Highlanders cleared from their old homes. A visitor said: 'If I was tempted to envy any of my fellow creatures it would be men such as Mr Dale for the good they have done to mankind.'

Dale's daughter Ann Caroline married Robert Owen, a young Welshman in the textile trade who had visited Glasgow on business and got to know the family. In 1800 he took over as manager of New Lanark. He saw it not just as an innovative enterprise but as the blueprint for an industrial society different from anything before. In a sense his insight was a true one; the modern world did break up the small communities where most people had always dwelt, and set them apart from the natural world which had ordered their existence with its slow seasonal rhythms. Owen believed that human nature had been formed by the traditional environment and that a novel environment would reform it. But at this crux there was also a chance for visionaries like himself to step in and make human nature better.

Owen extended his benevolent interest from the working conditions into the private lives of his employees. He wanted them cleaner and healthier. He made sure their children could read and write. He offered them all 'rational amusement': once workers finished their shifts they would be enticed into some self-improving activity, or at least be invited to dancing classes, instead of going off to get drunk in the usual Scottish fashion. Supervisors kept 'books of character' on each one, which Owen inspected in efforts to stamp out 'bad and inferior conduct'. He reminded fellow capitalists that they made sure to keep their machinery in good working order: 'Now, if the care which you bestow upon machinery can give you such excellent results, may you not expect equally good results from care spent upon human beings, with their infinitely superior structure?' New Lanark became a showplace to politicians and industrialists from home and abroad, admiring its unique blend of philanthropy and profitability. It also made of Owen an arch-bore, forever harping on about his answers to all the world's problems.

America was too tempting a target for Owen. There in the New World lay a new nation – what better place to realise *A New View of Society*, as he called the book on his theories which he published in 1813? After 1820 he withdrew from the management of New Lanark because he was looking for a place in the US to conduct an experiment yet more radical, a true secular utopia to be run on a system of socialism. He discovered what he was looking for at New Harmony by the banks of the Wabash River in Indiana. It had been founded as a co-operative community by a group of Germans some years before, but never prospered.

In 1824 Owen offered to take it over, with 20,000 acres of farming land round it, to bring in more capital and people, to devise better rules and ensure the experiment worked. The basic principle of New Harmony was to be the abolition of private property. Everyone was to be equal to everyone else. There would be no money – or rather it would be held in a communal treasury for dealings with the outside world. But all would by their labour acquire the same rights to share its fruits. They would wear the same clothing. They would eat the same food. Unfortunately, no rule made work compulsory. Owen, so imperious in other ways, thought such a rule would amount to tyranny. He believed all men wanted to work out of self-respect.

After drawing up a constitution, Owen invited 'the industrious and well-disposed of all nations' to come to New Harmony. Hundreds did, but not every one of them was industrious or well-disposed. They squabbled over who was to get what and, if disgruntled, refused to work; they preferred discussing the rights of man for hours on end. Owen meanwhile went off to lecture the rest of America on the marvels of New Harmony and one of his sons, William, wrote to him: 'We have been much puzzled to know what to do with those who profess to do anything and everything: they are perfect drones and can never be satisfied here.' Still, they managed to grow crops and produce timber, hats, shoes, soap, candles. Nothing made money except the town's tavern, always full of visitors wanting to see socialism in action. New Harmony lasted three years, as long as Owen had money to run it. Luckily for him he had kept the title to the land and sold it off at a profit when the community collapsed.

It is easy to smile at the human foibles of such idealistic schemes, yet they were in tune with the times. Capitalism remained as yet an imperfectly formed system and nobody could tell how it would turn out. It was never a monolith but assumed different patterns from the start, for the most part culturally conditioned. That has continued, so that today Japanese capitalism is different from German capitalism which in its turn is different from American capitalism, though this last is the dominant form worldwide. The distinguishing features of American capitalism reflect the development of the US, in its individualism, its corresponding rejection of collectivism, its stress on the primacy of consumers' interests, its offer of mobility as the answer to social problems, its lack of respect for historical antecedents. With hindsight it seems obvious that

Owen's utopia did not have much chance of survival in this sort of environment. But other Scottish contributions to American capitalism have proved to be of more lasting value.

Owen's children became Americans. They had gone with him to the US and most stayed there to lead successful professional and political lives. The family made a fresh fortune out of Texan oil which today enables them to maintain New Harmony as a historical monument. They illustrate the true role Scots could play in the development of America. This was a land of limitless resources but, as with the gold and silver of old, it was not enough just to possess them. Resources had to be set in motion in order to produce wealth. It was done by carrying across the Atlantic Ocean the labour and capital necessary to exploit them.

Scots enjoyed an advantage here. As a mobile people from a small, poor country they had discovered the options either of going out into the world and making money to bring back, or of emigrating to settle distant continents, while other Europeans were still tied to the soil of their forefathers. This mobility and enterprise attained an altogether different scale in Victorian times. Compared to perhaps 50,000 Scots who left for North America during the eighteenth century, more than a million left during the nineteenth century (the numbers fell during the twentieth century, especially the second half). This large exodus of the population is often deplored today, but in fact the emigrants were not all lost to Scotland: one in three of them came home again, temporarily or permanently. The movement back and forth proved, on the contrary, to be of great benefit to the country. The most mobile men (they were nearly always men) brought back not just money but also skills and knowledge of the conditions in faraway places invaluable to friends or relations who might seek opportunities there. The Scottish economist, Sir Alec Cairncross, described how in the Victorian heyday the English-speaking countries round the North Atlantic Ocean more or less formed a free-trade area where capital, labour and technology could easily be shifted about. It was open alike to the capitalists, to their companies and to ordinary workers. The cycles in the international economy did not move so much in unison in those days. So if there was a recession in Glasgow there might be at the same time a boom in New York, and when that petered out Montreal could take up the slack. A skilled or resourceful or hard-working man could go from place to place, and once he prospered in one or the other settle down with a local girl or bring over his family from Scotland.

Scottish workers were in demand, for the period from about 1870 saw the second stage of the industrial revolution, when the textiles of the first stage gave way to the heavy industries of coal, steel and shipbuilding, especially in Glasgow and the West of Scotland. The region sat on resources of the raw materials large enough to last into the twentieth century. Through trade in textiles, international shipping links had developed. The combination made Clydeside one of the world's great industrial centres, and the world's very greatest centre for shipbuilding and everything associated with it, including rapid development of new methods, technologies and organisations. The fact that these were transferable would work ultimately to Clydeside's detriment, as it allowed the rise of foreign competition. But meanwhile it worked to Clydeside's advantage, and to the advantage of Scotland and Britain as a whole. An example came in 1914 on the outbreak of the First World War. At once many skilled men in Glasgow joined up, leaving a shortage of labour. Ships crossing the Atlantic that autumn brought hundreds of Americans to fill their jobs, Americans who were perhaps of Scots blood or had learned their skills as apprentices to Scots in the US. Unfortunately the virtual free-trade area which made this possible was not to survive a war followed by depression, protectionism and restrictions on immigration to America. Only during the late twentieth century did the old mobility re-emerge, now in finance and technology rather than in heavy industry.

These workers moved within an economic framework that was also largely a Scottish creation. The shipping line is one of Scotland's gifts to the world. In earlier times intercontinental trade went either in convoy, so ships could give each other help and protection, or else individual captains sailed about from port to port picking up cargoes or passengers as they could. Haphazard habits of the past had to be rationalised in a period which saw a vast expansion of oceanic traffic in goods and in people. The development of steamships instead of sailing ships meant, too, that the traffic was no longer so much at the mercy of the elements. All the same, it took a while for the idea to emerge of regular and reliable voyages, so that in Glasgow passengers might know they could embark or merchants might be sure of sending their freight to Montreal every Tuesday, or to New York every Friday. Perhaps the idea was copied from the railways, another contemporary innovation in transport, which had to work to timetables. In any event, co-ordination on such a scale could only be managed by companies of corresponding size.

The new oceanic traffic soon came under the dominance of the magnificent shipping lines formed in Victorian times. In the western seas the greatest was Cunard, founded in 1840. Samuel Cunard himself hailed from Nova Scotia, to which his first service ran. But he could have done little without his managing partners, two pairs of Glaswegian brothers, George and James Burns and David and Charles MacIver; soon Cunard's ships were calling at all the major ports in the Americas with which their native city did business. They carried millions of tons in trade between the Old World and the New, and millions of passengers.

The investment needed to create a system of intercontinental transport was enormous. Cunard, for example, would not have got under way without an initial subsidy from the British Government to run the royal mail to Canada. Shipping lines have always had to operate in a commercially unstable, financially insecure environment. That makes them typical of the global economy they helped to form. In its enrichment of the human race, it required novel means of handling capital of a complexity unimaginable before. This brought greater opportunities, but opportunities where greater rewards were matched by greater risks.

The Americas offer a case in point. They could never have been developed without huge amounts of foreign money. The inflow continued through the nineteenth century and beyond: not till after 1918 did a booming US become for the first time a net exporter of capital. In the early days land lay there in abundance, with untold natural resources beneath it. A never-ending flow of people disembarked from the emigrant ships. Capital had to follow them if the potential of the Americas was to be realised. But capital needed to come from investors who wanted some assurance they were not throwing it away. Sometimes they did throw it away. Those false friends, gold and silver, could be found in the New World, yet many prospecting and mining efforts came to nothing. The Wild West was being divided up into vast ranches while railways crossed from the Atlantic to the Pacific Oceans: who could say if these pioneering enterprises would ever produce a decent return on money invested in them?

It fell to canny Scots to deal with the situation. Scots are notoriously thrifty, yet it is often forgotten how willing they have been to accept risk and how good at handling it. Their country had by now risen from poverty to plenty. Development was fostered by their own banking system, marked by two outstanding features: that it had emerged free from any control by the state and that it had relied on paper money, not on gold and silver which, in any case, could not be kept in Scotland. The banks solved Law's problem, of finding a self-policing mechanism which provided all the credit necessary for the economy while keeping inflation under control. With this level of financial genius, it is no surprise that Scots now discovered means to persuade the many little people who in Victorian times first started to accumulate some capital – shopkeepers and sea-captains and widows – that they ought to invest their money in places they had never heard of and in activities they could scarcely imagine.

The key was an instrument for sharing risk. The inventor of the instrument was Robert Fleming, son of a tradesman in Dundee who went to work aged 13 in the offices of the Baxters, one of the city's textile dynasties. He rose to be private clerk to the senior partner, proving himself astute and reliable enough to be entrusted with the family's private shareholdings. He came to understand the value of a diverse portfolio, where different risks could be offset against one another to maintain an average yield. Then he realised this might be a basis for collective capitalism, where many people pooled their resources and controlled risk through the scale of their joint investments.

From his insight Fleming launched in 1873 the Scottish American Investment Trust. The idea caught on at once and before long Fleming had the, for the time, enormous sum of £500,000 deployed. He liked American railways and mortgages on land being opened up in the West, but he made it a rule to stake no more than 10 per cent of the assets on a single enterprise. His brainwave was at once copied in the Scottish American Investment Company, set up by a firm of fuddy-duddy lawyers in Edinburgh, William J. Menzies, till then specialists in clergymen's lawsuits generated by the obscure but ferocious religious disputes of Victorian Scotland. Hard on its heels came a third trust, the Scottish American Mortgage Company. Others soon followed.

Fleming had created a craze in Scotland, which drew all sorts of unlikely people into the tingling excitement of a flutter not only in stocks and shares but also in real physical assets changing and improving the world. From it arose a permanent addition to the modern range of financial institutions. The investment trust proved its worth and remains to this day an effective means of mobilising funds from modest investors for enterprises which cannot always rely on more conventional forms of finance. At the outset it played in particular a huge role in bringing capital to the American frontier, by nature a risky place which has in the long run amply repaid investment in it.

Once labour and capital were mobilised, they could be applied to new technology. And new technology was needed to match the challenges of American development, while linking the New World to the Old and laying the foundations of a global economy. Again, Scots had equipped themselves to play a powerful part. Their educational system absorbed science into its curriculum while universities elsewhere were still teaching medieval metaphysics. Yet pure science divorced from the world, as often pursued today, was unheard of, almost unthought of, in Scotland.

Scottish science boasted as its triumph James Watt's steam engine, patented in 1769 though supposed to have originated in a boy playing with a spoon and a kettle. It was a functional discipline, concerned with problems thrown up by technology, related to ordinary life, something for everybody. Scotland was full of scientists who would today be called amateurs, from James Black, the doctor who discovered carbon dioxide, to Hugh Miller, the stonemason turned geologist. Much science was becoming mathematical, but Scots tried to stop it getting diverted too far away from demonstration, discovery, experiment and invention.

Even in academic posts, Scottish scientists remained practical men in the nineteenth century. The most famous was William Thomson, appointed a professor at Glasgow in 1846, at the age of 22. He is better remembered as Lord Kelvin; his was the first noble title granted to a scientist, especially for his formulation of the two Laws of Thermodynamics. Still, when in 1896 his university celebrated his professorial jubilee, it did not thank him for his theories but filled an entire gallery with his inventions. The first electric meter was his work; his house, at Largs on the Firth of Clyde, was the earliest in Britain with electric light. He was a partner in the firm of Kelvin & White which made more than two hundred electrical, optical and navigational instruments. At that jubilee in Glasgow in 1896, before 2,000 guests from around the world, a telegram of congratulations was sent from the library of the university. Travelling across the Atlantic by way of Newfoundland and New York to California, then all the way back, it returned to him in seven and a half minutes. It was a fitting tribute to the practical genius of a man who had done more than any other to invent the submarine cable and join Europe to America by this first modern means of intercontinental communication.

No task so tested the burgeoning technology of the age. Telegraphs had been invented in 1837 by the American, Samuel Morse, along with the Morse code. Cables were soon laid over long distances, but the time of transmitting a message increased with their length. Electric currents were not then fully understood, but Kelvin knew more about them than most and he solved the problem by his invention of the mirror galvanometer. It remained a formidable job to link both sides of the Atlantic by a telegraph transmitting impulses along a copper cable under the ocean. The British and US navies set out, in their first co-operative venture, to lay a cable from each end which was to be joined in the middle. This did not go well: the cable kept snapping or going dead, and when almost laid it was lost deep in the ocean. The solution came in laying the whole cable from a single vessel, but that had to be done by the largest then afloat, Isambard Kingdom Brunel's *Great Eastern*. Final success in 1866 owed a debt to many men, with Kelvin to the fore. He was a professor but also a successful businessman: his income from patents increased his academic salary six times over. He remained good-natured and unassuming about his worldwide fame. The German physicist, Hermann von Helmholtz, said of him: 'He far exceeds all the great men of science with whom I have made personal acquaintance in intelligence, lucidity and nobility of thought, so that sometimes I felt quite wooden beside him.'

There are parallels between the careers of Kelvin and of Alexander Graham Bell, inventor of the telephone. Both came from an academic background. Kelvin's father had been professor of mathematics at Glasgow while Bell's father taught elocution in Edinburgh, taking the discipline to a higher level and inventing a system of 'visible speech' by which deaf-mutes could learn to lip-read. Bell continued that work when, after his own studies in Scotland, England and Germany, he became a professor of vocal physiology in Boston. He went to New England because he thought the air would be cleaner for his weak chest, and there he fell in love with a deaf girl, Mabel Hubbard. It was for her sake he sought to devise a machine which would enable the deaf to hear. This put him on the track of a different but greater invention.

'If I could make a current of electricity vary in intensity precisely as the air varies in density during the production of sound, I should be able to transmit speech telegraphically,' Bell wrote. In other words, a technological task lay before him, though at first he lacked the skills to undertake it and produce the required undulating current. He studied the workings of the ear. He produced sound from an empty coil. But the means of linking dead matter to living organs eluded him. He went with his problem to Joseph Henry, the son of Scottish immigrants who was secretary of the Smithsonian Institution in Washington.

Henry at once recognised 'the germ of a great invention'. As Bell reported their conversation, 'I said I recognised the fact that there were mechanical difficulties. I added that I felt I had not the electrical knowledge necessary to overcome the difficulties. His laconic answer was "Get it".' American optimism gave the final push to Scottish practicality.

Bell would patent his invention in February 1876, just ahead of others racing to turn telegraphy into sound. So cutthroat had the competition been that afterwards he was forced to defend his patent rights to the telephone in hundreds of lawsuits, all of which he won. For now, working fast at home in Boston, he still had to perfect the concept. He carried out the experiments with the help of a friend, Thomas Watson. On 10 March 1876, this friend was in the basement with the receiver at his ear when he heard Bell say from another room: 'Mr Watson, come here, please. I want you.' They had the whole apparatus ready just in time for the Centennial Exposition in Philadelphia, celebrating the hundredth anniversary of the Declaration of Independence. There Bell caused a sensation by reciting Hamlet's soliloquy 'To be or not to be' over the telephone to the Emperor of Brazil.

So Bell won the battle to be recognised as inventor of the telephone, which had been so fierce because all understood its practical potential. He wrote: 'The great advantage it possesses over other electrical apparatus is that it requires no skill to operate.' This was the Scottish ideal of science for the common man. He owed to America his appreciation of how to exploit the invention commercially. Telegraphs could only be sent from one receiving station to another, but Bell thought telephonic cables might be 'laid underground or suspended overhead communicating by branch wires with private dwellings'. And it need not be just a local service, so that 'a man in one part of the country may communicate by word of mouth with another in a distant place'.

Bell, the inventor of the telephone was also the first to curse it. He often kept his own receiver stuffed with paper to stop it ringing. 'I hate the beast,' he said. He was content to leave its development to his partners in the forerunner of the modern Bell Telephone corporation and of its long-distance subsidiary, AT&T (American Telephone and Telegraph). He felt happiest pottering about at the home he bought for himself and called *Beinn Bhreagh* (Beautiful Mountain in Gaelic) in the bracing climate of Nova Scotia, where he endlessly tried out more new inventions. Like Kelvin, Bell had a taste for gadgets: a graphophone to record sound, a photophone to transmit sound by means of light. He retained an interest in teaching the dumb to speak, and hoped his skills might be of benefit to animals.

One of the rivals in invention whom Bell just beat to win the patent for the telephone was Thomas Edison: it is worth recalling he had an American Scot, Mary Elliot, for a mother. To an equal if not greater extent, he kept up the Scottish tradition of experiment and discovery. Known as the Wizard of Menlo Park (from his home in New Jersey), he took out over a thousand patents. In 1877 he created the gramophone and in 1878 the first wax record to play on it. In 1879 he invented incandescent lighting. His mastery of light and sound led on to movies and talkies. He was also an astute businessman, a founder in 1892 of the eventually giant US corporation, General Electric.

There was nothing of the absent-minded inventor about another Scot who found his destiny in America. Andrew Carnegie absorbed the ethos of the New World, or rather found there the scope to push to an ultimate conclusion two aspects of Scottish capitalism, of making money and then of using it for the benefit of mankind. He could never have done the same at home, as he himself realised: 'If I had been in Dunfermline working at the loom it is very likely I would have been a poor weaver all my days, but here I can surely do something better than that.' Rich and indeed ruthless as he became, he still suffered the sadness many exiled Scots feel at having to leave their small country behind because it cannot offer opportunity to all its sons. He, however, was able to come back to it, trailing clouds of glory.

Carnegie was a slight, blond boy, born in 1835, who spent his childhood at Dunfermline in Fife. It was not a happy time or place. The workers of the town lived off weaving, a trade in decline as mechanisation displaced craftsmen toiling at their looms in their own homes. They were overtaken by the Hungry Forties, a depression in the British economy so prolonged that by 1848 it seemed to threaten revolution. In that year many left for America, including the Carnegies, who went to Pittsburgh.

For immigrants to the US, things were seldom easy either. When young Carnegie had to find a job, he worked first as a drudge in a cotton factory, then as an engine tender, then as a telegraph operator and messenger, all humble occupations. Still, he worked hard at them and by dint of that rose during his twelve years with his final employer, the Pennsylvania Railroad Company, to become its general manager, after sterling labours in using its tracks to supply the Union's army during the Civil War. Now the moment had arrived for him to branch out on his own. He sank his personal savings into a company set up by George Pullman to build sleeping cars for passenger trains. It was a brilliant success and earned for Carnegie too some quite serious wealth. He could then found his own business, the Carnegie Steel Company.

Till this time most steel in the world was produced in Britain, not least in Scotland, under the impetus still of James Watt's steam engine and James Neilson's blast furnace. There had been a recent technological advance when the English scientist, Henry Bessemer, developed a novel method of forging steel out of molten pig iron, which increased production while cutting the workforce. Carnegie set up the first Bessemer plant in North America. He bought out other steelworks and converted them to the same process. His was what is known today as an integrated operation which mined its own iron ore, made its own steel and transported its own products by its own private railway or by its own fleet of steamers on the Great Lakes – all this during the huge economic expansion in a US on the rebound from the Civil War. By 1892, after twenty years in the business, Carnegie was producing steel equal to half the total British output.

It was an American achievement, yet the Scottish side of it should not be overlooked. Carnegie felt proud to call himself a Scotchman (to use the term he used himself) and never lost his love for his homeland: he read Adam Smith and quoted Robert Burns. More to the point for his business, he carried forward the native tradition that technology, rather than pure science, should be the driving force behind innovation. The technology was driven by the demands of production. Carnegie urged his managers to make it simpler, faster, cheaper, to monitor every stage so that efficiency could be raised and costs cut. He had discovered economies of scale, a key to success of modern industry. 'Cheapness is in proportion to the scale of production,' he said. 'To make ten tons of steel a day would cost many times as much per ton as to make one hundred tons . . . Thus the larger the scale of production the cheaper the product.'

Carnegie also remained a Scot in the good conceit he had of himself, in the vernacular phrase. He needed no prompting to go into raptures over his life's work. Like Owen, if in different form, Carnegie saw 'a new industrial world' arising. His vision went further: it would be a world 'without war or physical violence, in which through the genius of invention and the miracle of mass production, the fruits of industry would become so abundant that they could be made available to all.' This is a vision of the world, at least the western world, we live in – except that war and violence have not vanished. That his vision would encounter problems came home to Carnegie in his own lifetime. The workforce was to him a disposable element. If higher efficiency made men redundant, or even recalcitrant, they were sacked. In 1892 in Carnegie's steel mill at Homestead, Pennsylvania, this led to the most violent strike in American history. Armed police were summoned. The disturbance got out of hand and they fired on the strikers, killing nine of them. But it was Carnegie who stood condemned in the eyes of America, and he went into agonies of remorse: 'The pain I suffer increases daily. The works are not worth one drop of human blood. I wish they had sunk.' A few years later he sold his business to the financier J. P. Morgan.

Carnegie now had $300 million in his pocket. The real problem in his vision was how to get from abundance of production to availability for all. He had his own answer, already published in a book, *The Gospel of Wealth*: men should make as much money as they could, but then give the surplus away. For his remaining years he followed that gospel. The list of his benefactions is extraordinary, and they have made him even better remembered as philanthropist than as businessman – which would have pleased him. He paid for 7,700 pipe-organs in churches, for parks, swimming pools and auditoriums, such as Carnegie Hall in New York. He built 2,800 free libraries in North America and Great Britain. He set up the Carnegie Foundation for the Advancement of Learning providing pensions for academics. He aided the Negro College at Tuskegee, Alabama. He established the Temple of Peace at The Hague in Holland and the Carnegie Foundation in New York, dedicated to 'the advancement of civilisation'. He did not forget Scotland. The Carnegie Trust for the Scottish Universities still finances research in them. The plutocrat recalled how he had once been poor and he wanted 'to bring into the lives of the toiling masses of Dunfermline some sweetness and light'. Here, in the place whence he had risen so far, he restored the historical monuments and commissioned Patrick Geddes, the father of town planning, to lay out a public park. Finally he bought Skibo Castle in Sutherland, where he liked to play the Highland laird during frequent visits till his death in 1919.

Foreigners often condemn American capitalism for being ruthless and for letting its victims go to the wall. It is true that nobody, least of all any public body, will step in to save a business or its workers in the US. On the other hand, it is accepted there that the natural development of capitalism will cause many to go under, and the fact does not carry with it the same moral taint as it does in Britain and Europe. An American bankrupt has learned a lesson of life in business, and will be better equipped to pick himself up and succeed next time. This is a civilisation with business at its core, not the state or the nation or any theory of society. That is why in principle it remains open to everybody, and Americans who arrived a few years ago from Palermo or Bangalore or Seoul can do just as well for themselves as those whose ancestors came on the *Mayflower*. Their failure need never be permanent because they can always try again; their recovery may start once they strike a single deal.

But while in the US money talks, business does accept obligations, if not in a European way. It would be interesting to go round Britain and ask big companies to found, say, a new university. They would reply that universities are a matter for the state, nothing to do with them: they pay taxes with good or ill grace, and it is for politicians to decide how to spend the money. In Scotland the tendency is especially marked and most Scots believe that no public purpose should be fulfilled except by the state, indeed that harnessing private resources to it would be morally dubious, because a profit might be expected.

Americans take profits without inhibition but that makes them readier to give profits away: it cannot be far-fetched to ascribe this to Carnegie's example. The Carnegie Foundation offered a model for others. One is the Mellon Foundation, set up by a banking family in Pittsburgh of Scotch-Irish origins; Andrew Mellon, who endowed it, was when he became US Secretary of the Treasury in 1929 probably the richest man in the country, with a fortune from Gulf Oil and the Aluminum Company of America. A second is the Rockefeller Foundation, endowed by John D. Rockefeller, under whom Standard Oil became the largest company in the world; he had a Scottish American mother, Eliza Davison. So did another oilman, Paul Getty, whose ancestors also on his father's side were Scotch-Irish Presbyterians and founders of Gettysburg, Pennsylvania; Getty gave his name to cultural institutions he financed in Los Angeles. Visitors to museums or concert-halls all over the US will see a prominent display of the benefactors, their names perhaps carved in stone for posterity to admire as long as the building stands: harmless enough monuments, in all conscience, to human vanity. They can also count as a mark Scotland has left on American capitalism.

12

CONTEMPORARIES

F or America the twentieth century was a great one, and it has
often been called the American century. As it opened the US
was just emerging from the wings of the global stage – in not too
creditable a fashion, being engaged in a war of aggression to
expel Spain from the last territories in the New World which
Christopher Columbus had claimed for King Ferdinand and
Queen Isabella in 1492. The Spaniards felt incensed at such perfidy, recalling that they had helped to win independence from
Britain for the Americans. But the Americans, to all appearances, entertained no doubt that they were in the right: self-evidently the Cubans or Puerto Ricans would be better off by having an old imperial yoke lifted from them. That the people of
Havana or San Juan might merely see themselves as being obliged
to shoulder a different one did not occur to their liberators.

Americans would for a long time ahead find it hard to see
themselves for what they were, the youngest of the great imperial powers. The US had been born by secession from the British
Empire, and its ethos remained anti-imperialist. Only slowly
did it come to face the realities of the twentieth century. This
helps to explain the many ambivalences of its position. While its
intervention won the First World War for the Allies, it then
retreated into isolationism. Its intervention was again decisive
in the Second World War, yet the following forty years of Cold

War often only reinforced ideological simplicities without giving Americans a firmer grasp of *Realpolitik*. The US was unprepared to be left as the sole superpower after the collapse of Communism in 1989. It is still trying to find out how best to use its wealth and might.

The Scottish story in the twentieth century is almost the reverse of the American one. At its opening Scotland stood at an imperial pinnacle. By some accounts this was then the richest country in the world, and well content with its leading role in Union and Empire. For more than half of the fifty years on either side of the turn of the century the Prime Ministers of the United Kingdom were native Scots or men of wholly Scottish blood or representatives of Scotland in Parliament: William Gladstone, the Earl of Rosebery, Arthur Balfour, Henry Campbell-Bannerman, Herbert Asquith, Andrew Bonar Law. Their contribution was matched by that of hundreds of thousands of Scots out in the Empire: governors, merchants, missionaries, doctors, engineers, sailors, soldiers, settlers. Britain, too, was fighting a war of imperial expansion in 1900, to bring the Boer republics of South Africa into allegiance to Queen Victoria. War always stirs the spirit of Scotland. This one saw her regiments taking their usual heroic part. But it was also a war which pricked the Scottish conscience. A good many Scots thought the Afrikaners to be much like themselves: a God-fearing, hard-working people fighting against the odds to maintain their identity at the edge of civilisation. It shamed these Scots that Britain should want to conquer them. This was the first sign of disillusion with the destiny in Union and Empire which Scotland had sought.

The rest of the twentieth century would deepen the disillusion. Scottish valour brought horrific losses in the First World War. Of the 560,000 Scots who joined up, nearly 150,000 died – a rate of casualties exceeded only by Serbia and Turkey, but they had been invaded and crushed, whereas Scotland was supposed to be one of the victors. The peace proved no less tragic and wasteful. A slump overtook the great Scottish industries. It lengthened into the Depression. After that, prosperity returned to Scotland only in fits and starts. More Scots left their country than ever before, and at times its population actually fell. The

Scottish nation stopped growing not only in a physical but also in a moral and intellectual sense. Indeed it seemed for much of the period after the Second World War to be dying on its feet – poor, bleak and demoralised. One novelist, Gordon Williams, compared it to the land of dreams that America had become: 'We knew our country was a small-time dump, where nothing ever happened and nobody had a name like Jelly Roll Morton.' Not till towards the millennium did the gloom lift. For various reasons the revival emerged most successfully in the cultural sphere, and only afterwards in the political sphere. Its prime achievement was restoration of the Scottish Parliament in 1999. But in itself this has not been enough to reverse a century of decline.

At the threshold of the twenty-first century both the small, old country and the big, new country face an uncertain future, yet not without hope and freed of some earlier delusions. The enormous American influence on our age springs not only from the political power and military might of the US but at least as much from its culture. This is the main force in a universal culture, a culture of one world, where people, goods, money, fashions, ideas and creeds submerge frontiers and erode the distinct marks of nations, even of civilisations. The European civilisation out of which the US grew has itself been recolonised from America, so that Europeans watch American films, listen to American music, wear American clothes and eat American food. Scots, like any nation of their size, can only make a modest contribution to this universal culture. One way for them to do this has been to go to America.

The engine of American ascendancy during the twentieth century was the capitalist system. Because at home the Scots did not fare so well at its hands they became somewhat hostile to it, though the socialist alternatives they tried have proved far from successful. Scotland housed many millionaires at the turn of the century but few latterly, till the privatisation of nationalised industries in the 1980s and 1990s let the Scottish entrepreneur rise from the grave. Meanwhile anybody who wanted to make serious money had to get out. America was a magnet to them, of course, and they could join the previous generations of their countrymen who had found there a land of opportunity. When they did, they scarcely needed to employ their national talent for adapting to strange environments because so much already seemed familiar to them.

A key to this opportunity is the diversity of America: arrival there unburdens the immigrant of his cultural and historical baggage and gives him the chance to fulfil his own dreams. It is a country which best suits individualists, so it is hard to pick out any consistent course Scots have followed there. They feel no compulsion, like some other groups, to live in particular neighbourhoods or work in particular jobs. Since they are generally well educated anyway, all doors are open to them. If we can attach one label to what they have contributed, it might be that they have helped to keep open the means of communication which allow an ever more complex society to function. Certainly they play a role in the many modern forms of the media. This role, with its confidence in the capacity of the common man to absorb useful knowledge, is faithful to Scottish tradition.

A peculiar aspect of the modern media is that they tend to be owned by dynasties, with inevitable ups-and-downs according to the varying abilities of successive generations. One of the most prominent of these dynasties in America is the Forbes family, which hailed from Maud in Aberdeenshire. Bertie Charles Forbes, the grandfather of the three brothers who today run its interests, emigrated to the US in 1917 and set up a publishing company, of which the flagship is *Forbes* magazine, aimed at businessmen. Malcolm Forbes, who succeeded his father in the business and died in 1990, made so much money that he could devote a good deal of it to a lifestyle owing nothing to his humble Scottish ancestors but matching the most flamboyant standards of a pleasure-seeking age. He loved to throw parties on his yacht or at his palace in Morocco or at his opulent home in the countryside of New Jersey. Clad in a kilt, he might serenade Princess Margaret or Elizabeth Taylor, while other guests were regaled by bands of pipers as they picked at Scottish salmon garnished with caviare. He also enjoyed feats of derring-do and in 1973, with his son Robert, made the first crossing of North America by balloon. But the third generation has generally turned out more sober in every sense. Steve Forbes, the present head of the dynasty, has tried his hand at politics and twice run for the Republican presidential nomination, advocating a flat tax and a much-reduced role for government. Despite his lavishing millions of dollars from his personal fortune on the campaigns and greatly outspending his opponents, his political ambitions have yet to be rewarded.

Across the northern border of the US, the normally self-effacing Canadians have shown a remarkable capacity to produce press barons of titanic stature. The most famous was William Aitken, Lord Beaverbrook. The son of a Presbyterian minister who emigrated from Scotland to New Brunswick, Beaverbrook had already made a fortune on the Montreal Stock Exchange by the age of thirty. He took it to the imperial capital of London, where he got himself elected to Parliament and set up a publishing group which eventually included the *Daily Express*, the *Sunday Express* and the *Evening Standard*. These became famous campaigning newspapers, especially on everything which might advance the interests and unity of the British Empire. Beaverbrook was an intimate of Winston Churchill and served in the Cabinet in both World Wars, as Minister of Information in the First and as Minister of Aircraft Production in the Second: without his stupendous energy the Battle of Britain could not have been won. Till his death in 1964 he retained a journalist's instincts: his editors would be phoned up out of the blue and hear a gruff voice abruptly demanding, 'What's the news?'

Different in personality though no less important to his industry was Roy Thomson, the son of a Scottish barber in Toronto who ended up owning 150 publications, more than anyone else in the world. The first he bought in Britain was *The Scotsman* in 1955. The paper's palatial offices overlooked a staid, provincial Edinburgh, its later liberating boom undreamed of, which lay still in the grip of a smug and gloomy Presbyterianism. The Findlays of Aberlour, the proprietors for over a hundred years, had responded to an alarming decline in circulation by taking to drink. Into this hag-ridden northern air now swept a gale of North American consumerism. *The Scotsman* was picked up, shaken about and turned around, soon to become a major vehicle for the cultural and political revival of Scotland. Thomson also set up Scottish Television, a commercial station which he described as a 'licence to print money'.

Thomson meant his foothold in Scotland to be the springboard for much deeper penetration of the British media. Eventually he became the owner of *The Times* and the *Sunday Times*, national institutions which had likewise been faltering under fuddy-duddy management. For his rescue of them, he too got a peerage. Unlike Beaverbrook, however, Thomson had no wish for personal influence in politics. He was interested only in making money or, as a Scotsman at heart, in saving it: when in London, he usually travelled by underground and, if he had to take a taxi, he never gave the driver a tip. He certainly impressed on Britain's newspaper industry the need to become commercially viable. But the obstacles to this in its outdated technology and restrictive practices remained great. After Thomson's death, his son Kenneth withdrew and confined himself to his North American interests – which include the governorship of the Hudson's Bay Company, an outfit still largely manned by Scots.

Scots blood linked Thomson with the man who would finish his work in Britain, and have a yet greater impact on the media worldwide, Rupert Murdoch. He was born in Australia, partly educated in England and is now an American citizen: but he does not give the impression that nationality means much to him at the global level on which he operates. His grandfather, a minister, emigrated from the north-east of Scotland and in Australia became Moderator of the General Assembly of the Presbyterian Church. His father, Sir Kenneth Murdoch, distinguished himself as an editor, then a proprietor of newspapers.

So Rupert Murdoch was born into the business. After expanding the group he inherited in his homeland to comprise twenty-seven titles, he turned to Britain. He bought *The Times* and *Sunday Times* from Thomson. He took over two tabloids, the *Sun* and *News of the World*, and shamelessly encouraged them to titillate a swelling readership. Within them all he broke the power of the trade unions, a millstone round the neck of the British press. In the US, too, he acquired a string of publications. From 1985 he set himself to build a new empire in broadcasting. He then purchased the Twentieth Century Fox Film Corporation and six other major American television stations. Afterwards he became the joint owner of British Sky Broadcasting, the largest satellite service in Europe. More recently he has bought Star Television in Hong Kong, ready to exploit the largest consumer market of the future in China. His is the first truly global media network with the potential to reach two-thirds of the world's population.

A controversial feat of Murdoch's is to have blurred the difference between the newspaper and entertainment industries. Scots had long ago done much to set the standards of modern quality journalism. The *Edinburgh Review* founded in 1802, intelligent, fearless and questioning, was the first periodical magazine to reach a mass, intelligent readership on both sides of the Atlantic Ocean. It found a worthy successor in the US when the *New Yorker* was set up in 1925 by Harold Ross and made its name for sophisticated wit with Ellin Mackay's early articles, written up from her own experience, on the louche and expensive nightlife of the Big Apple; both writers were of Scottish descent. A later doyenne of women's journalism in the city was Diana Vreeland, born Dalziel, the daughter of a Scottish stockbroker in Paris. The Empress of Fashion, as she was known, worked for over thirty years for *Harper's Bazaar* and then as editor of *Vogue*.

Still, New York was, as it remains, rather alien to the all-American values out in the rest of the continent. Yet there too a demand emerged for reading which would entertain while it instructed – especially from the growing numbers of college graduates, which had more than doubled since the turn of the century. During the First World War an infantry sergeant by the name of DeWitt Wallace, the son of a Presbyterian minister of Scottish origins, had been wounded in France. During his convalescence, he began to clip interesting articles out of magazines sent to him from his family in St Paul, Minnesota. It struck him that too much was being published for people who did not happen to be in hospital with time to wade through it all. Even important features often seemed wordy, and capable of being reduced with advantage to something the reader could more easily digest. Once he was discharged and returned home, Wallace went to work on his cuttings till he had distilled them into thirty-one short essays that he thought had something important to say. He had these set in a common typeface and laid out as a magazine, which he called *Reader's Digest*. He ordered 200 printed copies and sent them to more than a dozen publishers in New York, who all sent them back. So Wallace and his wife, Lila, used their personal savings to launch the project themselves. Today the *Reader's Digest* has the largest circulation of any magazine in the world.

Scotland meanwhile continued to produce great journalists: in Britain, James Cameron was, with his work in the dying days of Empire, probably the finest foreign correspondent of all while, in the US, James 'Scotty' Reston, who emigrated as a child from Clydebank, became the leading political writer on the *New York Times*. President Eisenhower once said: 'Who does Scotty Reston think he is, telling me how to run the country?' What these journalists have brought to the trade is a refusal to let its commercial imperatives compromise the moral duty of telling the truth in terms understood by a man on a commuter train or his wife with their children round her feet. It is a distant modern descendant of the philosophy of Common Sense.

Not even Scots always rise to the high demands of this Presbyterian seriousness, however, and they have been just as ready to offer lighter fare. The expression 'yellow press' was coined to describe the *New York Herald*, founded by James Gordon Bennett, a failed candidate for the Roman Catholic priesthood who then went from his native Aberdeenshire to try his luck in the US. It was the first paper to print gossip about high society and the first to publish a sexual scandal. But Bennett's son, who bore the same name, redeemed his father somewhat by founding in 1887 a European edition of the paper, which continues even yet under the respected title of the *International Herald Tribune*, from 1966 owned jointly by the *Washington Post* and *New York Times* and since 2002 by the *Times* alone. We get a better idea of the original *Herald* from today's equivalent, yellower still, which is the *National Enquirer*, based in Florida. The Scotsman who edits it, Iain Calder, has won for it the biggest circulation in America with endless scoops about starlets' couplings and other high jinks among those famous for being famous. The stories are eagerly gathered by Calder's largely Scottish staff. Their prurience, heated by the sun of Palm Beach, must owe something to the national sin of hypocrisy but is justified, not least in financial terms, as what the readers want.

So Murdoch was not breaking with Scottish tradition by bringing the two extremes of the journalistic craft together under one corporate roof. Or indeed under one editorial roof – the archbishops and high officials of the state who used to form the staple readership of *The Times* will have become quite accustomed to the spicy stories it carries nowadays of actors, models and pop stars, and there will be no more red faces at them in the Athenaeum. It is another change from an earlier era that a good many of such stories may be about Scots.

Today the world's most famous Scotsman is Sean Connery. From his first job as a milkman in a dingy suburb of Edinburgh he rose to global celebrity in the character of James Bond, the secret serviceman – also supposed to have been a Scot – created for his thrillers by Ian Fleming, a scion of the financial family from Dundee. Connery has played an immense range of other roles, from a forensic monk in *The Name of the Rose* to an Irish American cop (with an oddly Scottish accent) in *The Untouchables*. He lives in Hollywood, but from his frequent visits is still a familiar figure in his homeland. Indeed he takes part in its affairs as if he had never gone away. He has generously donated to charities intended to give young Scots with no advantages their chance in life. More controversially, he supports independence for Scotland and makes large financial contributions to the Scottish National Party. This seemed to inhibit the Labour government from according him the official honour which many believed he richly deserved. But at last in 2000 he was knighted by the Queen. Connery has always been quick to refute the allegation that living in exotic locations in Spain and the Bahamas shows a lack of patriotism. In a series of interviews with *The Herald* in 2003 he let it be known that he had paid a total of £3.7 million in tax to the United Kingdom exchequer in the preceding six years.

Nowadays Hollywood houses quite a Scottish colony at all levels in the movies. It is older than we think: classic actors such as David Niven and Alastair Sim were born in Scotland, while Warren Beatty, Stewart Granger, Alan Ladd, Robert Mitchum, James Stewart, John Wayne, Mickey Rooney, George C. Scott, Rod Steiger, Ava Gardner, Katharine Hepburn and Audrey Hepburn, Shirley MacLaine, Marilyn Monroe and Elizabeth Taylor all claimed Scottish ancestry of some kind, if usually remote. James MacDonald from Dundee was the voice of Mickey Mouse: for forty years he did voice-overs and sound effects for Walt Disney, who could also claim some Scottish ancestry. So could a leading figure in the older generation of directors, John Huston, who made *The Treasure of the Sierra Madre* and *The Maltese Falcon*.

As the art of the cinema evolved, John Grierson from Kilmarnock invented the genre of the documentary – a word he coined himself. He worked for the Empire Marketing Board Film Unit and also founded the Canadian National Film Board, which was developed by his brother Scot, Norman McLaren. Both showed that films sponsored by public bodies need not be dull. Grierson had been partly educated in the US and was impressed by the creative skills of its young advertising industry. Like the admen he wanted to portray real life on the screen, not for the sake of sales but to convey the drama and heroism in the lives of ordinary people, which could be brought home all the more once sound-tracks became technically possible. Some of the films Grierson made or promoted, on fishermen, potters or miners, are today mainly of historical interest but others do attain the status of art, such as *Night Mail* directed by Harry Watts. It follows the nightly run of the train carrying the mails from London to Scotland, set to poetry by W. H. Auden and to music by Benjamin Britten. The poem conveys through the lyrical rhythm of the train both the urgency and the routine of the operation, with the final twist of the effect a letter can have on people:

And none will hear the postman's knock
Without a quickening of the heart.
For who can bear to feel himself forgotten?

The visual impact of film could be turned to the benign purposes of education, or to the malign purposes of propaganda in Soviet Russia and Nazi Germany, but the dream factory of Hollywood still bestrides the industry. There, Scots are now more visible than ever before. Another cinematic idol of the present day, Robert Redford, says his father was a milkman in Edinburgh too. In a younger generation are two brothers Macdonald, Andrew who appeared in the film of Irvine Welsh's novel, *Trainspotting*, and Kevin, an Oscar-winning producer. Ewan McGregor was also in *Trainspotting*, playing the lead, and has since won several new roles, most recently in Star Wars. The versatile Alan Cumming is a veteran of the James Bond films as well, and stars in *Sex and the City* on television, but also had a long and successful run on Broadway in the comedy *Cabaret*. Craig Ferguson is another comic actor who has moved to Hollywood and into movies. Julianne Moore, the daughter of a social worker from Dunoon, achieved stardom in *Hannibal*.

Among directors, Michael Caton Jones, born at Broxburn, made Robert de Niro's recent film, *City by the Sea*. A leading screenwriter is Alan Sharp, who started off working in a shipyard but found greater fulfilment in writing his fine novel, *A Green Tree in Gedde*, 'dedicated to Greenock, to its buildings and chimneys and streets and the glimpses they have afforded me of the river and the hills'. Published in 1965, it came out long before Irvine Welsh and James Kelman had made Scottish novels fashionable; it contains no scatology or swearwords, but a rather intense study of sex and guilt, of homosexuality and incest, composed at a time when these subjects had not yet become at all easy to discuss in print. So, while the book found many admirers, it did not provide young Sharp with a livelihood and he went to seek it in America, a loss to Scottish literature. It was Hollywood's gain. Probably Sharp's best script was for *Rob Roy*, the film of Sir Walter Scott's novel on the conflict between Highlands and Lowlands.

When *Rob Roy* burst on to the silver screen in 1996, it was in competition with a movie which grew into a still more spectacular hit, *Braveheart*, starring Mel Gibson, who was also the director; there can have been no previous year when two Scottish films vied to fill the world's cinemas. *Braveheart* is best described as an imaginative recreation of the life of William Wallace, the hero of Scotland's Wars of Independence in the fourteenth century. Historians despaired of the liberties taken with the actual events, but it was in vain for them to point out that, for example, no Scot still painted himself with woad at the relevant period. The emotion and excitement of the film carried all before it, and even the most flint-hearted unionist must have thrilled when Braveheart rode back and forth before his ragged Scottish army to proclaim, of the grim English host opposite, 'They can take away our lives, but they can never take away our freedom!' The defiance moved not only Scotland, but the rest of the globe too.

Medieval Scots did not wear tartan either, but *Braveheart* also had the effect of creating tartan chic, as a fashion statement for the rich and famous. Actually, some had been sporting the kilt for a good while. The actor Charlton Heston wore his grandfather's. The pop singer Rod Stewart, born in London to Scottish parents, wore his as a member of the Tartan Army, following the too often dismal fortunes of Scotland's national football team, which he had once hankered to join. Yet these older figures never succeeded in making a cult of the kilt. After *Braveheart*, Robbie Williams and Samuel Lee Jackson took to wearing one, or some version of it, in public, as did even Madonna. They brought a reproach from Deirdre Kinloch Anderson, whose family have for five generations been traditional makers of kilts, about their 'being worn simply for media attention and commercial gain. This is now commonplace with pop stars and personalities, most of whom have no Scottish ancestry. They tend to wear it in an unorthodox manner, again to increase attention. And, even worse, to lift it up for photographers.'

Another consequence of the cult of the kilt was to encourage people to come out as Scotsmen when it had never been suspected of them. Since Scots have been in the US such a long time, there are many Americans who can discover a Scottish ancestor. And since Scots form only a small minority in the US, their daughters are more than likely to marry husbands of a different ethnic origin and so conceal the Scottishness of their children. An example is David Duchovny, star of *The X Files*, whose

Slavic name hides that he has a mother from Aberdeenshire. Another is the author of *Lake Wobegon Days*, Garrison Keillor, whose work, more usually associated with the Scandinavian community of Wisconsin, formed the basis for the most popular programme in the history of American public radio. It turned out that Donald Trump, who with his huge interests in New York's real estate and his casinos in Atlantic City became in the 1980s a symbol of success – or of excess when they later slumped in value – had been born to Mary MacLeod from Lewis.

The enrichment of life in a melting pot of various and disparate cultures from round the world is a reward the US reaps from its openness to people from anywhere and everywhere. The Scottish element blends easily, as can be seen from the case of the talkshow king, earning $14 million a year, Jay Leno (full name: James Douglas Muir Leno). He had an Italian-American father and a Scottish mother, Cathryn. He says: 'I'm a half-breed of the oddest sort. My Scottish side is practical, analytical, even a bit frugal. My Italian side is loud, outgoing, ready to laugh.' And he recalls that 'when I was growing up, at the Italian functions there would be hundreds of meatballs for maybe a dozen people. More food than anyone could possibly eat. And my Aunt Nettie would say, "Oooh, look at all the food that's going to weeste".'

The dream factory of Hollywood is to the outside world the emblem of California, the US state which boomed most in the later twentieth century. But it is a powerhouse of other economic activities too, not least because talented people can be readily persuaded to settle there for its sun and its surf and its easy-going lifestyle. With deserts made to bloom in the south, giving way to a lush kingdom of nature in the north, it could hardly be more different, except perhaps when fog comes down, from the bare, gloomy landscapes of Scotland. The Mediterranean climate of southern California has proved especially attractive to the footloose. More than 50,000 Britons are reckoned to be living in the region, and the odd pub or fish-and-chip shop has sprung up to cater for them. If past experience is anything to go by, a high proportion will be Scots. 'We have seen the future and it plays,' Californians are wont to say.

So it comes as no surprise that one of the Scottish success stories on the Pacific seaboard is that of Richard Tait, the Glaswegian inventor of Cranium, which in 2000 was the world's biggest selling board-game. He first took to the local lifestyle as a shepherd. His breakthrough came after he joined Microsoft and won its award for employee of the year. This was for his work on the *Encarta* encyclopaedia, on the strength of which he left to follow up his own ideas and, with a partner, created Cranium. The game entails a demanding range of skills from its teams, such as sketching, spelling, sculpting and whistling, among others.

Tait is an instance of the sort of talent a region can attract once it reaches critical mass in technological innovation. California achieved that across the whole range of electronic industries, in an expansion which reached its climax during the late 1990s and which the recent crash of dot.com stocks may not have completely stopped in its tracks. In any event, Scots had made their contribution here too, in people like Bill Elder who in 1968 left Glasgow for San Francisco with £500 in his pocket and rose to head one of the largest computer companies. The contribution is visible also among the many auxiliary industries and their personnel which then gather round centres of excellence, as in the case of the Scotsman, Kevin Sneader, who in California runs McKinsey's, the management consultancy which has been voted the company most desirable to work for by MBAs in the US.

Modern business would be impossible without the computer, which today is also becoming ubiquitous in ordinary households on both sides of the Atlantic. This revolution in our everyday lives began in 1916 when James Johnston, born in Scotland, and Thomas Watson, of Scotch-Irish ancestry, developed the prototype of a practical tabulating machine. The company which they went on to set up, International Business Machines (IBM), burgeoned into one of the greatest global corporations and remained till the crisis of the 1990s the single most profitable enterprise on earth. Johnston brought it back to his homeland when he opened its plant at Greenock in 1951. Watson eventually handed the business over to his son, also Thomas, who remained its chief executive officer till 1971; he later served as US ambassador to the Soviet Union. Other early Scottish American contributions to this revolutionary industry included those of Howard Aiken, maker of the first automatic sequence computer in 1939, assisted by Grace Murray Hopper, who was serving in the US navy; she only retired in 1986, at the age of 80, as a rear-admiral, being then the oldest officer and highest-ranking woman in the American armed forces. More to the point Amazing Grace, to use her nickname, was the co-inventor of the early computer language Cobol and coined the word bug to mean a fault in a machine or system.

IBM has also brought to the fore Bill Gates, who in the 1990s became the richest man in the US. He was born to a mother of Scots blood, Mary Maxwell, who herself had a successful career in business and served on the boards of several large companies. She helped her son to get his first contract with IBM, producing the software for its computers. This was the start of Microsoft. The company came to dominate its market and has had to fight a series of huge and expensive lawsuits aimed at stripping it of what threatened to turn into a monopolistic position; the Supreme Court eventually ruled that it should be split in two. Other American Scots who have made a contribution to this most revolutionary of modern industries include Ross Perot, best known because he ran for president in 1992 on a programme of shrinking the government; he had made the money for his campaign from a company which provided a range of computer services.

These examples remind us that American Scots have not only figured in showbiz and the more glitzy kinds of innovation. In fact such activities are, for a normally sober people, rather the exception than the rule. The often unsung presence of canny, practical, determined Scotsmen has made itself felt in many other industries of the modern US: such familiar brand-names as Armour Meats, Black & Decker, Dow Chemical and Kellogg's Cereals are owed to Scottish founders of the companies producing the goods concerned. In the late twentieth century, native Scots who made their fortunes in North America included William Blackie, a chartered accountant who turned the

Caterpillar Tractor Company into a multinational corporation (with a plant at Cumbernauld in Scotland); Ian MacGregor, who returned from Lazard Brothers in New York to head British Steel and British Coal; James McLeod, in the Canadian oil business; and David Ogilvy, who built up his advertising company in New York into the most valuable in the world. The biggest single symbol of American civilisation in today's world is the Big Mac, the hamburger from the restaurants founded by Richard and Maurice McDonald, whose parents came from County Kerry in Ireland but ultimately from some distant branch of a Scottish clan.

Nothing is more typical of consumerism than the car, and the economic system of the modern age has sometimes been called Fordism, after the methods developed by Henry Ford for the mass production of sophisticated goods. Ford was not a Scotsman, but some of the early rivals he competed with were. They are largely forgotten now, but deserve notice for their part in creating an industry that has been a driving force in the US economy. Alexander Winton, an immigrant from Scotland, built one of the first cars in America in 1896, though his models were of too high a quality to find a wide market. They made their reputation in their time from their speed. Winton himself established a world record when in 1900 he drove fifty miles in an hour and seventeen minutes, and another of his cars was the first to exceed seventy miles an hour, in a race with a Mercedes. In 1903 he was the first man to drive across America, making the trip from San Francisco to New York in two months; the vehicle he used is now in the Smithsonian Institution. Winton eventually sold out to General Motors. The same company absorbed the business of David Buick, who emigrated from Scotland to the US and in 1903 built the first car bearing his own name, with advanced innovations in the engine. The trademark was to survive, but illness forced Buick himself to give up his career.

The US also took the lead in flight from the outset, when the Wright brothers launched the first machine capable of carrying a man through the air at Kittyhawk, North Carolina, in 1903. They were almost beaten to it by Alexander Graham Bell who, with his partner Samuel Langley, built a manned, powered aircraft which took off on the Potomac River in Washington DC a few days before, but immediately crashed. Even so, right till 1948 the Smithsonian Institution displayed the Bell-Langley plane as the first to fly. Till his death in 1922, Bell continued trying to improve his model at his home in Nova Scotia, where he ran an Aerial Experiment Association. It was from there in 1909 that the Scottish Canadian, James McCurdy, made the first successful flight in the British Empire.

The flop on the Potomac was far from the end of Scottish presence in American skies. In fact, by the end of the Second World War three out of the four major US aircraft-building companies had been created by Scots. The first was Lockheed, a word which appears to be a feeble attempt to help Americans to get their tongues round the Scottish name of Loughead, borne by the two brothers, Allan and Malcolm, who founded the company in 1926. The era of commercial aviation opened when in 1935 Donald Wills Douglas inaugurated the DC-3 (known affectionately as the Gooney Bird) which became the first plane to make money carrying only passengers. At one time it accounted for 95 per cent of all passenger traffic in the US. It was also the most durable plane ever built. Out of more than 10,000 produced in the company's first decade, more than 1,500 were still flying in the 1980s and one had logged 87,000 hours, equivalent to ten years in the air. Another American Scot, James McDonnell, set up his company in 1939 and made it famous in 1946 by producing a jet that could land on and take off from aircraft carriers. After the war the two companies produced rapid developments in the technology of jet aircraft, of missiles and eventually of spacecraft. In 1967 they merged, with the next generation of the founding families taking over the management. Amid testing economic conditions in the 1990s, a further merger took place with Boeing, their great rival. McDonnells and Douglases still play a leading role in the new, giant corporation.

McDonnell had built the Mercury spacecraft which carried the first American into orbit, and Americans themselves would probably consider their country's achievements in space to be the greatest of the twentieth century. They reached their climax on 20 July 1969, when Neil Armstrong teetered down a flimsy ladder from his spacecraft, where Edwin Aldrin remained inside, and became the first man to impress his footprints on the dusty surface of the moon. Both men could claim Scottish blood and, as they were later feted round the world, sometimes wore the kilt – Armstrong, for example, when he headed a parade through his ancestral home of Langholm in the Scottish Borders in 1972. The Scottish presence in America's cosmic feats has been a strong one. Four others of the men who have walked on the moon – Alan Shepard, Alan Bean, James Irwin and David Scott – were American Scots. John Glenn was the first American in orbit and Bruce McCandless the first to fly free in space. These men have flown high, but it seems unlikely that they reached the limit of achievement for American Scots.

CONCLUSION

The style of Scottish politics is more decorous than that of American politics, and Scottish politicians are not expected to be so demonstrative, let alone clownish, as their American counterparts. So those Scots who fly over to the US for National Tartan Day on 6 April, a growing event since the first one was celebrated in 1998, may experience a culture shock. That clearly happened in 2001, when the day was marked by a ceremony on the steps of the Capitol in Washington DC. Among others, Henry McLeish, the First Minister of Scotland, and John Swinney, leader of the Scottish National Party, gathered there with the world's most famous Scotsman, Sir Sean Connery. They found themselves under the orders of the Chaplain to the Senate, the Revd John Ogilvie, a Presbyterian minister born in Wisconsin and educated at New College, Edinburgh, the school of divinity in the city's university. As the proceedings got under way, he instructed them first to shout 'Tartan!', then to shout 'Freedom!'

Connery, an old stager, did so without a blush. For McLeish the performance was more tricky. The Scottish Labour Party which he then headed is not given to exuberant patriotic displays. On the contrary, it stresses that the Scottish Parliament set up in 1999 is a limited exercise in the devolution of power within a United Kingdom still firmly united. It is meant not to inspire nationalism but to contain it. McLeish had come primarily to tell Americans what they could buy in or from Scotland: golf, whisky, woolly jumpers. He must have calculated that shouting 'Tartan!' and 'Freedom!' might reasonably be defined as a promotional gimmick, and did what he had to do. The moment was a bit awkward for Swinney too. For years his party has been trying to move away from a tartan image, from a vision of Scotland where people leave off tossing cabers, playing bagpipes or dancing reels only to fortify themselves with another plate of haggis. The aim is rather to present Scotland as part of modern Europe, industrious and progressive, fully worthy of independence, a serious nation in other words, not one of kilted buffoonery. Still, Swinney found it in himself to obey the Chaplain to the Senate and shout 'Tartan!', then 'Freedom!'

The source of embarrassment lay in the fact that this ceremony, just like those Highland games in the Old South, was not really about Scotland but about America. It did not convey what Scots think about themselves, but what Americans think about them: and in both cases the thoughts may be a little confused, which does not help.

National Tartan Day was the brainchild of Senator Trent Lott of Mississippi, leader of the Republican majority in the Senate at the relevant point. His grandmother was a Buchanan from the shores of Loch Lomond and he wears a kilt of her tartan. In 1997 he introduced Senate resolution 155 which his colleagues approved just a few months later – with extreme rapidity by their august standards – so as 'to recognise the outstanding achievements and contributions made by Scottish Americans to the United States'. The resolution named 6 April as National Tartan Day because this marked the anniversary of the Declaration of Arbroath in 1320. That sonorous expression of Scottish sentiment was the first claim to national rights ever written in Europe. All leading Scottish patriots of the time signed it to make clear they would never submit to the rule of the English, who had been engaged in aggression against Scotland for more than twenty years.

Senator Lott is a Southerner. His campaign for National Tartan Day may well have been meant to please the moderate end of the constituency which, back home in Mississippi, likes to sport the Confederate tartan. This was perhaps something he could not declare openly to the Senate. So he invented for its benefit a strange interpretation of history. The American Declaration of Independence in 1776, according to Resolution 155, was 'modelled on that inspirational document', the Declaration of Arbroath.

In his speech proposing the resolution, Lott went into greater detail: 'On a hot steamy day, a group of men stood in a building in the British colony of Pennsylvania . . . debating and then signing their own declaration of independence. They used the

Arbroath Declaration as the template for their own thoughts, their own words.' And once he had won his fellow senators over, he explained that:

> National Tartan Day is about liberty. It is about the demand of citizens for their freedom from an oppressive government. . . . By honoring April 6, Americans will annually celebrate the true beginning of the quest for liberty and freedom, Arbroath and the declaration for liberty. . . . The Scottish clansmen who met on that cold day and declared their independence were our clansmen, no matter what nation we hail from, they were our brothers.

Whatever the Senator's future since he lost the leadership of his party in 2002, it does not lie in history. By the Scots' conceptions of 1320, their independence had existed time out of mind. The Declaration of Arbroath was not about Scottish independence as such, but about persuading the Pope to recognise that it had never been extinguished by English claims to the contrary. With their crushing victory over the invading army of King Edward II of England at the Battle of Bannockburn in 1314, the Scots had as a matter of fact secured their independence and, six years later, only needed others to stop acknowledging his absurd pretensions to reign over them.

To some, admittedly, the language of the Declaration of Arbroath and of the American Declaration of Independence may seem so alike that it could not be there by accident – in other words, the Americans of 1776 must somehow have copied the Scots of 1320. There is no evidence at all for this. While the American declaration was written in English, the Scottish one was written in Latin, so any linguistic parallels are bound to be far-fetched. People who have never done any translation often naively assume that each word in one language has an exact equivalent in another, yet the norm is for the translator to face a choice of words, none of which may precisely overlap with the original. The Declaration of Arbroath could as well be put into English in a way which produces no parallels with the Declaration of Independence. And even where the parallels appear exact, they may be deceptive. The fact is that the Latin word *libertas* just did not mean the same to a medieval Scotsman as the English word liberty meant to a colonial American. Anyway, most such declarations cry up the virtues of those who write them while crying down the vices of their enemies. We need look for little meaning beyond that. Not a single reputable historian sees parallels between the concepts enshrined in the two declarations, because parallels do not exist. In reality, and with apologies to Senator Lott, there are no grounds for thinking that any American gathered on that steamy day in Pennsylvania gave a moment's thought to the Declaration of Arbroath; with the possible exception of John Witherspoon, none had probably heard of it. Even if they had, it would have been hard to imagine a place or time less relevant to the aspirations of the Thirteen Colonies in 1776 than the Scotland of the fourteenth century.

That said, there is no need to underrate the real exchange which has taken place over the last three or four hundred years between the small, old country and the big, new country. The contribution of the Scottish nation to America has, here as elsewhere, been remarkable and out of all proportion to its size. And, as we saw in the last chapter, America today exerts a huge influence on the Scots, in the guise of the universal culture in a global economy which the wealth and might of the US have formed and which for all the past, present and future setbacks to it has steadily made this into one world.

A question for everybody is whether the universal culture and the global economy are to develop solely on American terms. At the outset of the twenty-first century the US faces deep dilemmas over how to use its vast imperial power. It needs to do so without generating revulsion against its own values, the values of freedom and democracy, and allowing tyranny to stage the sort of comeback which made the twentieth century such a terrible one for humanity. Americans have come only slowly face to face with the fact of their imperialism: it does not sit well with their origins as a revolutionary society which itself had to throw off an imperial yoke.

Inside the US, though, a cultural effect of external imperialism is already to be seen: its counterpart is internal multiculturalism.

If all the world can come to America and make a fresh start differing only in a greater degree of liberty and prosperity from the former life led in Guayaquil or Guangzhou, or indeed in Glasgow, then it is hard to accuse Americans of browbeating others. The trouble with multiculturalism is its shallowness. Life in Guayaquil, Guangzhou or Glasgow is of its own time and place. It arises out of societies which are deeply rooted and strongly bonded in a way the society of Galveston, Texas, or of Gary, Indiana, never has been and perhaps never will be. That life cannot be packed into a suitcase and flown to the US. Its roots will have been torn up and it will wither: sooner or later, the migrants follow the imperatives of their new life and become Americans. Multiculturalism is then reduced to meaningless gesture or to style without substance.

Nothing shows that better than the way Americans deal with Scotland, those who are interested, however generous their attitude may be. The Scotland making an appearance in recent years at Stone Mountain or on the steps of the Capitol is not the Scotland that Scots know (which, surely, must count as the only genuine Scotland). The American Scotland is on the contrary a caricature, which might indeed be taken as offensive if Scots were not themselves such a good-natured people, or perhaps so flattered at all this attention paid to them in the mighty US. It displays little understanding of Scotland or readiness to take the Scots on their own terms, because it is an exercise in make-believe. It displays rather a desire to assimilate Scotland and the Scots into an American construction of the world and into the American requirements for multiculturalism. In the Americans' relations with different, less kindly nations, this is just what leads to misunderstanding and mistrust, or worse. An imperial power has to see realities.

It can be said in mitigation that Scots are not good at making outsiders understand them. The state of the nation remains uncertain, though this is nothing out of the ordinary. Arguably the oddest fact of Scotland's messy history is the re-emergence after 300 years' assimilation to Union and Empire of a country capable in some degree of self-determination, when others which seemed more secure in 1707 – the Kingdom of Prussia, the Republic of Venice – have vanished for ever. Today, while more and better Scottish history is being written than at any time since the eighteenth century, it has yet to produce really satisfying explanations. We can point to Scotland's strong institutional structure and tenacious popular memory. Into the Union the Scots built defences against English imperialism, while they turned the British Empire to their own purposes, of making money and spreading enlightenment. The independent US also was a hardly less important safety valve for emigration and investment.

Even so, all these seem to be necessary rather than sufficient conditions for the turn of events which has seen a nation rise again and advance into a future which, to say the least, appears open. Now nobody can say what the end of Scottish history is going to be. Most western countries may be reasonably sure that, even while times move on, they will in ten or twenty years look much as they do now. Scots have no idea how their country will look by then, the potential extremes ranging from dingy province to hare-brained republic (though several more pleasant possibilities lie in between). At any rate, kilts and tartans obscure, rather than clarify, the prospects.

Perhaps a final plea for Scottish history will be in order, at least for the kind of Scottish history that deals in realities rather than make-believe. The historians of the eighteenth century wrote Scottish history because it seemed to them exemplary. It laid out in the context of a particular nation the progress of humanity, seen here more clearly because it was accelerated: Scotland passed within a couple of generations from burning witches to building the New Town of Edinburgh as a sort of machine for rational living. If more and better Scottish history is being written today than at any time since, perhaps this is because of some inkling that Scottish history has again become exemplary, or at least of a little significance to people other than the Scots themselves. When they entered the Union in 1707, they consciously exposed themselves to the global economy. They felt they had no choice if they were not to starve in their remote and chilly corner of Europe. They took the plunge, saving what they could from the past yet knowing their country was going to be changed beyond all recognition. This indeed happened: we see it on every hand from the empty glens of Sutherland to the now silent shipyards of the River Clyde. Yet despite the transformations of those three centuries, Scotland is still Scotland, visibly separate and distinct from all other nations.

In other words, Scottish experience shows it is possible for community to survive in the global economy, even against the odds. This is not a history that should be casually forgotten, because it may have its uses for the twenty-first century. The global economy has today attained a new and apparently all-conquering dynamic. From North America and Europe it has already caught up the more fortunate peoples of the Orient, while it snatches enticingly at the tardier societies of China and India. Latin America, Russia, the Islamic world may be carried away by it, or perhaps not. Africa has been left hopelessly behind. The allure of the global economy is that it can bring people wealth beyond their wildest dreams. If not, it is likely to reduce them to grinding poverty. But whether its effect is enriching or immiserating, it works by the same means, by what has been called creative destruction. In other words it constantly rips community apart, tearing the fabric of our traditions and habits and twisting our lives into conformity with the demands of the market. This can be hard to take even by those who benefit from the process.

Since the US is the powerhouse of the global economy, it becomes also the focus for the resentments aroused. Even as they enrich themselves, the French or Arabs or Hindus cling all the more passionately to their own civilisation and despise the new American consumerism of hamburgers, baseball caps and rock music. It seems hideous that everything they treasure might succumb to such superficiality. They turn anti-American. And anti-Americanism, as we saw on 11 September 2001, can descend into barbarity. The US responded to that with force, as it had to. But in the longer run Americans would do well to appreciate that not every other nation actually wishes to be assimilated into their construction of the world. Many peoples take part in the global economy and cultivate friendly relations with the US, but also want to remain themselves and not become what Americans think they are or ought to be. One good historical example of how the destructive forces in the global economy can be withstood is Scotland, the Scotland which might have vanished after 1707, as the Kingdom of Prussia or the Republic of Venice vanished, but which has survived, indeed risen again. In the lessons from that resilience the small, old country may still have something of mutual benefit to offer to the big, new country.

INDEX

Cortes, Hernan, 11
Covenanters, 14, 15, 16, 32, 89, 184
Craig, David, 162-3
Craig, Elijah, 172
Creeks, 68, 69, 118, 137, 139, 140, 141, 142, 143, 145, 146, 147, 148
Crockett, Davy, 69, 147
Cromwell, Oliver, 14, 48, 96, 102
Cuba, 58, 59, 76, 171, 206
Cumming, Alan, 216
Cunard, Samuel, 195

DABNEY, Robert, 178
Dale, David, 190
Dalziel, Diana, see Vreeland, Diana
Darien, 16, 17-18, 138, 187, 188
Darwin, Charles, 110
Davidson, G.C., xiii
Davis, Jefferson, 179
Davison, Eliza, 205
Declaration of Independence, American (1776), 32, 35, 36, 38, 42, 49, 59, 104, 107, 155, 200, 225, 226
Delaware, 35
Democratic Party, 58, 60
Devine, Tom, xii
Dickens, Charles, 85, 90
Dickinson College, 104
Dinwiddie, Robert, 64
Disney, Walt, 215
Dixon, Thomas, 184
Douglas, David, 128, 129, 130, 131
Douglas, Donald Wills, 222
Duchovny, David, 217
Duff, William, 178
Duncan, King of Scots, 1

Dundas, Robert, Viscount Melville, 123, 124
Dundee, 173, 196, 214, 215

EDINBURGH, 21, 32, 56, 68, 72, 81, 85, 90, 99, 102, 103, 104, 105, 108, 109, 173, 175, 188, 199, 210, 214, 224
Edison, Thomas, 201
Eisenhower, Dwight D., 61, 213
Elder, Bill, 219
Elgin, Earl of, see Bruce, James
Eliot, Charles, 111
Elliot, Mary, 201
Emerson, Ralph Waldo, 85, 95, 96
Empire, British, ix, 5, 17, 18, 19, 25, 27, 30, 38-9, 63, 81, 83, 86, 98, 104, 120, 135, 157, 160, 167, 175, 176, 181, 206, 207, 222, 228, 229
England and the English, x, 2, 11, 12, 13, 14, 15, 17, 18, 19, 23, 27, 29-30, 43, 47, 58, 62, 71, 81, 83, 87, 90, 93, 96, 98, 99, 100, 107, 112, 114, 115, 117, 135, 136, 152, 153, 154, 162, 173, 188, 199, 211, 217, 225, 226
Enlightenment, Scottish, 21, 32, 46, 72, 83-4, 90, 109, 114, 140, 154, 165
Erskine, Henry, Lord Cardross, 16
Eskimos, 123-4, 126

FERGUSON, Craig, 216
Ferguson, Patrick, 28
First World War, 60, 77, 159, 194, 206, 207, 210
Fleming, Ian, 214
Fleming, Robert, 196-7